The Rhythm Image

New Approaches to Sound, Music, and Media

Series Editors: Carol Vernallis, Holly Rogers, and Lisa Perrott

Forthcoming Titles:

Musical New Media by Nicola Dibben
David Bowie and the Art of Music Video by Lisa Perrott
Popular Music, Race, and Media since 9/11 by Nabeel Zuberi
Popular Music and Narrativity by Alex Jeffery

Published Titles:

Transmedia Directors by Carol Vernallis, Holly Rogers, and Lisa Perrott
Dangerous Mediations by Áine Mangaoang
Resonant Matter by Lutz Koepnick
Cybermedia: Science, Sound, and Vision edited by Carol Vernallis, Holly Rogers, Jonathan Leal, Selmin Kara
The Rhythm Image: Music Videos in Time by Steven Shaviro

The Rhythm Image

Music Videos and New Audiovisual Forms

By Steven Shaviro

BLOOMSBURY ACADEMIC
NEW YORK • LONDON • OXFORD • NEW DELHI • SYDNEY

BLOOMSBURY ACADEMIC
Bloomsbury Publishing Inc
1385 Broadway, New York, NY 10018, USA
50 Bedford Square, London, WC1B 3DP, UK
29 Earlsfort Terrace, Dublin 2, Ireland

BLOOMSBURY, BLOOMSBURY ACADEMIC and the Diana logo are trademarks of Bloomsbury Publishing Plc

First published in the United States of America 2023

Cover photograph: FKA Twigs performs at the Alexander McQueen: Savage Beauty Fashion Gala at the V&A © David M. Benett/Getty Images for Victoria and Albert Museum

A catalogue record for this book is available from the Library of Congress.

Library of Congress Cataloging-in-Publication Data
Names: Shaviro, Steven, author.
Title: The rhythm image : music videos and new audiovisual forms / by Steven Shaviro.
Description: New York : Bloomsbury Academic, 2022. | Series: New approaches to sound, music, and media | Includes bibliographical references and index. | Summary: "Analyzes recent music videos in depth, and considers how they reflect new technologies and new cultural conditions, from an audiovisual perspective"– Provided by publisher.
Identifiers: LCCN 2022015186 (print) | LCCN 2022015187 (ebook) | ISBN 9781501388552 (hardback) | ISBN 9781501388569 (paperback) | ISBN 9781501388576 (epub) | ISBN 9781501388583 (pdf) | ISBN 9781501388590
Subjects: LCSH: Music videos–History and criticism.
Classification: LCC PN1992.8.M87 S537 2022 (print) | LCC PN1992.8.M87 (ebook) | DDC 780.26/7–dc23
LC record available at https://lccn.loc.gov/2022015186
LC ebook record available at https://lccn.loc.gov/2022015187

ISBN: HB: 978-1-5013-8855-2
PB: 978-1-5013-8856-9
ePDF: 978-1-5013-8858-3
eBook: 978-1-5013-8857-6

Series: New Approaches to Sound, Music, and Media

Typeset by Integra Software Services Pvt. Ltd.

To find out more about our authors and books visit www.bloomsbury.com and sign up for our newsletters.

For Adah and Roxanne, as always.
And in memory of David Bernstein and of Bill Kennedy

Contents

List of Figures

List of Table

Preface

This book has a double focus. On the one hand, it offers close, detailed readings of a number of pop commercial music videos. But on the other hand, drawing on and extrapolating beyond Gilles Deleuze's writings on cinema from over a third of a century ago, it also proposes a framework for thinking more generally about the aesthetics of audiovisual media in the twenty-first century. I write both on a micro-level and a macro-level, because I think that both levels of focus and attention are necessary. Individual works of art and culture, even short ones like music videos, often contain such a wealth of detail as to frustrate any effort to categorize them. Yet without theories to guide and even generate our categorizations, we are left at the mercy of bland and complacent commonplaces. Without calling on theory, we will fail to note the ways that the particulars of singular works often point us beyond the confines sketched out by theory. Kant famously said that "thoughts without contents are empty, intuitions without concepts are blind" (Kant 1998, 193–4). In the same way, theory without close reading is empty, but close reading without theory is blind.

Though most of the videos discussed in this book were created quite recently, the ideas here are ones that I have been pondering for decades. Deleuze's two *Cinema* volumes were written and published in the 1980s, and I was actively responding to their suggestions as early as my second book, published in 1993. MTV started broadcasting in 1981, and I have avidly watched and thought about music videos right from the beginning. My first published academic essays on music videos date from the late 1990s and early 2000s. My ideas have changed, as audiovisual technologies have evolved, as music videos have moved from cable television to YouTube, and as more and more music videos have been produced. It is challenging, but also rewarding, to try to write about subjects that keep changing faster than you are able to figure them out and write about them. This book is one result of my efforts to keep up.

Several sections of this book have previously been published in different forms. I wrote about Massive Attack's "Splitting the Atom" in the online-only volume *Post-Cinema: Theorizing 21st Century Film*, edited by Shane Denson and Julia Leyda. My musings on Tierra Whack were published as a pamphlet in the online only *Flugschriften* series, edited by Dominic Pettman and Carla Nappi. My discussion of Bonobo was first published in a special issue of *Music, Sound, and the Moving Image*, edited by Mathias Bonde Korsgaard and Tomáš Jirsa. One section of my discussion of Moses Sumney was published in a special issue of the online-only *ASAP/Journal*, edited by Elizabeth Reich and Stephen Yeager. Another section was published in a special issue of the journal *Cinephile*, edited by Harrison Wade and Kate Wise. I give thanks to all these editors for letting me rework and reprint those passages here. I also give particular thanks to Carol Vernallis, the premier scholar of music videos working today, for her continual encouragement and feedback.

I would like to dedicate this book to two good friends who passed away while it was being written. David Bernstein (1953–2020), with whom I grew up in New York City, and Bill Kennedy (1960–2021), with whom I so often went to movies during the twenty years I lived in Seattle, were both approximately my age, and I wrongly presumed that they would both be around as long as I was, and that I would always be able to reach them.

But I also dedicate this book, as always, to my daughters Adah Mozelle Shaviro and Roxanne Tamar Shaviro. Gertrude Stein reputedly said, "I write for myself and strangers." Though this is largely true for me as well, I also always write for Adah and Roxanne.

1

The Rhythm Image

Some Starting Points

"In the beginning, there was rhythm." So sings the British feminist punk band the Slits (Slits 1980). The sentence is also attributed, however, to the nineteenth-century German pianist and conductor Hans von Bülow (Walker 2009, 7). In either case, this declaration is an apt motto for *The Rhythm Image*. I take it for granted that rhythm is fundamental, because—to quote Mark Abel, in turn quoting Victor Zuckerkandl, who himself refers to Henri Bergson—rhythm "is not an event *in* time, but an event *of* time." That is to say, "time happens; time is an event .... Change does not create time; time literally creates change" (Abel 2014, 51; Zuckerkandl 1973, 181–5). Rhythm both enacts change and provides the background of continuity through which change is experienced. Digital audiovisual expression is always, as Maurizio Lazzarato writes, "a duration, a rhythm that enters into relation with other durations and other rhythms" (Lazzarato 2019, 104). Music (moving sounds) and cinema (moving images) are arts of duration, and thereby also arts of rhythm. Their entanglement, not in a rarefied form, but emerging through the hustle and bustle of marketing and publicity, is the basis of the contemporary music video.

In this book, I look closely and intensively at a small number of commercially produced music videos from the English-speaking world, all of them made in 2010 or later. I explore the ways that the visual and sonic rhythms of these videos fascinate and derange us. Music video is a hybrid and impure medium, in several ways. It is the bastard offspring of pop music singles and television advertising. It is a highly collaborative medium as well, since the musician or band usually works with a video director. The director might well have different expressive aims than the musicians do, but their differing perspectives must somehow coalesce. "To make a video," Saul Austerlitz writes, "the performer and director enter into a symbiotic relationship, one best compared to that between an architect and his or her client" (Austerlitz 2007, 8). In addition, both the musician and the director usually have large crews of technicians and assistants. Often the artist's record company, or management, pays for the video, and demands a say in how it is made and what it shows. All this makes for a lot of people, a lot of perspectives, and a lot of disagreements and crossed signals.

The ostensible purpose of a music video is to promote an already existing song, as well as to establish or embellish the persona of the performing musical artist. The music has already been recorded before the video is conceived. Where filmmakers generally seek sounds that suit and amplify a primary image track, music video directors must seek to create images that match a pre-given soundtrack. And yet, even within these constraints, music videos are often highly inventive and independent artistic expressions in their own right. Their rhythms give rise to different perceptions, feelings, and ideas than the music alone does—or for that matter, than movies and television generally do. As I have written elsewhere, music video is an intrinsically *post-cinematic* medium, with its own tendencies and forms (Shaviro 2010, 2017a). In this book, I seek to describe, in particular cases, both how music videos give us small doses of what Carol Vernallis calls "audiovisual bliss" (Vernallis et al. 2019, 181), and how music videos "work us over completely," as Marshall McLuhan says that new media do, changing our relation to the world by altering the "ratios" of our "sense perceptions" (McLuhan and Fiore 1967, 41).

Rhythm is an informing force, and an organizing principle, for music videos visually as well as sonically. As the brilliant music video director Calmatic puts it in a video interview:

> I treat editing like I'm making a beat. I do all my cuts on the little in-between intricate sounds that people don't even really hear. To me, the edit has its own beat to complement the beat of the actual song.
>
> (Calmatic 2018)

Kodwo Eshun, whose work on music videos—as well as on Black popular music more generally—is absolutely foundational to any discussion of the medium, similarly writes about how sound and image work in entangled counterpoint. In Hype Williams's late-1990s videos for Missy Elliott, Eshun says, "choreography, effects processing and musculature all fuse in an angular fluidity." A music video is "a slice of time that enthralls and appalls in rapid succession." Rhythms cross over between the soundtrack and the image track, so that "new slownesses, new speeds, new fermatas, new polyrhythms, new dynamic events emerge from the elastic reality and softimages of broadcast entertainment culture" (Eshun 2000,

116). Eshun epitomizes these synesthetic transfers in the "sleek equation" of a phrase he takes from George Clinton: "the rhythm of vision is a dancer" (Parliament 1978). Rhythm involves the eyes as well as the ears; and even further, beyond sight and hearing, it resonates proprioceptively through the entire body.

The film theorist Vivian Sobchack argues that this sort of "cross-modal sensory exchange" already takes place in conventional filmviewing. The viewer/listener is a "*cinesthetic subject*," who feels the intensities not just of sight and sound, but of the other senses as well (Sobchack 2004, 69–70). This still applies to music videos, if anything in more concentrated form. Of course, music videos today are usually accessed online, on YouTube and other sites—rather than in large theaters as movies used to be. Also, we encounter them on a much wider variety of screens than was the case in the age of MTV (the 1980s and 1990s), when music video was part of the ongoing flow of cable television (Goodwin 1992, 134). Today, music videos appear on monitors of all sorts and sizes, from gigantic home theater screens all the way down to the tiny viewing areas of mobile phones. And instead of having to wait for a certain video to come up in the course of MTV's rotation, we can watch it whenever we want, and as often as we want.

The ubiquity and everydayness of the circumstances in which we currently watch and listen to music videos might seem to de-intensify them, in comparison both to blockbuster, large-screen cinema, and to the ways that certain videos used to be orchestrated as big media events (like Michael Jackson's "Thriller" in 1983). But in recent years, both the availability of new digital tools and the need to adopt new media strategies have led music video directors to sharpen and heighten their skills, honing their productions to degrees that are never matched in feature-length movies and television series. As I write this chapter, The Weeknd has had to pull one of his videos from being shown in IMAX theaters, due to worries that its "intense strobe lighting" might be triggering for epileptics (Bloom 2021). In contemporary music videos, editing, camera movement, and close-ups all happen on a severely compressed micro-level. As Eshun already said two decades ago, a music video works as "a five-minute hypersyncopated landscape in which everything has rhythmelodic properties," from the "camera angles" to "the limbs, the faces, the gestures, the expressions" (Eshun 2000, 123). One of the aims of this book—and the reason it pays such close, descriptive attention to the second-by-second formal movements of particular videos—is to untangle these new sensory synergies, these changing McLuhanesque ratios of the senses.

My choice of precisely which music videos to discuss at length in the following chapters should be understood as *exemplary*, rather than representative. That is to say, I do not claim to give a comprehensive survey of music video production today as a whole, or to catalog all the important recent trends. Also, I do not discuss fan-made or noncommercial work; I do not look at music videos outside the sphere of the Anglo-American music industry; and I do not discuss the ways that online sites like Twitch and Instagram have recently come to influence video production. The music videos that I discuss here are simply ones that spoke to me in a powerful way, and appealed to my aesthetic sensibility. In all the chapters of this book, I work to analyze the videos in question as closely and carefully as possible. I pay attention to their formal strategies, as well as to the pop culture allusions that they include. I also consider the role the videos play in the overall multimedia construction of the musician's persona. But in addition to such close analysis, I also look for affinities and continuities among the different videos; and I consider ways in which these works are pushing against the limits, or enlarging the affordances, of music video as a medium. Music videos are second only to pornography in their rush to employ the most cutting-edge technologies. And music videos often register, with particular acuteness, the powers and tendencies of digital audiovisual production more generally. Music videos often stand at the most intensive intersections of an overdetermined multiplicity of social, cultural, and technological forces.

When I say that the videos I discuss are exemplary, I am also thinking of Immanuel Kant's aesthetics. Kant says that great works of art are always original; they cannot be imitations of previous works. They are not made by following any preexisting rules; and yet they are sufficiently orderly and nonrandom that they seem to be made according to rules of their own invention. In this way these works seem like powerful examples; but that *of which* they are the examples does not exist anywhere apart from them or prior to them. This means that such works are also exemplary in the sense that they invite us to imitate them in turn. But the only way to create something genuinely powerful and expressive, Kant says, is not to imitate previous great works, but rather to *emulate* the ways in which they reject previous rules and models, and create new procedures of their own (Kant 2000, 193 and passim).

As commercial products of what Horkheimer and Adorno call the culture industry (Horkheimer and Adorno 2002, 94–136), music videos might not seem to be appropriate objects for this sort of high-minded approach. Music videos are fully ensconced within the realm of mass culture, as it is produced and promoted by large media corporations. They are also rarely self-contained; they most often allude to, parody, and render homage to a plethora of previous works—including other videos, movies, television shows, commercials, internet memes, and fashion trends. As I have insisted before, music video is unavoidably an impure and highly compromised medium (Shaviro 2017a, 7). Still, just as McKenzie Wark argues for the value of *low theory* as opposed to academic high theory (Wark 2021; Webb 2011), so I argue for the low culture of music videos presented on YouTube and commented upon by fans and haters, as opposed to the high culture of video installations in art galleries and museums. As Wark explains,

> High Theory is the grand tradition of philosophy, claiming to legislate for other domains of thought and practice, whereas low theory is the organic concept-forming practices of everyday life, which might borrow from High Theory but really doesn't care about its desires … It is about inventing new practices of knowledge, hopefully more interesting ones.
>
> (Wark 2012)

My claim in this book is that commercial music videos are engaged in inventing new practices of expression, more broadly and exuberantly than conceptualist high-art works are able to do. My invocation of Kant's Romantic aesthetics is unlikely to please either high-minded theorists of modernism and after, or popular-culture scholars and critics. Nevertheless, I think that my invocation of Kant here is relevant and justified, given the ways that—in the words of Lev Manovich—"the genre of music video has been a laboratory for exploring numerous new possibilities of manipulating photographic images made possible by computers" (Manovich 2001, 261; see also a similar passage quoted by Eshun 2000, 116). Formal experimentation and formal innovation, even or especially in the context of a race to rack up the maximum number of views on YouTube, can lead to new, technologized versions of the beautiful and the sublime.

In any case, I am not trying to create a canon of music video masterworks, or to assert that the videos I discuss in this volume are necessarily superior to others that I could equally well have chosen. I only maintain that, more than two decades on from Eshun's and Manovich's observations, music videos have continued to push forward their explorations of the affordances for audiovisual expression that are opened up by new digital technologies. This is as much a process of aesthetic invention as it is one of commercial calculation. Stanley Cavell, writing about film, points out that the affordances of a new technology are not intrinsically inscribed in the technology. They cannot be known in advance. They need to be both discovered and invented—here, these words are closer to being synonyms than alternatives—in the experimental process of creation. "The aesthetic possibilities of a medium are not givens . . . Only the art itself can discover its possibilities, and the discovery of a new possibility is the discovery of a new medium" (Cavell 1979, 32). All the music videos I discuss here are engaged in such a process. They all move beyond prior accomplishments, in order to explore new and "extreme possibilities" (to use the phrase made famous by David Duchovny's character Fox Mulder in *The X-Files*).

Scholarship on music videos has only recently caught up with many of the genre's developments. Since the videos themselves are characterized by such rich hybridity, the criticism and scholarship on them has also been scattered among different fields: music and sound studies, film and new media studies, popular culture studies, and so on. This can easily lead to confusion and contradiction. My own background is in film studies; when I have presented my work on music videos at popular music conferences (most notably the Pop Conference, which used to be located in Seattle, but which now takes place, post-Covid, in New York City), I am almost oppressively aware of the contrast between my own cinematically based work, and that of music scholars who probe musical form in ways that I could never manage. This divergence goes back to the very beginning of academic discussion of music videos. Back in the last century, the first Anglo-American book-length study of music videos, *Rocking around the Clock*, was written by the film scholar E. Ann Kaplan (Kaplan 1987). The second, *Dancing in the Distraction Factory*, was written by the pop music scholar Andrew Goodwin (Goodwin 1992). Kaplan writes about music videos from the perspective of feminist film theory, as well as in terms of the then-popular discourse of postmodernism. Goodwin, in contrast, describes his own approach as "rooted in the sociology of popular music, and in musicology itself"; he writes that he "view[s] music television very much from *within* the field of pop consumption" (Goodwin 1992, xviii).

These different starting points lead to strikingly different readings of the same videos. Kaplan sees Madonna's "Material Girl" video (Madonna 1985) as a disruptive, postmodern feminist work in which "the usual hierarchical arrangement of discourses in the classical realist text is totally violated" and deconstructed (Kaplan 1987, 125). Goodwin rather argues that the video works to construct Madonna's "star identity"; in order to accomplish this, the video is in fact "a highly conventional narrative that moves through an initial lack, via action, to (romantic) resolution" (Goodwin 1992, 99–100). More generally, Goodwin says that Kaplan and other film-studies-based scholars fall short because of the "*visual bias* of [their] theories," which "necessarily neglect the analysis of sound" (Goodwin 1992, 20). They "have tried to analyze music television in iconographic, semiotic, and narrative terms, while paying insufficient attention to the sound track ... Strangely enough, very few analysts have thought to consider that music television might resemble music" (Goodwin 1992, 3).

Though my own work is based in film theory, and especially in Gilles Deleuze's two *Cinema* volumes (Deleuze 1986, 1989), I have tried to keep Goodwin's warnings in mind as much as possible. I have drawn upon the often undervalued—but insightful and crucially important—strain of film scholarship that focuses on cinematic sound. And I have endeavored, to the extent that I am capable of it, to engage with academic musical scholarship, as well as musical journalism, as closely as I do with film studies and film-philosophy. Above all, I have attempted to compensate for my unavoidable cinematic bias by attending, as carefully as I can, to the sonic and musical aspects of all the works that I discuss. Of course, it is up to the reader to decide how well I have succeeded in this.

In any case, I am fortunate that academic scholarship with regard to music videos, much of it from a music-based perspective, has expanded and flourished in recent years. Carol Vernallis has led the way with two rich volumes (Vernallis 2004, 2013), and a third one forthcoming (Vernallis 2022b). Mathias Bonde Korsgaard has also published important work on the recent, post-televisual mutations of music video (Korsgaard 2017). There have been a number of rich anthologies as well, containing essays by a wide variety of authors (Arnold et al. 2017; Burns and Hawkins 2019; Vernalllis et al. 2019). I have learned from all of these sources, even when I do not cite them directly in what follows.

All the music videos that I discuss in this book start out from familiar positions in contemporary Anglo-American popular culture. But the directions in which these videos then move, and the aesthetic, emotional, and political perspectives that they propose, are singular inventions. I discuss videos by musical artists who have had massive popular success (The Weeknd), ones who have gained considerable critical respect but less sales (Massive Attack, FKA twigs, Moses Sumney), ones who have established something of a niche following (Dawn Richard, Bonobo), and ones who are just at the start of their careers (Tierra Whack, Tkay Maidza). In all cases, though, these artists' music videos (sometimes self-directed, but more often made in collaboration with other directors) add new dimensions to the music, expanding its effects, rather than just illustrating it.

Deleuze's two regimes of audiovisual expression

In order to think about the rhythms of music videos, and the relations between sounds and images that they explore, I draw inspiration from Gilles Deleuze's account of cinema in his volumes *Cinema 1: The Movement-Image* (Deleuze 1986) and *Cinema 2: The Time-Image* (Deleuze 1989). Deleuze discusses the ways that time and duration are produced and expressed in the movies, and how this results in the creation of audiovisual worlds. Deleuze distinguishes between the *movement-image*, in which time is expressed through movement and action, and the *time-image*, in which time is freed from movement and subsists "in its pure state" (Deleuze 1989, 17).

Deleuze's two "images" of cinema are both ideal conceptual types. But they also correspond to roughly historical distinctions. The movement-image is characteristic of classical silent and sound cinema, whereas the time-image is grounded in the modernist cinema that emerged after the Second World War (Italian neorealism in the late 1940s, the French New Wave in the late 1950s and early 1960s, the New Hollywood in the early 1970s). Deleuze wrote and published his *Cinema* volumes in the 1980s; so he barely touches on the digital technologies that were only starting to be developed in that decade, and that have radically transformed audiovisual media—in ways he could not foresee—in the years since his death in 1995.

Deleuze says that his overall aim, in the two *Cinema* volumes, is "to isolate certain cinematographic concepts" (Deleuze 1986, ix). Though these concepts seem to reside in images, they have to do, most fundamentally, with *duration*. Even an entirely motionless image in a movie lasts for a particular amount of time; this is part of what differentiates cinema from still photography. I can look at a photographic image for as short or as long a time as I wish; the photograph itself has no intrinsic duration. But as Justin Remes argues, though movies can do entirely without motion, they cannot exist without time (Remes 2015, passim). Maurizio Lazzarato similarly maintains that audiovisual technologies do not unfold *within* the passage of time, so much as they "accumulate and produce duration and time" in the first place (Lazzarato 2019, 73).

Deleuze's typology of cinema—despite his wildly and beautifully poetic language—is actually far more systematic, and even schematic, than it might appear to be at first glance. In the two *Cinema* volumes, he carefully delineates a series of systematic contrasts between the classical movement-image and the modernist time-image. Classical cinema, like classical philosophy, subordinates time to movement, and imagines time only in the linear, serial form that Deleuze elsewhere calls *Chronos* (Deleuze 1990, 77). It is Aristotle who first argues that time can only be conceived as the measure of movement: "when the state of our minds does not change at all, or we have not noticed its changing, we do not think that time has elapsed" (Aristotle 1995, 1:371). The idea that time cannot be experienced, or even noticed, independently of change or movement persists in Western thought for two thousand years thereafter. The corresponding priority of movement in classical cinema is reflected both in the characters' moment-to-moment behavior, and in their progression through the narrative as a whole. Relations in time and space are established through montage, continuity editing, rational (motivated) cuts, and the actors' presentation of character types by means of easily legible bodily motions and facial expressions. Classical cinema unfolds in a Euclidean space, Deleuze says, and its forms mimic the operations of sensory-motor circuits in the brain (Deleuze 1986, 155–9).

All this changes in modernist or postclassical cinema. Or more accurately, while the structures and techniques of the classical movement-image are never abandoned by filmmakers, they are joined, and sometimes replaced, by procedures of a radically different sort. We will never be entirely done with the movement-image, because our sensory-motor circuits remain essential to all mental functioning. But other patterns may arise as well. Yasujiro Ozu's movies are punctuated by *pillow shots*: "seemingly random shots, held for several seconds, of everyday life: of seas and mountains, boats and train tracks, public buildings and private rooms," that have no narrative function of their own, but are interpolated between scenes showing characters and action (Singer 2016). Italian Neorealism leads us to moments when the protagonist is unable to respond to the situation that he or she encounters. In Roberto Rossellini's films with Ingrid Bergman, such as *Europa 51* (1952) and *Journey to Italy* (1954), Bergman's character "discovers something unbearable, beyond the limit of what she can personally bear" (Deleuze 1989, 2). Her paralysis interrupts the time of movement and action, so that we are given over to "time in its pure state," or what Deleuze elsewhere calls *Aion* (Deleuze 1990, 162–8). Italian Neorealism thereby gives us "a cinema of the seer and no longer of the agent" (Deleuze 1989, 2).

This breaking forth of unbearable images also defines the political sensibility of time-image cinema. In *Europa 51*, Bergman's character witnesses the sufferings of the poor in slums, jails, factories, and other such spaces of confinement. This experience transforms her, so that she is no longer capable of worldly action. As a witness, she is compelled to "pass through every state of an internal vision, affliction, compassion, love, happiness, acceptance, extending to the psychiatric hospital where she is locked up" (Deleuze 1989, 2). Her breakdown, culminating in this imprisonment, is also a way of freeing herself from her social role as a wealthy housewife, and more generally from the entire bourgeois-patriarchal order. Rossellini forces us to contemplate both sides of this paradox. The cinema of the time-image gives us harsh visions of social oppression. But its exaltation of time unhinged, or "time in its pure state," is the liberating underside of this oppression (Deleuze 1989, 17).

In Pier Paolo Pasolini's *Teorema* (1968), made some fifteen years after Rossellini's film, the arrival of Terence Stamp's mysterious Visitor similarly awakens all the members of a bourgeois household (father, mother, son, daughter, and servant) from the torpor of their self-imposed confinement. But they are all abandoned to the extremities of existential despair when the Visitor just as mysteriously withdraws. The ruptures of the time-image adumbrate an image of freedom, even though we are then returned to the social reality of capitalist exploitation. While one might describe both *Europa 51* and *Teorema* as movies that negate the principles of post-War capitalist society, it is more accurate (as well as more Deleuzian) to say that they both illuminate a liberating potentiality, indeed a *positivity*, that is implicit within the otherwise oppressive reigning social order. Both movies offer us moments of illumination, against the background of continuing subordination. These moments stand out from the background that immediately re-absorbs them; I am thinking here of Deleuze's lovely description of how lightning "distinguishes itself from the black sky but must also trail it behind, as though it were distinguishing itself from that which does not distinguish itself from it" (Deleuze 1994, 28).

When time thus emerges in its own right, the sensory-motor circuits that underlie action cinema are interrupted, and break down. Instead, we are exposed (along with the characters in the movie) to "pure optical and sound situations" (Deleuze 1989, 9) that cannot be resolved through action. Narrative and character development are suspended. They become open and indeterminate, in the expanded perspective of deep time. In Orson Welles's films, a new articulation of time breaks out from the old, familiar one. Some sequences in

Citizen Kane (1941) still give us the classical passage of time through montage, as in the breakfast-table sequence with Kane and his first wife, which tells us the entire sad story of their marriage and ever-increasing estrangement. But other sequences in *Citizen Kane* convey duration directly, through long takes in deep focus, usually combined with unusual camera placement. Consider the scene in which Kane is reproached by Leland after losing the election, with the camera located almost at floor level. Or even better, consider the scene of Susan's attempted suicide, with the empty glass and medicine bottle right in front of the camera, and the door to the room, through which Kane enters, all the way in the back, in forced perspective. Throughout *Citizen Kane*, Deleuze says, "the images in depth express regions of past as such, each with its own accents or potentials" (Deleuze 1989, 106).

Where continuity editing was a mainstay of the movement-image, it gets disrupted in the cinema of the time-image. Instead of smooth editing that confines action within a homogeneous space, we get irrational cuts, resulting in "false continuity" and "aberrant movement." The jump cuts and deliberate continuity violations in Godard's *Breathless* (1960) are one good example of this (Deleuze 1989, 9). Camera movements also become autonomous and nonfunctional. Think of that moment in Antonioni's *Red Desert* (1964), evoked by Pasolini, in which the camera drifts away from the action, indulging instead in "an insane pan from the bottom up along an electric blue stripe on the whitewashed wall of the warehouse." Antonioni thus "allow[s] himself the greatest poetic freedom, a freedom which approaches—and for this it is intoxicating—the arbitrary" (Pasolini 2005, 178). The movie thus transforms the boredom and neurotic alienation of its protagonist into an unmotivated experience of pure duration.

Deleuze, following Bergson, privileges time over space. But in the time-image, just as time is emptied of action in order to emerge "in its pure state," so space becomes indeterminate as well. Think of the "emptied spaces" in the famous final minutes of Antonioni's *L'Eclisse* (1962), where we see a sequence of shots from the location of the lovers' planned rendezvous, even though neither of them ever shows up. This series of empty spaces, Deleuze says, "might be seen as having absorbed characters and actions, retaining only a geophysical description, an abstract inventory of them" (Deleuze 1989, 5). More generally, in films of the time-image, Euclidean space gives way to Riemanian space, "when the connecting of parts is not predetermined but can take place in many ways: it is a space which is disconnected, purely optical, sound or even tactile." For instance, space becomes tactile or haptic, constructed through gesture rather than given to us as a whole, in the scene in Bresson's *Pickpocket* (1959) where the camera follows the movements of stolen watches and wallets as the pickpockets transfer them from hand to hand (Deleuze 1989, 129).

In Deleuze's schema, the emergence of the time-image in modernist cinema is correlated with the liberation of time from movement in modern Western philosophy. This liberation is first accomplished by Kant, and then pushed further by Bergson. Kant defines time as "the form of inner sense" (Kant 1998, 163 and passim). This means that time can no longer be understood as the measure of motion, as it was for Aristotle, nor even as an indifferent, external container for events, as it was for Newton. Instead, time "increasingly appears for itself" in the form of duration (Deleuze 1989, xi). This is why we say that rhythms *produce* time, rather than merely taking place *in* time. Kant is the first to associate time with interiority; Bergson radicalizes this, by demonstrating, in Deleuze's words, that "time is not internal to us," so much as "we are internal to time" (Deleuze 1989, 82).

Deleuze's philosophy as a whole—and not only in the two *Cinema* volumes—is largely focused upon time and duration. Being is not substantive for Deleuze, but consists in processes of becoming. Nothing in the world is given all at once; everything is in process. Things continually change. This does not mean that there is no stability or identity. Rather, stability and identity must themselves be produced, and reproduced, through ongoing processes. For Deleuze, as for Whitehead according to Isabelle Stengers, the *endurance* of an entity through time "is an accomplishment and an achievement," and should not be taken for granted (Stengers 2011, 156). In particular, living entities can only maintain themselves by means of unceasing far-from-equilibrium flows and dissipations of energy. When these flows cease, the entity dies. It is only by continually renewing itself that an entity can persist in being—what Spinoza calls *conatus* (Deleuze 1988c, 21 and passim). "Continuity and heterogeneity" are therefore necessarily intertwined, as "the two fundamental characteristics of duration" (Deleuze 1988a, 37).

One shortcoming of Deleuze's theorization of cinema is that he privileges the ocularcentric term *image*, and thereby underplays the degree to which film is also "a sound art," as Michel Chion rightly insists (Chion 2009). This is all the more perplexing when we consider how intimately sound requires duration. You can make a still of an image, but you cannot make a still of a sound. Deleuze does not ignore cinema sound entirely; he attends to it in many discussions of particular directors and films. But even when he does so, Deleuze still refers to sonic matter, on the model of visual matter, as a kind of *image*. It would be better and more accurate to speak, not of different types of images, but rather of different *regimes of audiovisual expression*.

In any case, Deleuze argues that the emergence of "time in its pure state" also gives rise to what he calls the "autonomous sound-image" (Deleuze 1989, 262). Just as time is liberated from movement, so sound is freed from its subordination to naturalistic speech acts. Deleuze unfortunately says very little about musical soundtracks and other non-diegetic uses of sound. But he does insist that, when time is disengaged from narrative in order to stand out in and by itself, so "the sound must itself become image instead of being a component of the visual image" (Deleuze 1989, 278). In classical cinema, as Michel Chion describes it, the soundtrack is supplemental, giving *added value* to the images while making it seem as if the images contained this value by themselves (Chion 1994, 5). But in the regime of the time-image, the soundtrack separates itself from the image track. In the 1970s films of Marguerite Duras, for instance, we are given "two 'heautonomous' images, one visual and one sound, with a fault, an interstice, an irrational cut between them" (Deleuze 1989, 251ff). Deleuze takes the idea of *heautonomy* from Kant's *Critique of Judgment* (Kant 2000, 28), where it refers to components that are not entirely autonomous from one another, but also not systematically determined by one another. As David Rodowick explains the term, "image and sound are distinct and incommensurable yet complementary" (Rodowick 1997, 145). The principle of the "irrational cut" applies not just to the heterogeneous visual assemblages of modernist cinema, but equally to the ways that this cinema creates a "complex link between the two heterogeneous, non-corresponding disparate [realms of vision and sound]: this new intertwining, a specific relinkage" (Deleuze 1989, 253).

Toward a Third, Digital Regime of Audiovisual Expression

Deleuze does not say much about the rise of digital media. This is not only because he was writing before digital technologies became anywhere near as ubiquitous as they are today. More crucially, digitization *per se* is barely thinkable for Deleuze. Duration, or pure time, is a continuum, which is to say that it is analog. It "cannot be divided without changing in nature at each division" (Deleuze and Guattari 1987, 483). To digitize a continuum, sampling it at regular intervals in order to extract discrete bits or pixels, is therefore to destroy it. For Deleuze, as for Bergson, the *spatialization of time*—its reduction to homogeneous quantity—is the original sin of Western science and technology. As far as Deleuze is concerned, therefore, we cannot get beyond the time-image, which already frees time to its maximal extent. This is why Alexander Galloway presents Deleuze as "a philosopher of the analog paradigm alone … the analogical philosopher par excellence" (Galloway 2014a, 104).

Nonetheless, it seems increasingly obvious that we cannot understand audiovisual media today without taking digitization into account. Digital tools can readily replicate older analog forms; it has never been easier and cheaper to make either a movement-image film or a time-image film. But these new tools also provide us with new affordances, which allow new media techniques and forms to be invented. We are misled when we think of new technologies as mere extensions of older ones. Marshall McLuhan reminds us that the automobile was originally called the "horseless carriage," and that radio was originally called the "wireless" (telegraph or telephone). But both of these inventions quickly pushed into quite different dimensions than those of the older media that they replaced (McLuhan 1964, 292). The same is true for more recent media forms. When MTV first broadcast music videos on cable television in 1981, one of their advertising taglines was that the service combined "the best of TV with the best of radio" (Speedster 2020). Today, of course, it is evident that music videos are no more a form of radio, or even of broadcast television, than automobiles are a form of the horse and buggy.

Given these developments, a number of theorists have attempted to extend Deleuze's typology of cinema by extrapolating a third type of image—or a third audiovisual regime—beyond the two that he himself describes. Patricia Pisters proposes the *neuro-image* (Pisters 2012); Sergi Sánchez proposes the *no-time-image* (Sánchez 2013); Nick Davis proposes the *desiring-image* (Davis 2013); Cesare Casarino proposes the *life-image* (Casarino 2011); Alexander Galloway proposes the *space-image* (Galloway 2014a, 65; Galloway and Salemy 2013); Elie During proposes the *volume-image* (During 2010); and Steen Ledet Christiansen proposes the *morph-image* (Christiansen 2019). Though I am indebted to all of these formulations, I will adopt none of them, but instead add to the list by proposing what I call the *rhythm image*.

Despite his anti-digital bias, Deleuze does in fact start to consider the radical changes wrought by digitalization in some of his last writings, and especially in his essay "Postscript on Control Societies" (written and published in French in 1990, and translated into English in Deleuze 1995, 177–82). Galloway goes so far as to suggest that this essay might well be "Deleuze's most lasting legacy." For it proposes "a new image of society and the self that can not simply be reduced to Deleuze's previous tropes like the body without organs, the rhizome, or even the virtual" (Galloway 2014a, 96 and 108). Rather, through an engagement with the work of Michel Foucault—following on from his previous book on Foucault (Deleuze 1988b)—Deleuze begins to speculate, in strikingly new ways, on an emerging third regime both of social organization and of aesthetics.

In much of his work, Foucault traces the transformation of modern Europe from a sovereign society to a disciplinary society. The sovereign society is ruled by a king or despot, and it is largely grounded in prohibitions and public spectacles of power. The disciplinary society is ostensibly democratic, and it is ruled by bureaucratic regulations concerning every aspect of private life. The sovereign society tells you what you *must not* do, and it punishes you spectacularly for violating these prohibitions. The disciplinary society is more concerned with what you *must* do, and it pushes you in all sorts of subtle ways to get you to do it. In Deleuze's words, sovereignty is about "condemning to death," whereas discipline is about "ordering life" (Deleuze 1995, 177). Foucault illustrates this contrast by opening his book *Discipline and Punish* with two descriptions of the treatment of criminals. One is a spectacle: the public torture and execution of a prisoner in 1757. The other is a set of regulations: the minute-by-minute organization of the lives of prisoners, kept away from the public eye, just eighty years later (Foucault 1977, 3–7). Foucault is concerned with the social transformations that led from the former sort of practice to the latter. He shows how the disciplinary society that emerges in the nineteenth century is organized around institutions of confinement—not only prisons, but also factories, schools, military barracks, hospitals, insane asylums, and so on—within which bodies are constrained, and behavior is regimented, on a micro-level.

Deleuze regards the shift from sovereignty to discipline in Foucault's account of European society as congruent with the shift, in his own account of cinema, from the movement-image to the time-image. The emergence of time in itself, first envisioned by Kant, accompanies the disciplinary society's invention of the rigidly determined scheduling of behavior, played out in spaces of confinement, along with its massive expansion of surveillance as figured in the model of the Panopticon (Foucault 1977, 200ff). Deleuze underlines this parallelism, in his "Postscript on Control Societies," by once again citing the nervous breakdown of Ingrid Bergman's character in *Europa 51* at the sight of her husband's factory, which she sees as a place of confinement not much different from a prison

(Deleuze 1995, 177). The disciplinary confinement of populations—their paralysis in space—coincides with the emergence of "pure optical and sound situations" that solicit contemplation, but exceed our powers of action (Deleuze 1989, 9 and passim).

Deleuze extends Foucault's schema, however, by discerning the beginnings of a new, third social formation: the *control society*. In the late twentieth century, Deleuze says in his "Postscript," the "sites of confinement" central to the disciplinary society begin to break down. For instance, mental patients are released from hospitals, and consigned instead to "community psychiatry, day hospitals, and home care" (Delueze 1995, 178). Similarly, workers are no longer assured factory jobs for a lifetime; instead, they are compelled to demonstrate "flexibility" by continually "re-inventing" themselves, in order to get precarious short-term positions. Such changes seem to promise release from confinement, and new degrees of autonomy and self-realization, as neoliberal propagandists incessantly proclaim (Boltanski and Chiapello 2018, passim). But Deleuze argues that these seeming "new freedoms" actually involve new "mechanisms of control as rigorous as the harshest confinement" (Deleuze 1995, 178).

Deleuze schematizes the differences between these two sorts of social regimes. The long-term confinement of the disciplinary society gives way to the continual variations and short-term placements of the control society. Where the logic of the disciplinary society is "analogical," that of the control society is "digital." Where the disciplinary society seeks to concentrate and centralize everything by establishing strong vertical hierarchies, the control society is networked, horizontal, and "dispersive." Where the disciplinary society addresses both specific individuals and large populations, the control society breaks people down into "dividuals," tranches of data that can be aggregated in multiple ways. Where capitalism in the Fordist disciplinary society is "directed towards production," capitalism in the control society is "directed toward metaproduction … What it seeks to sell is services, and what it seeks to buy, activities. It's a capitalism no longer directed toward production but toward products, that is, toward sales or markets" (Deleuze 1995, 181). As Deleuze sums it up in one of his densest formulations,

> confinements are *molds*, different moldings, while controls are a *modulation*, like a self-transmuting molding continually changing from one moment to the next, or like a sieve whose mesh varies from one point to another …. Control is short-term and rapidly shifting, but at the same time continuous and

unbounded, whereas discipline was long-term, infinite, and discontinuous. A man is no longer a man confined but a man in debt.

(Deleuze 1995, 178–9)

Although Deleuze dwells mostly on the horrors of the new control society, he also hopes that at least it "will not prove worse than its two previous forms" (Deleuze 1988b, 132). His point is that, when these social regimes change, it is not really a question of better or worse; rather, "there's a conflict in each between the ways they free and enslave us" (Deleuze 1995, 178). Every form of oppression also generates its own corresponding potentialities, or "lines of flight" (Deleuze and Guattari 1987, 222ff and passim). The time-image is both a symptom of the disciplinary society, and a possible way out from that society. The question Deleuze leaves us with, but does not answer, is this: What sort of media form, or audiovisual regime, might stand in a similar relation to the digital formations of the control society as the time-image does to the institutions of the disciplinary society?

New Audiovisual Media

A number of media theorists, both pre- and post-Deleuzian, give us clues toward theorizing a new digital audiovisual regime. While the disciplinary society seems to involve the unleashing of deep time—a time that is, in the words that Deleuze likes to quote from *Hamlet*, "out of joint" (Deleuze 1989, 41)—the control society seems to involve the inverse movement, one that is summarized in William Burroughs's call for us to move "out of Time, and into Space" (Burroughs 1987, 252). This inversion is especially worth noting, given that Deleuze takes the very idea of *control* from Burroughs (Deleuze 1995, 178). Many theorists follow Burroughs in seeing new articulations of space as crucial to the globalized capitalism of the late twentieth and early twenty-first centuries. Fredric Jameson observes that, whereas high modernism was obsessed with time, late capitalist or postmodern culture is "increasingly dominated by space and spatial logic" (Jameson 1991, 25). More specifically, Galloway tells us that "the computer is a space-based medium," for which "time is just a variable like any other" (Galloway and Salemy 2013). Lev Manovich similarly notes that computer technology "mak[es] time just one dimension among a number of others"; for Manovich, the aesthetic of the database, will all combinations simultaneously available, replaces that of the narrative extending linearly through time (Manovich 2001, 147). All these thinkers have contributed to a "spatial turn" in critical theory and the humanities over the past half-century (Soja 1989).

David Rodowick gives us another clue to the new audiovisual regime when he notes that "through digital screens our relation is not to an image, but to function or force." Rodowick means this as a pejorative comment. He rejects digital media because, he claims, they annihilate duration, replacing it "with another conception of time … the time of calculation or computer cycles" (Rodowick 2007, 104). But this position ignores the ways that—as Beatrice Fazi puts it—even within computer science itself "the basic algorithmic model of computation has been challenged by new conceptualizations of the computing machine." Fazi argues for "the contingency of computation" as it interacts with "the unpredictability of the environmental input, so as to bring the indeterminacy of the real world into the computational system" (Fazi 2018, 3). But Rodowick only sees one side of the picture; he ignores the full potentiality of the "function or force" that he attributes to digital media and screens. The control society is indeed grounded in the instrumentalized, bureaucratic "management of information" that Rodowick decries (Rodowick 2007, 141). But when image becomes force, something else also happens. Audiovisual media are no longer experienced in terms of identification and recognition—crucial terms in the modernist film theory championed by Rodowick—but rather in terms of pulsations and rhythms.

This leads to an important philosophical distinction. Bergson describes duration as having "the uninterrupted continuity of melody" (Bergson 1946, 173). But today, we would probably do better to think in terms of a different musical metaphor. Contemporary genres of popular music like hip-hop and EDM (electronic dance music) tend to be organized around "rhythmic and timbral intensity" more than around melody and harmony (James 2015, 33). Rhythms are at the center: as they cross one another in syncopation, they express multiple temporalities at once, encompassing both stability and change. The Marxist musicologist Mark Abel traces the steady meter of modern groove music to the Taylorist rhythms of the assembly line; he agrees with both Adorno and Deleuze that such music "uses as its raw material the abstract, alienated time of capitalism rather than an ideal liberated time." But Abel also insists on something that neither Adorno nor Deleuze is able to recognize: "polyrhythm and syncopation … suggest alternative pulses and tempos which nonetheless remain integrated within the metrical framework"; these alternative rhythms open up the possibility of "an emancipated, collective temporality" (Abel 2014, 255–6).

What does this mean for Bergson's and Deleuze's "time in its pure state"? As early as the 1930s, Gaston Bachelard, under the influence of the Brazilian philosopher Lúcio Alberto Pinheiro dos Santos, sought to revise Bergson by defining duration in terms of rhythm rather than melody. For Bachelard, "the concept of rhythm is the fundamental concept of time … to have duration, we must entrust ourselves to rhythms" (Bachelard 2000, 20–1). Deleuze himself does not seem particularly interested in this sort of approach; instead, he privileges "the 'nonpulsed time' of a floating music" that he finds in Pierre Boulez and John Cage (Deleuze and Guattari 1987, 262 and 267). But Steve Goodman notes that rhythmic time, as championed by Bachelard, and as featured in the music released by Goodman's own Hyperdub record label, has the Deleuzian virtue of treating time *intensively*, as a force irreducible to spatial extension: "by emphasizing rhythm over melody, Bachelard is emphasizing intensity over duration, arguing in fact that duration is merely an effect of intensity" (Goodman 2009, 86).

Lev Manovich, one of the first theorists to seriously consider the unique traits of digital media, offers us yet another clue to the new audiovisual regime. Manovich describes how the modernist logic of disjunction is replaced, in digital art, by a new "aesthetics of continuity" (Manovich 2001, 135–6). In the formal terms of audiovisual media, this means that the classical cinematic practice of montage (featured in different ways in both the movement-image and the time-image) gives way to the digital technology of compositing:

> Montage aims to create visual, stylistic, semantic, and emotional dissonance between different elements. In contrast, compositing aims to blend them into a seamless whole, a single gestalt … In digital compositing, the elements are not juxtaposed but blended, with their boundaries erased rather than foregrounded.
>
> (Manovich 2001, 136 and 145)

Other theorists have made similar observations about digital technology. Galloway argues that the new digital media present us with "*a multiplicity of vision*," with images "all captured simultaneously, each from its own vantage point" (Galloway 2014a, 66). In philosophical terms, this is not far from Leibniz's *Monadology*, according to which

> The same town, when looked at from different places, appears quite different and is, as it were, multiplied in perspectives. In the same way it happens that, because of the infinite multitude of simple substances, there are just as many different universes, which are nevertheless merely perspectives of a single universe according to the different points of view of each monad.
>
> (Strickland 2014, 25)

Elsewhere, Galloway notes how a computer's "GUI creates spatial continuity through the simultaneous windowing of different spaces .... Fusing cuts within the frame replaces fusing cuts in time" (Galloway 2014b). Elie During, for his part, writes about "the co-existence of images" in digital broadcast media: the most disparate scenes, drawn from the most various times and spaces, are all able to be present on the screen at once (During 2010, passim). These sorts of formulations cannot be found in Deleuze; but they are congruent with his overall claim that the spacetimes of control are "short-term and rapidly shifting," but also "continuous and unbounded." This stands in contrast to the "long-term" but "discontinuous" spacetimes of confinement in the disciplinary society (Deleuze 1995, 181).

All these effects—simultaneity, multiplicity, combinatorial logics, and so on—point up the fact that machines do not see, hear, and feel the world in the same ways that human beings do. Digital computation has its own aesthetic and its own phenomenology, both of which are quite different from ours. One might object to this statement on the grounds that, at least as far as we know, computers are not yet sentient, and therefore do not have an aesthetic or a phenomenology at all. But I think that my extravagance here is justified, because it points up just how *alien* computers are to the anthropocentric modes of perception, thought, and experience that we take for granted.

One reason why computational experience is different from, and incommensurable with, ordinary human experience is that computational media are *procedural* and *generative*. They produce output by running algorithms repeatedly and recursively, with the results each time feeding into the next iteration. Ian Bogost defines *procedurality* as "the computer's special efficiency for formalizing the configuration and behavior of various representative elements" (Bogost 2006, 13). The human mind does not operate in this way. According to Bergson and Deleuze, human perception, or so-called natural perception, is *subtractive*: it "subtracts from the thing whatever does not interest it," creating a simplified and manageable picture (Deleuze 1986, 63). André Bazin praises the analog (chemically based) cameras of his own time because when they are used "an image of the outside world takes shape automatically, without creative human intervention, following a strict determinism" (Bazin 2009, 7). But this is still ultimately a subtractive process; even without human selection coming into play, the camera's images give us less than the world itself does.

In contrast, computation is ultimately additive. Digital image capture starts out with a reduction, albeit in a different manner from human perception or analog photography. Digital devices *sample* various aspects of the world, taking instantaneous readings at predefined intervals. But this is only the beginning of the process. Computation subsequently works over its sampled material, through iterative processes of mutation and recombination (and sometimes interpolation as well). In this way, digital processing gives us far more information than we started out with. Computational systems accumulate "big data" in multitudinous arrays with vast numbers of parameters. These extend far beyond the ability of any human being, or group of human beings, to parse. Though claims that "the data deluge makes the scientific method obsolete" (Anderson 2008) are silly and overstated, these arguments do point to the vast difference, both in scale and in kind, between computational and human-phenomenological ways of experiencing and understanding the world.

Computational processes also work according to a vastly different temporality than that of human perception. As Mark B. N. Hansen reminds us, new digital media "operate at microtemporal scales without any necessary—let alone any direct—connection to human sense perception and conscious awareness." And yet these "microtemporal processes … despite evading the grasp of our conscious reflection and sense perception, nonetheless impact our sensory lives in significant ways" (Hansen 2015, 37–8). Digital recording and playback devices are now ubiquitously present in our daily lives, in the form of mobile phones, RFID tags, and environmental sensors. These devices interact with us on a subliminal level. They can sense our subjective responses and decisions in their incipient state, as they are just being formed, and before we ourselves become fully conscious of them. Under the control of large corporations, these media can then "nudge" our responses in ways that are quite insidious—even though certain neoliberal thinkers celebrate them (Thaler and Sunstein 2008). Hansen is fully aware of these dangers, but he also expresses the hope that such "twenty-first-century media" can instead be turned to our benefit, through the "the *feed-forward* of data into consciousness," allowing us to access "*the power of potentiality*" (Hansen 2015, 252 and 260). In our current situation of corporate control, this is a very distant prospect; but it is very much worth cultivating as a Deleuzian line of flight.

Applying these insights about computation to audiovisual media in particular, Shane Denson looks at the ways that "post-cinematic cameras and screens" operate on the basis of "fine-tuned temporal events taking place in intervals fundamentally inaccessible to human perception." The temporality of these media "is no longer tuned to that of their human receivers." This leads to what Denson calls *discorrelation*: "a phenomenological disconnect between viewing subjects and the object-images they view" (Denson 2020, 33). In the rapid, unmotivated edits and jerky camera movements of a Michael Bay action sequence, for instance, we are *affected* by images and sounds without actually being able to track them on a conscious level; they pass by too quickly for full awareness. In the 1980s and 1990s, the use of "fast, nonlinear cuts" and other such devices in feature films and narrative television shows was often disparaged as "MTV-style editing" (Pascual 2021). But such techniques have only become more widespread in the twenty-first century, both in movies and in music videos, thanks to the continuing development of ever-more-powerful digital tools. We should also remember that discorrelation is not just a matter of high velocity. In the *Paranormal Activity* series of horror films, the human attention span is also frustrated by the slow loops and repetitive pans of surveillance cameras, the fixed gaze, complete with timecodes, of webcams, and the nonperceptual abstractions of devices like the Microsoft Kinect system. These movies never let us forget how our world is permeated by audiovisual recording and playback devices (Denson 2020; Shaviro 2017b). All of these technologies—not only depicted within these movies but also used to make them in the first place—display "the affective impact and bypassing of cognitive (as well as narrative) interest through video and computational imaging devices" (Denson 2020, 50).

All these developments effectively lead to the alteration of our sense ratios, as Marshall McLuhan foresaw half a century ago. McLuhan proclaims (even prior to digitization) that electronic media give us "a brand-new world of allatonceness" (McLuhan and Fiore 1967, 63). That is to say, electronic media—even ostensibly image-centric ones—unfold in a space that is no longer predominantly visual, but rather "audile-tactile" (McLuhan and McLuhan 1988, 33 and passim). Allatonceness is apprehended by the ear and by the finger, more than it is by the eye. Sound and touch—each in its own particular manner—are immediate, and intimate, to a far greater extent than vision can be. When sound and touch work together, "space is constituted of resonant intervals, dynamic relationships, and kinetic pressure," all of which are invisible, but directly felt (McLuhan and McLuhan 1988, 35).

Touch requires close proximity, while you have to move a distance away from an object in order to be able to see it clearly. McLuhan tells us that "tactility is the space of the significant bounding line, of pressure, and of the interval." When we explore a surface or a volume through touch, we do not observe these divisions (intervals and boundary lines) and stresses (pressure), so much as we physically feel them. We come as close to Others as possible, but without consuming or assimilating them: "when we touch something, we contact it and create an interaction with it: we don't connect with it, else the hand and the object would become one" (McLuhan and McLuhan 1988, 6).

When Deleuze writes about certain filmmakers (most notably Bresson, as I have already mentioned), and also when he writes about visual art (most notably Cézanne and Francis Bacon), he develops the idea (initially taken from the art historian Alois Riegel) of *haptic space* (Deleuze 2003, 133). As vision becomes extremely close-up, it operates more like touch: "one never sees from a distance in a space of this kind," but only locally, moving from point to point (Deleuze and Guattari 1987, 493). Laura U. Marks, following Deleuze, takes up this notion of *haptic visuality*, and applies it directly to digital audiovisual media (Marks 2000, 2002). Even sight no longer works panoptically, in the manner of what feminist film theorists call the male gaze (Mulvey 1989, 19). Instead, the eyes adapt themselves to a predominantly audile-tactile mode.

This audile-tactile media regime also gives us a new sense of process, becoming, and sensory multiplicity. This is what Steen Christiansen calls *animacy*, and what Deborah Levitt calls the *animatic apparatus*. Audiovisual media today work, as Christiansen puts it, by "articulating our liveliness as a form of mutability," so that "a positive generation of liveliness" extends beyond any traditional notions of the organic, and "disturbs the distinction between animate and inanimate" (Christiansen 2021, 85–7). Levitt similarly notes how "images possess their own forms of vitality" in contemporary audiovisual media (Levitt 2018, 15). Though both Christiansen and Levitt write most explicitly about the visual, their formulations take for granted the reordering of the sensorium that I am evoking here.

I have already noted that Deleuze says less than one might wish about sound in the movies and related media. But the deterritorializing power of sound is evident, since the ear hears from all directions, while the eye is unidirectional. As McLuhan puts it, "we hear from all directions simultaneously; acoustic space has the structure of a sphere in which things create their own space and modify and coerce each other" (McLuhan and McLuhan 1988, 35). Michel Chion similarly insists that hearing is unbounded: while the cinematic image must appear in a frame, "there is no auditory container for sounds" (Chion 1994, 67). This is what allows movies of all sorts to make such varied, extensive, and sometimes disorienting use of both off-screen sound and non-diegetic sound. Chion also notes that, even though light waves are physically faster than sound waves, in the movies sound tends to precede sight. At such close range, we cannot discern the speed difference; but sound predominates because "the ear analyzes, processes, and synthesizes faster than the eye" (Chion 1994, 10). Sound is experientially immediate and "allatonce"; but we should not forget that sound is also not punctual—it can only unfold in a rhythmic duration, however short this may be. Sound also echoes and prolongs itself through vibration; this is why McLuhan says that "resonance is the mode of acoustic space" (McLuhan and McLuhan 1988, 6).

These new arrangements are foreshadowed in the philosophy of Alfred North Whitehead, who is strongly influenced by Bergson, but not as loyal to him as Deleuze tends to be. The logic of multiple and scattered "digital events," pressed into continuity through compositing, is similar to what Whitehead calls *actual occasions*: finite, singular processes, each with its own specific spacetime location. Every occasion has its own particular duration, but there is nothing like a wider "block of duration" that includes them all. Rather, the individual occasions are each discrete and autonomous. They are densely interrelated, however, through what Whitehead calls the *extensive continuum*. This is a web of connections and contrasts. Each occasion offers a range of potentialities to the others, but each also limits how far the others can go. For any given occasion, the other occasions provide a sort of environment that it has to come to terms with in some way. There is no unity imposed from outside or above, but there are all sorts of overlaps, cross-connections, and influences streaming among the occasions (Whitehead 1978, 51–82). In addition to Deleuze's models of linear, narrative time (Chronos) and of the suspended time of events in their purity (Aion), we have a third model of time as a multiplicity of polyrhythmic, cross-resonating vibrations.

The Rhythm Image

Pulling all these clues together, we get the outline of a third audiovisual regime, correlated both with digital technologies and with the control society. This is what I call the *rhythm image*: the subject for a third *Cinema* volume that Deleuze never wrote. The rhythm image cannot be described in terms of Bergsonian duration; but it is also different than the *spatialization of time* denounced by both Bergson and Deleuze. The rhythm image does not subordinate time to motion, as the movement-image does; but it also does not liberate time in its pure state, as the time-image does. Rather, the rhythm image renders time as pulsation and force, and as the play of multiple intensities. This new audiovisual regime is the product of digital machines, but it also has its roots in the powerfully embodied polyrhythms of African and Afrodiasporic music. It is linked to the oppressive mechanisms of the control society, but it also offers us potential lines of flight away from those mechanisms.

I have already mentioned how, in the cinema of the time image, camera movements through three-dimensional deep-focus space also provide us with a kind of passage through time. The time-image unfolds for us, Deleuze says, with "all the circles of the past constituting so many stretched or shrunk *regions*, *strata*, and *sheets*" (Deleuze 1989, 99). Think of the camera movement in *Citizen Kane* (actually two shots, but with a hidden dissolve) where we start outside, passing through a neon sign and a rain-soaked skylight in order to descend upon Susan Alexander Kane inside her club, sitting at a table and drinking alone. When the moving camera penetrates deep space, it also passes through these many layers of time, from the present moment of the news reporter trying to interview Susan, and back through her history of failures and humiliations. This is a kind of exploration unique to the time-image.

Movies and videos of the rhythm image offer us a different, but equally unique, mode of spacetime exploration. At a crucial point in the music video director Joseph Kahn's feature film *Detention* (2011)—a film as crucial for the rhythm image as *Citizen Kane* was for the time image—the teenage protagonists are all seated in a circle in the school library. One of the students recounts how he has been stuck in detention, without aging, every day for the past nineteen years. As he explains this, the camera tracks all the way around the circle of seated students. Each time the camera accomplishes one complete 360-degree rotation, we jump in time to a few years earlier. Different students are seated in the same chairs, mostly in the same postures, but wearing different clothes in different styles, and with different music playing on the soundtrack. In this way, we jump back, at several years' intervals, from 2011 to 1993. Time is explored, not through movement in depth, but rather through a superficial or lateral camera movement, accompanied by textual overlays on the screen, and with a continuous circular motion across abrupt cuts, smoothed out through digital compositing. Different moments of the past coexist, and even share a common space. They all occupy this space in similar ways, but with different surface details each time, as if they had been altered through a series of discrete digital transformations. All these occasions resonate without actually coinciding.

Similar explorations of space and time can be found in many music videos. We see it, for instance, in Marc Klasfeld's 2002 video for Scarface's song "On My Block" (Scarface 2002). The camera circles counter-clockwise around the urban block that Scarface describes as the heart of his neighborhood. As the song proceeds, the camera explores the past by panning through scenes of neighborhood life—pick-up basketball games, police brutality, drug deals, funerals, private homes, and crack dens—along with portraits of Scarface at different ages, from birth to childhood to adolescent sexual experiences to first attempts at rapping, and culminating with his return to the neighborhood as a star. The video goes in a 360-degree circle, ending at the same location as where it began, with a church on the corner, and sneakers slung over a power line. At the start, there is only one pair of sneakers, and the church's billboard reads: "And this too shall come to pass." At the end, there are many pairs of sneakers on the power line, and the billboard reads: "What is in the beginning will be in the end." The movement of the camera, along with the verse-chorus structure of the song, and its repeated piano-riff sample, reconciles linear progression with cyclical repetition, to give a rhythmic account of the lives of the poor Black people who live on the block, where "everything is everything."

This sort of lateral camera movement, in composited long takes—filled with multiple images, and making heavy use of CGI—is common in movies and videos of the rhythm image. Such a movement is used to explore a time that is without depth, but infinite in its extent and in the range of its variations, all of which seem to coexist in a common space. This form of temporality is indeed "short-term and rapidly shifting, but at the same time continuous and unbounded." It makes for a configuration of spacetime that is not a Bersonian-Deleuzian "block of duration," but rather what Rodowick calls "a combination of logically discrete elements completely open and available to changes in value, both perceptual and semantic" (Rodowick 2007, 172).

For yet another example of this configuration, think of Alexander Sokurov's 2002 movie *Russian Ark*, an eighty-six-minute single take in which the camera passes through hundreds of years of Russian history as it traverses the rooms of the Winter Palace in St. Petersburg. Rodowick complains that *Russian Ark* is not really a film about time passing, because it contains "more than 30,000 'digital events,'" which were added through compositing in postproduction (Rodowick 2007, 165). As "a highly composited artifact," Rodowick says that the movie "is not spatially uniform," and "cannot be considered a single long take" (Rodowick 2007, 173). I quote Rodowick here because I think his descriptions are accurate, even though I reject his pejorative judgment of the film. Sokurov's camera movement through time is indeed of a radically different sort than those we find in time-image movies like *Citizen Kane*. In the world of the control society, time is rhythmic rather than melodic; it is not a single, unified duration, but a pluriverse composed of scattered polyrhythmic "digital events" that interact in unpredictable ways.

And finally, for one more example, consider Grant Singer's music video for Lorde's song "Green Light" (Lorde 2017). The song is about a breakup; Lorde expresses both sadness and anger about being dumped by her former boyfriend, but looks for a "green light" that will allow her to move on to something new. The song starts in a melancholy manner, with Lorde's plaintive voice backed only by sparse piano chords. In the course of the song, however, the instrumentation becomes thicker and more percussive, and also more upbeat. Lorde pivots from mournfulness in the verse, and reproach in the refrain, to hopefulness and anticipation in the pre-chorus, and then to an ecstatic release in the chorus. The second time through each of these sections of the song, the cycle is repeated more emphatically, and at a higher energy level (in terms both of Lorde's voice and the instrumentation). The music video is set mostly at night; Singer gives a distinctive look to each section of the song, not only in terms of Lorde's actions, but also in terms of lighting and color, as well as cinematography and editing. We see Lorde staring into the bathroom mirror, dancing in a club, riding in an Uber, dancing on the car's roof, and strutting and dancing down the street (see Figure 1.1).

As the song proceeds, and as Lorde gets more energetic and positive, the editing becomes quicker as well. In the latter parts of the song, shots from all the earlier sections of the video are rapidly and continually intercut with newer shots. This creates a polyrhythmic visual mix, in which the different sections of the song seem to coexist. Lorde's changing moods, and her actions, are somehow simultaneous, as well as successive. In the course of the video, the upbeat shots gradually predominate over the melancholy ones, but this feels more like a

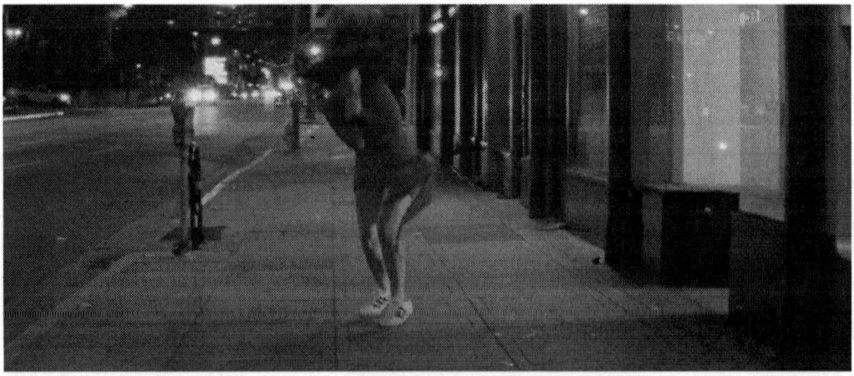

Figure 1.1 Lorde, "Green Light." Dir. Grant Singer, 2017.

statistical redistribution than like a linear progression. The video ends with the sky getting light behind Lorde, as the dark night, lit only in garish neon, gives way to the orange, purple, and pink layers of the horizon from which the Sun is about to rise. Change does happen; Lorde will not be stuck in her misery forever. But this change is not the result of any sort of linear or even dialectical progression. Rather, joy arises through the accumulation of multiple, discontinuous pulses of energy, all resonating at different frequencies and in rapidly shifting intervals.

The structure of the music video, including the ways that its images respond to and interact with the music, can be summarized in the form of a table (see Table 1).

All in all, the song has a four-part structure, with the four-part sequence repeated twice. The first and second parts are emotionally subdued, but the third and especially the fourth parts are more upbeat. The Chorus sounds positively jubilant, even though the lyrics still imply hesitation (Lorde sings that she is still waiting for a green light, not that she has gotten one). The second iteration of the four parts is musically denser, and thereby more emotionally intense, than the first. The video responds to this musical structure in the way that it moves from relatively longer takes to much shorter ones as the song proceeds. There is also a certain thickness or lack of definition to the images, because the video was initially shot on 16-mm film (Hogan 2017). The video exemplifies what I have elsewhere called a *post-continuity* style, appropriate to "the time of microintervals and speed-of-light transformations, that are characteristic of globalized, high-tech financial capital" (Shaviro 2016), but which here endeavors to transfigure this temporality in personalized, affective terms.

Table 1: Breakdown of Lorde, "Green Light" (dir. Grant Singer, 2017).

Time	Section	Music	Lyrics	Scenes	Visuals	Colors
0:00	Verse 1	Sparse piano	I do my makeup …	Close-up on Lorde's face in mirror	Single long take; cut at very end to side view	Bluish background
0:30	Refrain	Piano and percussion	But you're not in love …	Lorde's face as she dances; background blurry	Extreme close-ups, with several jump cuts	Bluish, a few greens, strobing
0:50	Pre-Chorus	Piano and percussion, louder and more upbeat	But I hear sounds …	Lorde exits club, enters car, leans out of car	Longer shot of entering car; close-up in car; close-up of driver; background blur; shot from outside car as Lorde leans out	Naturalistic nighttime lighting; Lorde's red/purple dress
1:18	Chorus	Heavier instrumentation, choral singing	That green light …	Lorde leans out of car, then she dances and lies on top of car	Camera is further away; Lorde's upper torso or whole body; camera circles ecstatically around her or pans down the length; some longer shots showing whole scene, with driver standing at distance from car	Reddish light on Lorde's body; urban night background
1:35	Verse 2	Thicker orchestration	Sometimes I wake up …	Lorde walks down street; back to dancing on car	Close-up of Lorde's face as she walks down street, with blurry background; similar when she is back on top of car	Naturalistic lighting as she walks; back to reddish glow on top of car

(continued)

Table 1 *(continued)*

Time	Section	Music	Lyrics	Scenes	Visuals	Colors
1:48	Refrain	Percussion and synthesizers	But you're not in love …	Lorde dancing down the street; turns around pole, twirls her hair, grabs pay phone	Two medium traveling shots, one from behind Lorde, one from front and side; we see more of her body; background in focus	More naturalistic night-street lighting; Lorde's dress stands out
2:08	Pre-Chorus	Back to piano and percussion	But I hear sounds …	Lorde dancing in street, enters door, bathroom as she looks in mirror and Jack Antonoff plays piano in background	Cuts between longer shots of Lorde dancing on sidewalk and in bathroom	Bathroom has contrasting sickly green and bluish haze
2:35	Chorus	Thickest orchestration, choral singing	That green light …	Lorde dancing and running, highest energy so far	Fast montage of all the scenes seen previously: street, in car, on car, dancing in club, dancing in bathroom	Rapid alternation of all lights we've seen before: blue, reddish, green
3:05	Outro	Repeated thick sound	That green light …	Lorde dancing in multiple venues, also walking over highway bridge; from 3:47, she is motionless on the highway bridge, looking toward the camera	Continued rapid montage, often blurry, moving camera, tracking shot right-to-left over highway bridge; camera moves in on her for a few more seconds after music ends	Continued color alterations; shots over highway show more naturalistic lighting of sunrise in background

Summary

The distinctions among the three audiovisual regimes, or "images," can be summarized in this way:

Movement Image	**Time Image**	**Rhythm Image**
Sovereign society	Disciplinary society	Control society
Fixed social roles	Individuals	Dividuals
Servitude	Confinement	Debt
Time via movement	Time in its pure state	Time as pulsation/force
Sensory-motor circuits	Pure optical-sound situations	Machinic microperception
Euclidean space	Riemannian space	Audile-tactile space
Continuity editing	False continuity	Compositing
Rational cuts	Irrational cuts	Concealed cuts
Normal movement	Aberrant movement	Suspended movement
Time in montage	Durations in deep focus	Occasions in lateral pan
Chronos	Aion	Polyrhythms
Classical cinema	Modernist cinema	Music videos

I take Deleuze's typology, and my extension of it, as a useful heuristic device, rather than as some sort of definitive formulation. It is rare to find a complete example of any one type of image; earlier formations persist in the midst of later ones, and later formations are anticipated in earlier ones. A movie like Tony Scott's *Domino* (2005) includes elements of the movement-image (in its action sequences), of the time-image (in its nonlinear chronology and its isolation of privileged objects and critical moments), and of the rhythm image (in its aggressive, speed-freak editing style, which divides even the simplest actions into clashing and overlapping multiple shots, often distorted in color and angle as well). Moreover, the temporal transitions that Deleuze layers on top of one another—among social formations, philosophical arguments, and cinema formalisms—do not necessarily coincide. For instance, the transition from the sovereign society to the disciplinary society according to Foucault took place before the invention of the cinema, so it cannot literally coincide with the passage from the movement-image to the time-image. Indeed, as Jacques

Rancière observes, Deleuze sometimes uses the very same films and sequences to exemplify both the movement-image and the time-image, so that "the passage from one book to the other would not mark the passage from one age of the cinematographic image to another but the passage to another point of view on the same images" (Rancière 2006, 107–23).

Despite all these reservations, however, I still find Deleuze's classifications both useful and informative. They allow us to draw crucial distinctions (even if these are unstable, and ultimately subject to deconstruction). And most importantly, these three "images," or regimes, allow us to notice and pick out important features of audiovisual works that would be much harder to discern otherwise. In spite of all its shortcuts and ambiguities, Deleuze provides us with a powerfully generative framework for thinking about audiovisual forms and how they have changed over the course of the past century. He provides many valuable suggestions for linking formal and technical devices to larger meanings and feelings. He also provides—albeit reluctantly—a broad sense of how historical changes in film production and reception are related to, and embedded within, larger social, political, and technological developments. If film study tends to be divided between formal analysis and ideology critique, Deleuze moves along a diagonal, offering insights and methods of approach that are reducible to neither of these approaches, but relevant to both of them.

In this book, I try to avoid over-generalizing my claims about the "rhythm image" as a third audiovisual regime in the history of cinema. My approach is by design tentative and experimental. Whatever can be said about twenty-first-century cinema, made with digital tools in general, I try to restrict my focus to characteristics to the particular digital music videos, produced in the context of the largely Anglophone music industry, that I analyze and discuss in depth. I am ultimately more interested in singular expressions and effects than I am in larger trends, even though I remain aware that context always matters. Obviously all the works I discuss in this book are defined to a great extent by the musical and cinematic conventions that they assume, refer to, and (to a large extent) adhere to. But I still seek to search for the points at which these works deviate from such contexts and frameworks, in order to express novel feelings and ideas.

In other words, my concern throughout this book is less to give a specifically Deleuzian account of music video as a genre or form, than to understand how music videos function as particularly dense nodes of expression for a series of transformations in contemporary social and cultural life. These transformations include:

1. aesthetic changes, or changes in the sensorium, having to do with our experience of relations of space and time, of sound and image, and of attention and distraction;
2. social and cultural changes having to do with the ways that things like race, gender, sexuality, and relative affluence or impoverishment are both lived in individual experience, and structured transpersonally in ways that are simultaneously constraining and liberating;
3. technological changes (in such things as screens and devices, data gathering and, digital processing) having to do with new modes of media production and distribution, and with new habits of personal consumption;
4. affective changes having to do with the ways that people (and particularly younger people) negotiate many of the issues that have traditionally been central to pop music (sex and romance, money and fame, questions about personal identity, and so on).

These are all, of course, issues that have been extensively discussed in recent years by philosophers, social scientists, media theorists, and scholars of popular culture. The driving idea behind my book is that we can *also* approach all these issues *intensively* (rather than *extensively*), in terms of the ways that they are compressed and enfolded in singular cultural productions like the videos I discuss. Most broadly, I seek to consider the ways that popular music culture in the Anglophone world today negotiates and explores the spacetime (and especially the temporal structures) of our contemporary world, and how it finds ways to express, within this world, new sorts of feelings, desires, and frustrations.

2

Post-Cinematic Articulations of Sound and Vision (Massive Attack)

The Audiovisual Contract

During the middle third of the twentieth century, sound cinema established what Michel Chion calls "the audiovisual contract": a basic paradigm for the relationship between sounds and moving images. In both classical and modern cinema, sound brings "added value" to the image: "a sound enriches a given image" in such a way that it seems to us as if the added "information or expression" were "already contained in the image itself" (Chion 1994, 5). That is to say, cinema sound is *supplemental*, precisely in Jacques Derrida's sense of this word: "an *addition* [that] comes to *make up for* a deficiency … to compensate for a primordial non-self-presence" (Derrida 1973, 87). We rarely pay attention to film sound in and of itself; we always regard it as secondary to the images of the film. And yet it turns out, again and again, that sound endows those images with a potency, a meaning, and a seeming self-sufficiency, that they never could have established on their own. "Added value," Chion says, "is what gives the (eminently incorrect) impression that sound is unnecessary, that sound merely duplicates a meaning which in reality it brings about" (Chion 1994, 5).

It can be plausibly argued that this was already the case, through a sort of anticipation, even in the era of silent film. As Mary Ann Doane suggests, silent film was understood even in its own time "as incomplete, as lacking speech." The missing voice plays a crucial role in silent film; for, denied any direct expression, it "reemerges in gestures and the contortions of the face—it is spread over the body of the actor" (Doane 1980, 33). In this way, speech already plays a supplemental role in cinema from the very beginning; by its very absence, it underwrites the seeming autonomy of moving visual images. In addition, most silent films were shown with live musical accompaniment. Chion discusses at length the way that soundtrack music and ambient noises *temporalize* the sound film, giving it a sense of forward movement, and of duration (Chion 1994, 13–16). But musical accompaniment already performs this service for silent film. (Indeed, most "silent" films are excruciatingly difficult to watch in actual silence.) We can conclude from all this that the audiovisual contract was already in effect, to a large extent, even in the silent era. When the talkies finally arrived, sound had a place marked out for it. It was already doomed to be supplemental. It immediately functioned—as Deleuze puts it, citing and extending Chion—not as an independent sensorial source, but rather "as a new dimension of the visual image, a new component" (Deleuze 1989, 226).

Mainstream cinema since the talkies has generally synchronized sound to image—as so many film theorists have noted and lamented. Despite the fact that sounds and images are recorded on separate devices, and that many sounds are added in postproduction, the dominant tendency has always been to create the illusion that the image track and the soundtrack coincide naturally: "the voice must be anchored by a given body," and "the body must be anchored in a given space" (Doane 1980, 36). Even non-diegetic soundtrack music is naturalized; for the role of the soundtrack's "unheard melodies" is to blend seamlessly into the visual action, and thereby subliminally instruct us in how to understand and feel the images (Gorbman 1987, passim). This demand for naturalism is the basis for sound's traditionally supplemental role in the movies.

Of course, every dominant practice inspires a counter-practice. The illusionistic synchronization of sound to image has long been opposed by radical filmmakers and film theorists. Already in 1928, when sound was not yet available in Soviet cinema, Eisenstein denounced the "adhesion" of sound to image in Hollywood film, and demanded instead "a contrapuntal use of sound … directed along the line of its distinct non-synchronization with the visual images" (Eisenstein 1949, 258). Eisenstein was never able to put his ideas about sound montage into practice; but, starting in the 1960s, directors like Jean-Luc Godard, Marguerite Duras, and Jean-Marie Straub and Danièle Huillet experimented with separating sound from image, and giving sound its own autonomy as a source of perceptions and of information. They demonstrated the arbitrariness of synchronization, and explored the possibilities of setting sounds and images free from one another, or even directly against one another. As Deleuze puts it, in the films of these directors "talking and sound cease to be components of the visual image; the visual and the sound become two autonomous components of an audio-visual image, or better, two heautonomous images" (Deleuze 1989, 259).

I do not wish to minimize the importance of these dialectical explorations. But we should not exaggerate their novelty either. Fundamentally, the films of Godard, Duras, and Straub/Huillet still belong to the traditional cinematic regime of the time image, in which images are primary, and sound only provides a supplemental added value. Modernist films may well call attention to the arbitrariness of sound-image relations, instead of dissimulating this arbitrariness. But these films do not actually alter the terms of the underlying audiovisual contract. In positing sound as an independent "image," and making the role of sound (as it were) "visible," they point up a certain way that cinema functions—but they do not thereby actually change this mode of functioning.

This is part of the general malaise of modernism. Twentieth-century aesthetics grossly overestimated the efficacy, and the importance, of alienation-effects, self-reflexive deconstruction, and other such demystifying gestures. Aesthetically speaking, there is nothing wrong with these gestures; they are often quite beautiful and powerful. I am second to no one in my admiration for *Two or Three Things I Know about Her* and *India Song*. But we should not deceive ourselves into thinking that these films somehow escape the paradigms whose mechanisms they disclose and reflect upon. They still largely adhere to the audiovisual contract—as Chion explicitly notes in the case of *India Song*, where "the sounds of the film congregate around the image they do not inhabit, like flies on a window pane" (Chion 1994). The audiovisual contract allows both for the seamless combination of sounds and images, and for their more or less violent disjunction. Sound can add value to a visual presentation, Chion says, "either all on its own or by discrepancies between it and the image" (Chion 1994, 158). The sound fulfills its supplemental function either way, energizing the images while remaining secondary to them.

From Film to Video

In the past few decades, however, post-cinematic media have altered the terms of the familiar audiovisual contract. Today, audiovisual forms no longer operate in the same ways that they used to. "In the cinema," Chion says, "everything passes through an image"; but television and video work instead by "short-circuiting the visual" (Chion 1994, 158). The technological transformations from mechanical to electronic modes of reproduction, and from analog to digital media, have accomplished what avant-garde cinematic practices could not: they have altered the balance between images and sounds, and instituted a new economy of the senses. The new media forms have affected what Marshall McLuhan (taking the term from William Blake) calls the "ratio of the senses." For McLuhan, new media always "alter sense ratios or patterns of perception." Indeed, "any invention or technology is an extension or self-amputation of our physical bodies, and such extension also demands new ratios or new equilibriums among the other organs and extensions of the body" (McLuhan 1964, 45). When media change, our sensory experiences also change. Even our bodies are altered—extended or "amputated"—as we activate new potentialities, and let older ones atrophy.

Specifically, McLuhan claims that, as mechanical and industrial technologies give way to electronic ones, we move away from a world defined by "segmentation and fragmentation" (McLuhan 1964, 176), and into "a brand new world of allatonceness" (McLuhan and Fiore 1967, 63). Mechanical technologies, from Gutenberg's printing press to Ford's assembly line, broke down all processes into their smallest components, and arranged these components in a strict linear and sequential order. But electronic technologies invert this tendency, creating patterns and fields in which processes and their elements happen all together.

This transition also entails a reordering of the senses. When we leave mechanical technologies behind, we move away from a world that gives itself to the eye, and that is organized around the laws of Renaissance perspective. We move instead into a world that no longer privileges sight: "an acoustic, horizonless, boundless, olfactory space" in which "purely visual means of apprehending the world are no longer possible" (McLuhan and Fiore 1967, 63). Of course, this doesn't mean that we will stop reading words and looking at images. But however much time we spend today looking at multiple screens, we can no longer privilege the model of a disembodied eye, detached from, and exerting mastery over, all it sees. Electronic media foster "audile-tactile perception," an interactive and intermodal form of sensibility, no longer centered upon the eye (McLuhan 1964, 45). This is one reason why video is significantly different from film, even when we watch movies on our video devices. Walter Benjamin famously wrote that "it is another nature which speaks to the camera as compared to the eye … It is through the camera that we first discover the optical unconscious" (Benjamin 2003, 266). But when cinematic mechanical reproduction is displaced by video-based electronic reproduction, such ocularcentrism is no longer valid. The sound recorder becomes as important as the image recorder (the camera). We discover, not an optical unconscious, but a thoroughly audiovisual one.

Of course, this change is not thoroughgoing or total. For one thing, the transformation of media forms is still in process. For another, new media and new sensorial habits do not usually obliterate older ones, but tend instead to be layered on top of them. For instance, very few people use typewriters any longer; but computer keyboards continue to be modeled after typewriter keyboards. Similarly, lots of people still go to the movies; and lots of newer video and digital moving-image works continue to be modeled after the movies. Traditional movies continue to be made, even as they increasingly rely upon post-cinematic (electronic and digital) technologies for production, distribution, and exhibition. In both contemporary Hollywood films and contemporary art films, sound still often functions as it used to, providing added value for the moving images.

Nevertheless, electronic media today work quite differently from how the movies used to do. Video and television tend to bring sound into greater prominence. Chion goes so far as to suggest that television is basically "illustrated radio," in which "sound, mainly the sound of speech, is always foremost. Never offscreen, sound is always *there*, in its place, and does not need the image to be identified." In these electronic media, the soundtrack takes the initiative, and establishes meaning and continuity. The televisual image, on the other hand, "is nothing more than an *extra image*," providing added value, and supplementing the sound (Chion 1994, 157–8). Images now provide an uncanny surplus, subliminally guiding the ways that we interpret a foregrounded soundtrack. In the passage from cinema to television and video, therefore, audiovisual relations are completely inverted.

Chion also argues that electronic scanning, the technological basis of television and video, changes the nature of visual images themselves. Where cinema "rarely engages with changing speeds and stop-action," video does this frequently and easily. "Film may have movement *in* the image"; but "the video image in itself, born from scanning, is pure movement" (Chion 1994, 162). The intrinsic "lightness" of video equipment replaces the "heaviness" of the cinematic apparatus. All this leads to yet more paradoxical inversions. For "the rapidity and lability of the video image" work to "bring [it] closer to the eminently rapid element that is text." There is a certain "visual fluttering" in video, a speeding up that makes it into "visible stuff to listen to, to decode, like an utterance." This means that "everything involving sound in film—the smallest vibrations, fluidity, perpetual mobility—is already located in the video image" as well (Chion 1994, 163). In other words, where classical cinema subordinated sound to image, and modernist cinema made sound into a new sort of image, in television and video visual images tend rather to approach the condition of sound.

From Analog to Digital

The ratio of the senses—the balance between eye and ear, or between images and sounds—has also been altered by the massive shift, over the course of the last several decades, from analog to digital media. Digitization undermines the traditional hierarchy of the senses, in which sight is ranked above hearing. On a basic ontological level, digital video consists in multiple inputs, all of which, regardless of source, are translated into, and stored in the form of, binary code. This means that there is no fundamental difference, on the level of raw data, between transcoded visual images and transcoded sounds. Digital processing treats them both in the same way. Digitized sound sources and digitized image sources now constitute a plurality without intrinsic hierarchy. They can be altered, articulated, and combined in numerous ways. The mixing or compositing of multiple images and sounds allows for new kinds of juxtaposition and rhythmic organization: effects that were impossible in pre-digital film and television. These combinations may even work on the human sensorium in novel ways, arousing synesthetic and intermodal sensory experiences. Digital technologies thus appeal to—and also arouse, manipulate, and exploit—what Catherine Malabou calls the fundamental *plasticity* of our brains (Malabou 2008). Digital electronic technologies can do this because, as McLuhan says, they do not just exteriorize one or another human faculty, but constitute "an extension," beyond ourselves, "of the central nervous system" in its entirety (McLuhan and Fiore 1967, 31–40).

Digitization reduces sounds and images alike to the status of *data* or *information*. Images and sounds are captured and sampled, torn out of their original contexts, and rendered in the form of discrete, atomistic components. Additional components, with no analog sources at all, may also be synthesized at will. All these components, encoded as bits of information, can then be processed and recombined in new and unexpected ways, and then represented to our senses. In their digital form, no source or component can be privileged over any other. Digital data conform to what Manuel Delanda calls a *flat ontology*: one that is without hierarchy, "made exclusively of unique, singular individuals, differing in spatio-temporal scale but not in ontological status" (Delanda 2002, 47). Digital information is organized according to what Lev Manovich calls a *database logic*: "new media objects do not tell stories; they do not have a beginning or end; in fact, they do not have any development, thematically, formally, or otherwise that would organize their elements into a sequence. Instead, they are collections of individual items, with every item possessing the same significance as any other" (Manovich 2001, 194).

Strictly speaking, Manovich's point is not that narrative ceases to exist in digital media, but that its role is secondary and derivative. All the elements deployed in the course of a narrative must first be present simultaneously in the database. The database therefore predefines a *field of possibilities* within which all conceivable narrative elements are already contained. And this is why, "regardless of whether new media objects present themselves as linear narratives, interactive narratives, databases, or something else, underneath, on the level of material organization, they are all databases" (Manovich 2001, 201). The temporal unfolding of narrative is subordinated to the permutation and recombination of elements in a synchronic structure.

This structural logic of the database has several crucial consequences. For one thing, digital sampling and coding takes precedence over sensuous presence. Not only do all sounds and images have equal status; they are also all subordinated to the informational structure in which they are stored. Images and sounds are stripped of their sensuous particularity, and abstracted into a list of quantitative parameters for each pixel or slice of sound. These parameters do not "represent" the sounds and images to which they refer, so much as they are instructions, or recipes, for reproducing them. As a result, sounds and images are not fixed once and for all, but can be made subject to an indefinite process of tweaking and modulation. In addition, sounds and images can be retrieved at will, in any order or combination. Even in the case of older media forms like classic films, digital technologies allow us to speed them up or slow them down, to jump discontinuously from one point in their temporal flow to another, or even—as Laura Mulvey suggests—to halt them entirely, in order to linger over individual frames (Mulvey 2006, passim). Databases allow in this way for random access, because their underlying order is simultaneous and spatial. In digital media, time becomes malleable and manageable; Bergson would say that time has been spatialized.

Out of Time and into Space

The movement from narrative organization to database logic is just one aspect of a much broader cultural shift. Along with the transitions from cinema to video, and from analog technologies to digital ones, we have moved (in William

Burroughs's phrase) "out of Time, and into Space" (Burroughs 1987, 252). The modernist ethos of duration and long-term, historical memory has given way to an ethos of short-term memory and "real-time" instantaneity. This shift has been widely noted by social and cultural theorists. Already in the 1970s, Daniel Bell argued that "the organization of space … has become the primary aesthetic problem of mid-twentieth-century culture, as the problem of time … was the primary aesthetic concern of the first decades of this century" (Bell 1976, 107). Fredric Jameson's early-1980s reading of "the cultural logic of late capitalism" similarly sees our culture as being "increasingly dominated by space and spatial logic"; as a result, "genuine historicity" becomes unthinkable (Jameson 1991, 25). Manuel Castells, in his survey of turn-of-the-century globalization, also argues that "space organizes time in the network society" (Castells 2010, 407).

Any audiovisual aesthetics must come to terms with the social logic of spatialization. How do relations between sound and image change when we move out of time and into space? In the first place, it is evident that images are predominantly spatial, whereas sounds are irreducibly temporal. You can freeze the flow of moving images in order to extract a still, but you cannot make a "still" of a sound. For even the smallest slice of sound implies a certain temporal thickness. Chion says that "the ear … listens in brief slices, and what it perceives or remembers *already* consists in short syntheses of two or three seconds of the sound as it evolves" (Chion 1994, 12). These syntheses correspond to what William James famously called the *specious present*:

> The practically cognized present is no knife-edge, but a saddle-back, with a certain breadth of its own on which we sit perched, and from which we look in two directions into time. The unit of composition of our perception of time is a *duration* … We seem to feel the interval of time as a whole, with its two ends embedded in it.
>
> (William James 1983, 574)

Such a *duration-block*, "varying in length from a few seconds to probably not more than a minute," constitutes our "original intuition of time" (William James 1983, 603).

Chion suggests, along these lines, "that everything *spatial* in a film, in terms of image as well as sound, is ultimately encoded into a so-called visual impression, and everything which is *temporal*, including elements reaching us via the eye, registers as an auditory impression" (Chion 1994, 136). Sound has the power to temporalize an otherwise static flow of cinematic images, precisely because "sound by its very nature necessarily implies a displacement or agitation, however minimal" (Chion 1994, 10). The logic of spatialization would therefore seem to imply a media regime in which images were dominant over sounds.

However, the fact that hearing is organized into "brief slices," or discrete blocks of duration, means that, according to Chion, hearing is in fact atomized, rather than continuous (Chion 1994, 12). William James similarly writes of the "discrete flow" of our perception of time, or the "discontinuous succession" of our perceptions of the specious present (William James 1983, 585 and 599). Many distinct sounds may overlap in each thick slice of time. In contrast, images cannot be added together, or thickened, in this way. We can easily hear multiple sounds layered on top of one another, while images superimposed upon one another are blurred to the point of illegibility. In addition, cinematic images imply a certain linearity, and hence succession, because they are always localized in terms of place and distance. You have to look in a certain direction to see a particular image. As Chion puts it, cinema "has just *one place for images*," which are always confined within the frame. Sound, however, frees us from this confinement; "for sound there is neither frame nor preexisting container." Although sound can have a *source*, it doesn't have a *location*. It may *come from* a particular place, but it entirely fills the space in which it is heard (Chion 1994, 67).

By entirely filling space, sound subverts the linear, sequential order of visual narrative, and lends itself to the multiplicity of the spatialized database aesthetic. McLuhan cites the linear progression of alphabetic writing as the basic form of visual dominance; in contrast, he always associates the predominance of sound with simultaneity, allover patterns, and "information" as the "technological extension of consciousness" (McLuhan 1964, 57). In acoustic space, McLuhan says, "Being is multidimensional and environmental and admits of no point of view" (McLuhan and McLuhan 1988, 59). Chion similarly notes that sound promotes a sense of simultaneity and multiplicity in post-cinematic media. In music video, for instance, "the … image is fully liberated from the linearity normally imposed by sound." This means that the music video's "fast montage," or "rapid succession of single images," comes to function in a way that "closely resembles the polyphonic simultaneity of sound or music" (Chion 1994, 167). Precisely because the music video's soundtrack is already given in advance, we are offered "a joyous rhetoric of images" that "liberates the eye" (Chion 1994, 166). In cinema, sound temporalizes the image; but under the post-cinematic regime of the rhythm image, sound works to release images from the demands of linear, narrative temporality.

The Death of Cinema

The movement out of time and into space has crucial ramifications for cinema as a time-bound art. In his recent, beautifully elegiac book *The Virtual Life of Film*, David Rodowick mourns what he sees as the death of cinema at the hands of electronic and digital technologies. Rodowick, joining Bazin with Deleuze, argues that cinematic experience is grounded in the closely related "automatisms" of (Bazinian) indexicality and (Bergsonian) duration. In both classical and modernist film, Rodowick says, every cinematic space "expresses a causal and counterfactually dependent relation with the past as a unique and nonrepeatable duration" (Rodowick 2007, 67). That is to say, for Rodowick the space of the film is indexically grounded in a particular span of time past, which it preserves and revivifies. Analog film "always returns us to a past world, a world of matter and existence"; and it thereby allows us to feel "an experience of time in duration" (Rodowick 2007, 121). Moreover, cinematic space is actively assembled through the time-dependent processes of camera movement and montage. For both these reasons, cinema presents to us the pastness, and the endurance in time, of actual things.

But according to Rodowick, digital media no longer do this. Where analog photography and cinematography preserved the traces of a preexisting, profilmic reality, digital media efface these traces, by translating them into an arbitrary code. Without the warrant of analog cinema's indexical grounding, Rodowick says, digital moving-image media are unable to express duration. They are only able to transmit "the expression of change in the present as opposed to the present witnessing of past durations" (Rodowick 2007, 136). Indeed, in digital works not only is time undone, but even "space no longer has continuity and duration," since "any definable parameter of the image can be altered with respect to value and position" (Rodowick 2007, 169). In sum, for Rodowick, "nothing *moves*, nothing endures in a digitally composed world. The impression of movement is really just an impression … the sense of time as *la durée* gives way to simple duration or to the 'real time' of a continuous present" (Rodowick 2007, 171).

I do not think that Rodowick is wrong to suggest that time plays a very different role in electronic and digital media than it did in the cinema. Indeed, this is why I argue that a new Deleuzian audiovisual "image" is needed to displace and supplement the movement image and the time image. I take it as symptomatic, in this regard, that Rodowick ignores the dimension of sound in cinema even more than Deleuze himself does. Rodowick's book has almost nothing to say about sound; it discusses cinema exclusively in visual terms. This is a problem; for even in the indexical, realist cinema valued by Bazin, Cavell, and Rodowick, sounds work quite differently than images do. Images may well be understood as indexical traces, or as perceptual *evidence* of a former presence, as Rodowick maintains, citing Roland Barthes (Rodowick 2007, 116 and passim). But sounds cannot be conceived in this way. This is because of sound's inability to be contained. Even the simplest and clearest sounds resonate far beyond the bodies or objects that have produced them, and thus can easily be separated from their origins. Also, as Chion reminds us, even the most direct or naturalistic cinematic sound is *rendered* rather than *reproduced* (Chion 1994, 109ff). The temporal thickness of even the slightest experience of hearing means that we cannot take recorded sound as a vestige of pastness in the way that we take recorded images to be. Cinematic sounds can never be indexical traces, and warrants of profilmic reality, in the way that analog cinematic images are.

Chion notes that even classical sound films are filled with "invisible voices" (Chion 1994, 127), or with what he calls the *acousmêtre*: a sound source that is "neither inside nor outside the image," neither onscreen nor off, but rather haunts the image without being manifested within it (Chion 1994, 129ff). Even when sound serves only as "added value," its phantasmatic effects complicate Rodowick's sense of "an image expressive of a unique duration that perseveres in time" (Rodowick 2007, 117). With sound's increasing prominence in electronic and digital media, the question of audiovisual temporality becomes even more convoluted and complicated. Post-cinematic media may not express Bergsonian or Proustian duration, just as they do not lay claim to indexical realism; but their "spatialized" temporalities may well be more diverse and fertile than Rodowick is willing to allow for.

"Splitting the Atom"

Edouard Salier's music video for Massive Attack's song "Splitting the Atom," from their 2010 album *Heligoland*, offers a new articulation of space/time and sound/image relations, one that is consonant with what I have been calling the rhythm image (Massive Attack 2009). "Splitting the Atom" is a trancy and mournful song, with a strong reggae-inflected beat that is just a bit too slow to dance to. The sparse, and mostly synthesized, instrumentation is dominated by an organ-like keyboard sound, whose repetitive minor-key chords reinforce the clap-like beat of the percussion. A second, more dissonant synthesizer line plays in the upper registers. The skeletal melody is carried by male vocals that scarcely go above a whisper. Massive Attack co-leader Daddy G sings the first two verses in his extraordinary deep bass voice; Horace Andy's quivering baritone sings the later verses. The song's lyrics are atmospheric, opaque, and generally bleak, speaking of decay and death in the course of time's "relentless flow."

Overall, "Splitting the Atom" is a contemplative, melancholy work. Its steady pulse implies stasis, despite the steadily increasing chaos of the dissonant upper synthesizer register. The song refuses both the dynamic churn of polyrhythmic dance music, and the forward movement of anything that has a narrative. The sound just drifts; it never reaches a climax, and it never really gets anywhere. Indeed, one reviewer, the usually reliable Tom Breihan, complained that "the song doesn't move toward anything; it just plods quietly along for five minutes" (Breihan 2009). I would argue that, while this is descriptively correct, it is not a bug, but a feature. "Splitting the Atom" is profoundly autumnal. It stands on the verge of incipient change, but without actually yielding to it. It seems to be poised at the moment of impending death, barely holding on in the face of oblivion. In the chorus, the singers exhort us to not give way to defeat and despair. But despite this suggestion of resistance, the overall sound of the song seems already resigned to loss. "Splitting the Atom" is dedicated to endurance in the face of pain, or simply to maintaining oneself in place—as if this were the best that we could hope for.

Salier's video does not attempt, in any direct way, to illustrate the song's lyrics, or even to track its musical flow. But in its own way, it responds to the song's dampened affect, its bleak vision, and its sense of stasis before catastrophe. The video is entirely computer-generated, and almost entirely in grayscale. It implies a narrative, without explicitly presenting one. And although the video simulates camera movement, the space through which the virtual camera seems to move is itself frozen in time, motionless. Something terrible has just happened, or is on the verge of happening; but we cannot tell exactly what it is. The director's own description of the video is cryptic in the extreme:

> The fixed moment of the catastrophe. The instant the atom bursts on the beast, the world freezes into a vitrified chaos. And we go through the slick and glistening disaster of a humanity in distress. Man or beast? The responsibility of this chaos is still to be determined.
>
> (Van Zon 2010)

The video consists of a long single take: a slow virtual crane shot, passing over a bleak and dense landscape. The (simulated) camera moves freely in three dimensions. Sometimes it tracks forward; at other times it pivots sideways, or spirals around slowly. At first, we pass over fracture lines running across a smooth surface, in which vague, blurry shapes are reflected. Then the camera rises, and swoops over a series of abstract geometric forms: multifaceted mineral crystals, or perhaps the polygons that are basic to 3D modeling. But shortly, the camera moves into an urban scene; the polyhedral crystals now congeal into the forms of buildings. We see heavy traffic on skyscraper-lined streets. Human figures are posed in upper-floor apartment windows, having sex or watching the traffic below. The camera then moves through a series of plazas and open squares. Here there are more human figures milling about; often, their forms are not completely rendered, but appear as masses of polyhedrons. There are also robots firing what seem to be huge laser guns.

As the song continues, the urban space through which the camera passes becomes increasingly dense; it is jammed with closely packed tall buildings, and crisscrossed by overpasses. There is also a lot of wreckage, suspended motionless in mid-air: falling bodies and vehicles, and shards of debris (see Figure 2.1). Nothing moves except for the camera itself, as it swings and swirls around the wreckage. Stabs of light occasionally penetrate the murk. Eventually the camera approaches what seems to be an enormous organic form. The camera circles and

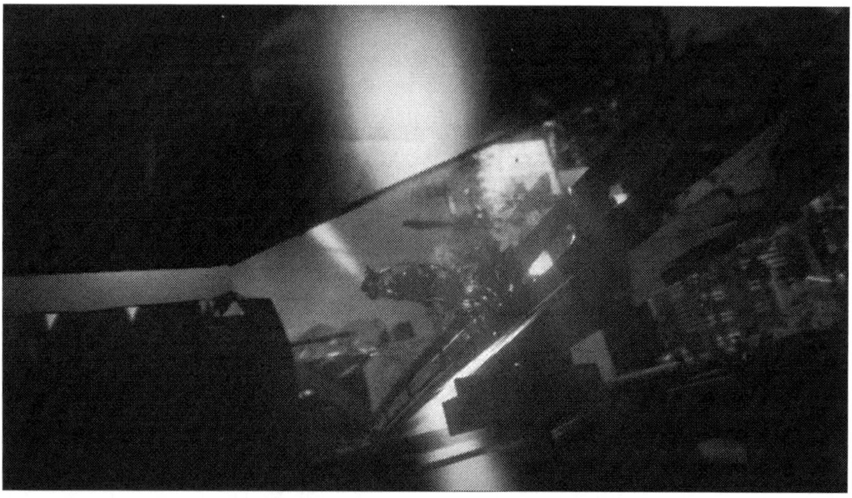

Figure 2.1 Massive Attack, "Splitting the Atom." Dir. Eduoard Salier, 2009.

pans around this form, and then moves back away from it. From a distance, the form looks vaguely cat-like, with a rounded body, uncertain limbs, and whiskers jutting out just above an open mouth filled with gigantic teeth. It is apparently dead, and surrounded by devastation. Is this the "beast" of which the director speaks? Perhaps the monster has attacked the city, though we do not know for sure. In any case, the video seems to have progressed from the inert to the mechanical to the organic, from sharp angles to curves, and from abstract forms to more concrete ones.

Twice in the course of the video, there is a burst of bright red light. This red is the only touch of color in "Splitting the Atom," which is otherwise composed entirely in shades of gray. The red first appears at around the 3:56 mark, where it seems to be reflected in, and to glimmer out from, the dead monster's eye. But the video ends with a second red flash; this time it originates in the eye or head of a distant, skeletal human figure. It glistens there, and then explodes outward to fill the screen. This pulse of red is the last image that we see, aside from the white-letters-on-black of the final credits. Strictly speaking, the explosion of red light is the only *event* in the course of the video, the only thing that *takes time* and actually happens. Its brief flashing across the screen is the only movement in the entire video that cannot be attributed to the implicit motion of the virtual camera. The flash seems like a nuclear explosion; it obliterates everything that has come before. Perhaps this is the "catastrophe" of which the director speaks, the "instant" in which "the atom bursts." In any case, the video is restricted to the "fixed moment," the "vitrified chaos," of the explosion's advent. We see the devastation, but not what leads up to it, nor what comes after. Just as the song refuses us any sense of progression, so the video suspends time in order to explore the space of imminent disaster.

Movies vs 3D Modeling

The video for "Splitting the Atom," like the song on which it is based, is five minutes and nineteen seconds long. But the time that passes within the video's diegesis is close to zero. "Splitting the Atom" explores a landscape that has been immobilized, frozen at a single point in time. All motion is halted. People are poised in mid-action. Things have been blown up into little pieces; but the fragments hover in mid-air, never falling to the ground. Each object in the video suffers the fate of the arrow in Zeno's paradox: arrested in mid-flight, unable to reach its goal. The catastrophe here, like the disaster evoked by Maurice Blanchot, is one that never quite arrives. But this also means that, as Blanchot puts it, "the disaster *is* its imminence" (Blanchot 1995, 1). It is always impending, always about to arrive: which is to say that it never ceases arriving. This also means that the disaster is never over. It is like a trauma: we can never have done with it, and move on. "Splitting the Atom" places us within a heightened present moment; and yet this present seems disturbingly hollow—precisely because it does not, and cannot, pass.

But there is more to the haunted, imploded temporality of "Splitting the Atom." For Salier's computer-generated landscape—given all at once, in a single moment of time—is hardly unique. Similar stop-time and slow-time effects have become increasingly common in recent movies, videos, and computer games. What's noteworthy about these effects is that they are no longer produced by means of traditional cinematic techniques like slow motion and freeze frames. Instead, they rely upon computer-based three-dimensional modeling. This makes it possible to move around within, and freely explore, the space of the slowed or stilled image. The most famous and influential example of this is *Bullet Time®* in the Wachowskis' movie *The Matrix* (1999). The flight of a bullet shot from a gun is slowed down to such an extent that we can actually locate the bullet, like Zeno's arrow, at a particular point in space for every moment of its trajectory. At the same time, the camera circles around Neo (Keanu Reeves) as he dodges the bullets. Within the diegesis, Bullet Time® exemplifies Neo's superhuman powers. But for the audience, the effect is to undermine what Deleuze calls the "cinematographic illusion" of continuous movement (Deleuze 1986, 1). Time is stopped, and the individual moment is isolated. The bullet or arrow is halted in mid-flight.

Bullet Time® is in fact achieved through the use of multiple cameras, deployed in a full circle around the action. Still images from these cameras are converted into individual movie frames; by choosing among these simultaneous images, the filmmakers are able, as Alexander Galloway puts it, "to freeze and rotate a scene within the stream of time," and to view the scene, at each moment, from any desired angle (Galloway 2021, 59). In this way, Bullet Time® commits the cardinal sin according to Henri Bergson: it *spatializes* time, undoing the "concrete flow of duration" by analyzing it into a series of instantaneous stills (Bergson 1912, 62). Deleuze argues that, contrary to Bergson's own prejudices, "cinema does not give us an image to which movement is added, it immediately gives us a movement-image" (Deleuze 1986, 2). That is to say, Deleuze argues that cinema is inherently Bergsonian, even though Bergson himself failed to recognize this. However, modeling techniques like Bullet Time®, in contrast to traditional cinematic techniques, actually do succeed in reducing duration to "an immobile section + abstract movement," just as Bergson feared (Deleuze 1986, 2). Reality is decomposed into a series of spatialized snapshots that are only secondarily put back into motion.

Fully computer-generated three-dimensional modeling systems—like the one used to create the "Splitting the Atom" video—go even further than Bullet Time®, as they allow us to move through the rendered space at will in any direction, and to take a view from any point within it. This means, not only that spatiality is unmoored from duration, but also that the presentation of space is no longer governed by, and no longer anchored to, any particular point of view. There is no longer any implicit ideal observer, as was the case in the whole tradition that started with Renaissance perspective and the *camera obscura*. There is no longer any such thing as a Kantian transcendental subject, for whom space would be the "form of outer sense," just as time would be the "form of inner sense" (Kant 1998, 157). More generally there can be no "metaphysical subject," defined by Wittgenstein as "a limit of the world," external to the "visual field" that it views (Wittgenstein 2001, 5.632 and 5.6331). Three-dimensional rendering, as Galloway says, "refuse[s] the monocular singularity of vision, dominant since the invention or renaissance perspective" (Galloway 2021, 51); instead it is fundamentally anti-phenomenological.

A Post-Cinematic Ontology

Galloway argues that cinema and three-dimensional modeling radically differ from one another in their origins, their presuppositions, and their effects. Cinema is primarily temporal, whereas modeling is primarily spatial. "By 1900, time had become the natural infrastructure of cinematic animation, while spatial representation and visual expression had become variables." But with Bullet Time®, in contrast, "time had become a variable, and space was suspended in synchrony" (Galloway 2021, 59). Cinema seeks to capture and preserve duration, and thence both the persistence and the mutability of appearances. But computational systems are focused, not upon duration, but rather upon "dimensional modeling" (Galloway 2021, 58). Computation works, not to capture fleeting appearances, but to grasp and reproduce the underlying structural conditions that have the power to generate and delimit all possible appearance.

Although three-dimensional modeling has become increasingly common in recent Hollywood movies, its fullest development comes in other, post-cinematic media, and most notably in computer games. In *The Matrix*, Bullet Time® is integrated within, and ultimately works in the service of, cinematic action. As Galloway notes, even as "the time of the action is slowed or stopped ... the time of the film continues to proceed" (Galloway 2005, 66). This means that however much the Bullet Time® sequences stand out by calling attention to themselves as what Tom Gunning calls "attractions" (Gunning 2006), or as spectacular special effects, they ultimately return us to the onward thrust of the narrative. But this is not the case with three-dimensional modeling in computer games. For games articulate space, and privilege space over time, in ways that films do not. The duration of a movie is preset. But most computer games do not have any fixed duration. They are organized, instead, around a series of tasks to fulfill, or a quantity of space to explore. They often contain optional elements, which a player is free either to take up or to ignore. To the extent that computer games still have linear narratives, they may have multiple possible endings; and even if there is only a single ending, getting there depends upon the vagaries of player input. The time it takes to play a game thus varies from session to session, and from player to player.

In other words, games take place in what Galloway calls "*fully rendered, actionable space*," which must already exist in advance of the player's entry into it. For Galloway, "game design explicitly requires the construction of a complete space in advance that is then exhaustively explorable without montage" (Galloway 2005, 63–4). Gamespace may in fact be composed of many heterogeneous elements; but these elements are fused together without gaps or cuts. As Lev Manovich puts it, the production of digital space involves "assembling together a number of elements to create a singular seamless object ... Where old media relied on montage, new media substitutes the aesthetics of continuity. A film cut is replaced by a digital morph or digital composite" (Manovich 2001, 132). Gamespace requires the use of digital compositing in order to produce continuity; as Galloway says, "because the game designer cannot restrict the movement of the gamer, the complete play space must be rendered three-dimensionally in advance" (Galloway 2006, 64). Gamespace is therefore abstracted, modeled, and rendered, rather than—as is the usual case in cinema—constructed or revealed through the montage and juxtaposition of indexical fragments.

How does this all relate to "Splitting the Atom"? The video is more like a movie than like a game, in that it does not allow for any sort of user input or initiative. Its presumptive audience is still the traditionally passive spectator-auditor of the cinema (even if one who is more likely to be seated in front of a video monitor than in a movie theater). Nonetheless, "Splitting the Atom" does not engage in cinematic narration, and does not employ montage. Instead, it presents and explores an abstract, seamless virtual space that has been wholly rendered in advance. Insofar as it freezes time, the video works—in the spirit of Galloway's post-cinematic ontology—by moving the camera and fixing the world. In "Splitting the Atom," time is neither expressed through action, as in the films of Deleuze's movement image (Deleuze 1986), nor presented directly as a pure duration, as in the films of Deleuze's time image (Deleuze 1989). Rather, time is set aside as a dependent variable. To this extent, "Splitting the Atom" conforms to Galloway's post-cinematic ontology.

However, this conclusion only applies to the images of "Splitting the Atom," ignoring the music. Galloway, like Manovich and Rodowick, and indeed Deleuze, makes his argument in predominantly visual terms, and pays little attention to sound. It is crucial to Galloway's claims that "rendered, actionable space" is entirely reversible: you can move through it at will, or have the camera "turn around the scene" in any direction. But even if this is the case for the space defined by the video images, it does not hold for the audio filling that space, or playing along with it. Chion reminds us that all sounds and noises, except for pure sine waves, are "oriented in time in a precise and irreversible manner … Sounds are vectorized," in a way that visual images need not be (Chion 1994, 19). I have noted that the song "Splitting the Atom" is largely static, without narrative or climax; but it still has a direction in time. The song does not *progress* on the macro-levels of melody, harmony, and rhythm; but its notes are oriented on the micro-level, moment to moment, by unidirectional patterns of attack and decay, resonance and reverberation.

This is where we come upon what I am calling, in an attempt to extend Deleuze's typology, the rhythm image. The ontology of audiovisual post-cinematic media is more complicated than Galloway's model allows for. Time is indeed suspended, or spatialized, in the diegetic world of "Splitting the Atom." We are presented with a "fully rendered, actionable space" that must be presupposed as existing all at once. But despite the suspension of time *within* this space, it still *takes time* for the virtual camera to explore the space. Paradoxically, it still takes time to *present* to the spectator-auditor a space that is itself frozen in time. This time of exposition is a secondary and external time, defined not by the visuals, but by the slow rhythms of the "vectorized" soundtrack. Just as the song is not heard within the diegetic world of the video, so the virtual camera movement does not "take place," or have a place, within this world. Instead of time as "inner sense," we now have an *exterior time*, one entirely separate from the time-that-fails-to-pass within the video's rendered space. It's telling that (as I have already noted) the only actual *event* in the course of the video is the explosion at the end. For this violent red flashing does not take place *within* the video's rendered space; rather, it obliterates that space altogether. The absence of time is the imminence of catastrophe. Time is eliminated from the world of the video—and more generally, from the world of three-dimensional modeling, which is also the world of "late capitalism," or of the network. But a certain sort of repetitious, yet irreversible, temporality returns anyway, acousmatically haunting the space from which it has been banished. We might think of this, allegorically, as time's revenge upon space, and sound's revenge upon the image.

Conclusions

"Splitting the Atom" is somewhat unusual among music videos, with its full-fledged three-dimensional modeling. But there are many other processes and special effects in current use in electronic and digital media that also work to generate new audiovisual relations. For instance, consider the *slitscan* technique, in which slices of successive frames are composited together, and put on screen simultaneously. The result is that the video's "timeline [is] spread across a spatial plane from left to right" (blankfist 2010). A slitscan video sequence looks something like a wipe, except that, instead of transitioning from one shot to another, this movement across the screen transitions from earlier to later segments of the same shot (41sttry 2009). In this way, time is quite literally spatialized, smeared across the space of the screen. The image ripples and flows, and the sound is divided and multiplied into a series of fluttering echoes and anticipations, slightly out of phase with one another. The result is almost synesthetic, as if the eyes were somehow hearing the images in front of it.

More generally, new audiovisual relations are even produced by music videos that use more common techniques, like "the stroboscopic effect of the rapid editing" described by Chion (Chion 1994, 166), and the manic compositing of images in a way that "openly presents the viewer with an apparent visual clash of different spaces" described by Manovich (Manovich 2001, 141). Consider, for instance, Melina Matsoukas's video for Rihanna's "Rude Boy" (Rihanna 2010), with its overt two-dimensionality, its fast cuts, and its deployment of multiple cut-out images of the singer against brightly colored backgrounds of abstract patterns and graffiti scrawls (see Figure 2.2). In this music video, as in so many others, we find what Chion calls "a joyous rhetoric of images," which "creates a sense of visual polyphony and even of simultaneity" (Chion 1994, 166). When time is apparently spatialized, as it is here through the song's verse-and-chorus structure and insistently repetitive beats, the images themselves are no longer linear, but enter into the configurations typical of McLuhan's acoustic space, with its "discontinuous and resonant mosaic of dynamic figure/ground relationships" (McLuhan and McLuhan 1988, 40).

Such is what I am calling the rhythm image. Beyond the movement image that Deleuze ascribes to classical cinema, and the time image (or pure duration, *un peu de temps à l'état pur*) that he ascribes to modernist cinema, we now encounter a new configuration: the *extensive time*, or *hauntological time*, of post-cinematic audiovisual media. In the last several decades, we have evidently passed what McLuhan calls a "break boundary": a critical point "of reversal

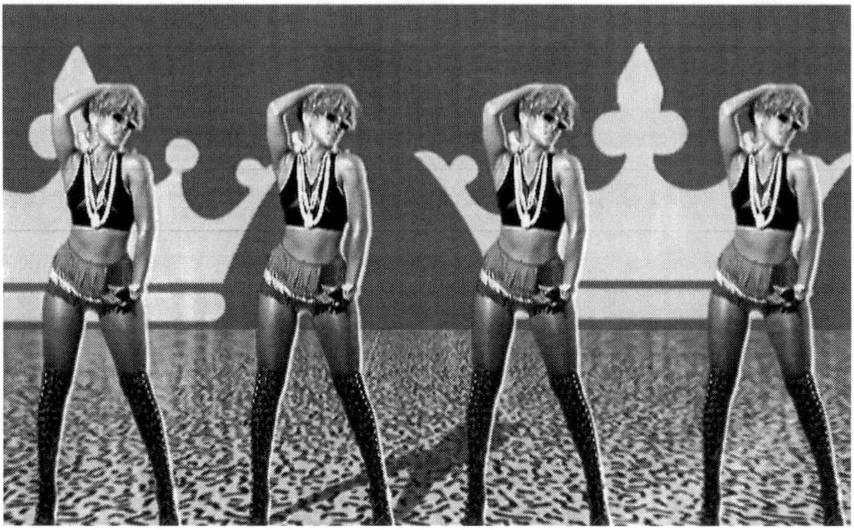

Figure 2.2 Rihanna, "Rude Boy." Dir. Melina Matsoukas, 2010.

and of no return," when one medium transforms into another (McLuhan 1964, 38–9). We have moved out of time and into space, but this transformation need not have such bleak consequences (homogenization, mechanization, reification) as Bergson and Deleuze both feared, and as film theorists like Rodowick still fear today. Instead, it may well be that the rhythm image permits a fully audiovisual medium "worthy of the name," as Michel Chion put it (Chion 1994, 156) to flourish as never before.

3

Cyborg Avatars (Dawn Richard)

Afrofuturism and Feminism

Kytten Janae's 2015 music video for the song "Calypso" by Dawn Richard (Dawn Richard 2015b) is an Afrofuturist vision of posthuman transformation. The video—set, as one critic puts it, in a "rainbow alien disco" (Mufson 2015)—clearly belongs to the century-long history of "sci-fi's obsession with sexy female robots" (Rose 2015). But "Calypso," with its black feminist assertiveness and its suppression of any place for the male gaze, turns this obsession inside out. Richard's "Calypso" has less to do with the line of fembots running from Fritz Lang's *Metropolis* (1927) to Alex Garland's *Ex Machina* (2015), than it does with the Black women *robo-divas* of recent R&B music (Robin James 2008), and with Donna Haraway's vision of the feminist cyborg (Haraway 1991).

"Calypso" also implicitly puts itself in dialogue with several earlier music videos that have related visions. These include, at the very least:

- Richard's own previous video for her song "Tide: The Paradox Effect" (Dawn Richard 2015a), co-directed by Richard and We Were Monkeys, in which she is an Afronaut striding across an alien planet, amid meteor strikes and explosions, and eventually confronting an enormous sun.
- FKA twigs' video for her song "Two Weeks" (FKA twigs 2014), directed by Nabil Elderkin, in which the singer sits on a throne, while smaller cyborg replicas of her dance in symmetrical formations around her.
- Beyoncé's video for her song "Video Phone" (Beyoncé 2009) directed by Hype Williams, in which Beyoncé and Lady Gaga invert the direction of the male gaze, gleefully dancing around men whose heads have been transformed into video cameras, as well as shooting toy weapons at them.
- Björk's video for her song "All Is Full of Love" (Björk 1999), directed by Chris Cunningham, in which two Björk-bots tenderly make love to one another, even as the surrounding machinery continues to construct their artificial bodies.

"Calypso" does not necessarily cite any of these other videos overtly (although its array of shiny cyborg dancers in front of a throne recalls "Two Weeks," and the gesture of a cyborg bowing her head resonates with a similar moment in "All Is Full of Love"). But "Calypso" shares many of the concerns of the older works. Like them, it insists upon a powerfully specific image of a Black woman augmented with cyborg powers. (Björk, of course, is white; but as I have argued elsewhere, her video self-consciously deuniversalizes whiteness, instead of taking it for granted as a default condition—Shaviro 2002.) All of these earlier videos also reject the hegemony of the male gaze, by foregrounding technologically enhanced female bodies who are unaffected by it, indeed indifferent to it, and concerned only with their own self-enjoyment. Richard, like these other artists, expresses a specifically women-centered vision of a science-fictional future.

"Calypso," like the entire album *Blackheart* from which it is taken, hybridizes twenty-first-century versions of R&B and of electronic dance music (EDM). The former genre, with its expressions of love and longing, clearly draws upon mid-to-late-twentieth-century African American musical genres like soul, as well as other forms of pop. But EDM, with its use of synthesizers and samplers rather than traditional musical instruments, is far less centered than soul and R&B are upon the expressive powers of the human voice. EDM tempers R&B humanism by drawing from an alternate electronic musical lineage that includes disco, techno, hip-hop instrumentals, jungle, dubstep, and other computer-based forms.

Kodwo Eshun, in his crucial 1998 book *More Brilliant Than the Sun*, describes this situation by distinguishing between "2 opposing tendencies" of Afro-diasporic music, "2 synthetic drives: the Soulful and the Postsoul" (Eshun 1998, 6). The Soulful is fundamentally humanistic: it is focused on the feelings and experiences of the singer, it draws upon basic emotions of pain and jubilation, and politically it demands inclusion and equality for people of color. The Soulful is very much oriented toward lived experience in the here and now. The Postsoul, however, is the musical form of that wider movement known as Afrofuturism (Womack 2013). It is anti-humanistic and science fictional, Eshun says; it "alienates itself from the human; it arrives from the future" (Eshun 1998, 5). Drawing upon the powers of electronic instruments and computers, the Postsoul envisions Black liberation as a radical, technologically enabled break from the oppressive actuality of the here and now. It rejects presentism, negates the constraints and limitations of immediate lived experience, and points up the inadequacy of our current pious (but still fundamentally racist) multiculturalism.

Even though these two poles cannot be reconciled, they also cannot exist in isolation from one another. Eshun polemically celebrates the Postsoul and scorns the Soulful; but he admits nonetheless that "all music is made of both tendencies running simultaneously at all levels" (Eshun 1998, 6). Indeed, much contemporary pop music can be understood in terms of the push and pull between the Soulful and the Postsoul. In the twenty-first century, these tendencies have entered into ever more complex and varying combinations. Sometimes, they are able to negotiate a precarious truce; at other times, one of them subsumes the other; and occasionally, the music is riven by their contradictions.

What can Postsoul, or Afrofuturism, mean in the twenty-first century? I would like to distinguish its striving from other versions of "how we became posthuman" (Hayles 1999). The currently popular doctrine of *transhumanism*—aiming, in the words of David Roden, at "the perfection of human nature and the cultivation of human personal autonomy by technological means" (Roden 2014, 9)—seeks to increase the human *power of acting* (to use Spinoza's term), but without upsetting hegemonic definitions of "the human." As such, it establishes an implicit hierarchy, with the highest place—the model or the norm—reserved for the affluent, white, heterosexual, cisgendered male. Transhumanist utopias, like Ray Kurzweil's vision of the Singularity, do not offer much to Black women and other people of color (Kurzweil 2005; see my discussion in Shaviro 2009). But Afrofuturism seeks to mobilize the resources of science and technology in a radically different way, one that questions and undermines traditional definitions of the *human*. This is what differentiates the feminist and Afrofuturist cyborg—so "resolutely committed," as Donna Haraway vividly puts it, "to partiality, irony, intimacy, and perversity" (Haraway 1991, 151)—from the dual fantasy of the transhumanist Singulatarians: omnipotent, immortal male machines on the one hand, and desirable/dangerous fembots on the other.

Mark Fisher makes a similar point when he argues that sonic Afrofuturism

> unravels any linear model of the future, disrupting the idea that the future will be a simple supersession of the past. Time in Afrofuturism is plastic, stretchable and prophetic—it is, in other words, a *technologised* time, in which past and future are subject to ceaseless de- and recompostion … in which it is no longer possible to securely delimit the present from the past, in which the traces of lost futures unpredictably bubble up to unsettle the pastiche-time of postmodernity. (Fisher 2013, 47)

Afrofuturism moves fluidly between traumatic pasts and visionary futures. It multiplies pasts and futures alike, and sets both of these dimensions of time against the constraints of a tyrannical present. Think of how Sun Ra simultaneously invokes ancient Egypt with its pyramids, and a conjectural future civilization on the planet Saturn with its spaceships. This is a soundscape that is deeply at odds with the linearity of the transhumanist vision.

We see this dissent from normative transhumanism not only in Richard's own work, or in Sun Ra's "myth science" before her, but also in that of the best-known musical Afrofuturist active today: Janelle Monáe. In the grand narrative of her *Metropolis* suite, Monáe adopts the persona of the cyborg Cindi Mayweather. The first music video from the suite, "Many Moons" (Monáe 2008), directed by Alan Ferguson, depicts an "android auction," in the course of which multiple iterations of Monáe/Mayweather appear as slaves for sale. As the suite progresses, Cindi Mayweather escapes from slavery, and leads a rebellion for equal rights. However, it is clear that, for Monáe/Mayweather, liberation does not just mean acceptance as normatively human. Rather than seeking integration into any conventionally human (or humanistic) category, Monáe/Mayweather hoists the freak flag of rebellion. This is shown most vividly in the music video "Q.U.E.E.N." (Monáe 2013), also directed by Ferguson.

Richard's songs and videos, like Monáe's, reject mainstream transhumanism as just more of the same. Instead, they invoke science-fictional visions of a radically different sort of *post*humanity—one that is not given in advance, but that still needs to be speculatively constructed. The empowerment of Black women can only come about by rejecting—rather than participating in—the norms of white patriarchy and the mechanisms of (neoliberal) capital accumulation. We live in a time when, as Eshun puts it, mainstream science fiction has been subsumed by capital, and become "a research and development department within a futures industry that dreams of the prediction and control of tomorrow" (Eshun 2003, 291). Against this, Afrofuturism seeks to reopen the future, to divert it from its preassigned and calculated path.

In pursuing this vision of liberation, Black women artists do not simply abandon, or reject, Soulful humanist affirmations. Rather, they amalgamate Soulful expressions with strange, Postsoul visions of cyborg hybridity, mutation, and radical emergence. Here I use the alchemical term *amalgamate* advisedly. If, in the words of Clarke's Third Law, "any sufficiently advanced technology is indistinguishable from magic" (Wikipedia 2021c), then the "black secret technology"—to cite the title of an album by A Guy Called Gerald (Wikipedia 2021a)—of feminist Afrofuturism is indistinguishable from alchemy. It's a true movement of "Ancient to the Future"—to cite the title of a famous album by the Art Ensemble of Chicago (Wikipedia 2021b). Afrofuturism conjugates an immemorial past together with an incipient future, in order to escape from, and transmute, the present—or better, as Deleuze puts it, to "elude [*esquiver*] the present" (Deleuze 1990, 1). Dawn Richard offers her own version of this strategy in "Calypso."

Extra-tonal Logic

These processes of transformation are not just played out in the songs' lyrics (and their associated videos' images), but also—and most importantly—in terms of their musical (and audiovisual) form. Most older genres of pop music (like Tin Pan Alley songs, or those of the Beatles) are organized tonally, on the basis of harmonic progressions that depart from the tonic key, and then eventually return back to it. In contrast, many more recent musical genres—including but not limited to EDM and hip-hop—display what Robin James calls an "extra-tonal" logic: one that "centers rhythm and timbre rather than harmony," and that is "modular rather than teleological" (James 2015, 26).

Extra-tonal musical forms are built around syncopated rhythmic patterns, and discontinuous variations in timbre and intensity. Different layers of pulsing sound are continually being added to, and subtracted from, the mix. Tonally organized pop music—much like sonata form in nineteenth-century Western classical music—suggests a linear narrative, with the final return to the tonic as a satisfying conclusion. Extra-tonal pop music, in contrast, suggests a kind of open, serial narrative structure. We hear multiple, massively ramifying iterations of a basic underlying situation. The series is indefinitely extensible and changeable, without ever reaching a point of finality or closure. In this respect, the difference between traditional pop and extra-tonal pop is roughly analogous to the difference between classical cinematic storytelling and long-form, episodic television or web-based narrative.

Extra-tonal compositional logic can be used to express a wide range of moods and visions. "Calypso" might be described, somewhat oxymoronically, as a frantically effervescent song. It is light and bouncy, but it also has a relentless forward drive. The beat pulses at 141 bpm, faster than most mainstream dance music (though slower than such mutant, futuristic genres as jungle and footwork). Looped and sampled beats—including the "Amen break" ubiquitous in recent hip-hop and dance music (Brown 2020a)—start and stop abruptly throughout the song. Synthesized burbles, squeaks, and percolation sounds emerge from this rhythmic background, sometimes crackling along with it, sometimes replacing it entirely for a few seconds with sustained tones. Melodic fragments are woven into the dense sonic tapestry, including (starting at approximately 2:31) the opening motif of Angelo Badalamente's theme for "Twin Peaks."

Vocal samples ride the top of this mix, but for most of the song they are so heavily processed that they do not register as subjective, emotional expression. We mostly hear babbling at a high pitch, like voices from a cartoon. Vocals are distorted by the vocoder, and in some cases, tone-shifted to sound like a male voice (although I believe that all these samples are taken from Richard's own singing). Many of the words are so shifted, scrambled, and bathed in reverb that they cannot be clearly understood. We do hear the name "Calypso" several times near the beginning. But for the most part, as one review puts it, Richard's voice "is used as a secondary instrument to the largely electronic orchestra" (Butterfield 2015).

"Calypso" starts out with bare synthesized percussion; but melodic layers are soon added to the mix. This creates a sense of increasing density and excitement. The song thus conveys a strong sense of anticipation—a common pattern in EDM. The music reaches its highest point of intensity at 2:00–2:11. But this is followed, at 2:11, by an actual pause, or moment of silence (matched, in the video, by a momentary black screen). This sudden interruption may be seen as an example of what James A. Snead calls the *cut*. A musical process is interrupted—but precisely in order to allow it to start all over again. This structure is ubiquitous in black music; Snead cites its prominence in African drumming, in the funk of James Brown, and in jazz improvisation. In all these cases, "the 'cut' overtly insists on the repetitive nature of the music, by abruptly skipping it back to another beginning which we have already heard" (Snead 1984, 69).

The cut in "Calypso" is far less pronounced than it is in the music of James Brown—or for that matter in much recent EDM. There's no orgasmic release in "Calypso"; it's more like the subtle recalibration of a steadily pulsing piece of machinery. Despite its occasional thickenings, and its fluctuations from moment to moment, the song remains for the most part on a single level of sustained intensity—what Deleuze and Guattari call a *plateau* (Deleuze and Guattari 1987). The pulse is continually changing and developing; but it does not tend toward any definable terminus or ending state. There is tension here, because the intensity level is well above zero; but the effect is more one of continually riding the waves (or the vibrations), than it is one of a drama with its crises and resolutions.

Part of the reason for this overall evenness of energy level in "Calypso" is that we don't really hear Richard's regular singing voice until more than halfway through the song. Belted-out female vocals are common in EDM; the singer's expressive voice adds a Soulful dimension to what is otherwise a Postsoul form of machinic pulsation. But in "Calypso," it is only in the last minute or so of the song, after the music has stopped and started again, that a voice clearly recognizable as Richard's emerges for the first time. We hear her at the 2:24 mark, repeating a single line of the lyrics: "I've been waiting so long." This line is a plaintive cry that almost seems to float free from the rest of the song. It's a Soulful expression, but one that does not really synergize with the Postsoul elements of the track. As Richard repeats the phrase, the song builds to what might be considered a second peak of intensity, at approximately 3:00 to 3:20. But this densification of the sound is fairly gradual, and therefore undramatic. And at the end, the song simply fades out in a haze of diminishing reverb.

The song title "Calypso" refers to the mythological character of that name in the *Odyssey* (Brodsky 2015). Richard seems to be both the magical ruler of the island of Ogygia, and the voyager who is trapped and imprisoned there. *Blackheart*, the album from which "Calypso" is taken, overall seems to be about the trials and tribulations of an unsuccessful relationship. The album displays an implicit, but not overly linear, narrative: the singer struggles to overcome emotional adversity, and achieve a sense of self-worth. "Calypso" is the second cut on the album, the first real song after a brief Intro; it stands at the very beginning of the process. In such a context, the mythological figure of Calypso might well indicate both the power of seduction (as Calypso originally entices Odysseus) and the condition of stasis, of being unable to progress (as Odysseus is mired in his relationship with Calypso, and stuck on her island, for seven years). These contrasting but interwoven impressions fit well with the music, which is propulsive and inviting, indeed seductive, but which nonetheless refuses us any real sense of movement toward a goal.

Cyborg and Goddess

Given all this, it is no surprise that kyttenjanae's music video for "Calypso" is a dance video, rather than a narrative one. It depicts a sustained condition of existence, or a process that might well loop back and repeat itself, rather than a clear progression toward a goal. Dance videos are of course one of the most common varieties of music video. But in "Calypso," the dancing mutates into strange new posthuman shapes. Richard's own figure is supplemented and multiplied by those of her cyborg avatars. The (virtual) camera is nearly always placed frontally, as these figures flex their muscles and dance.

We might well regard all of these bodies—the artist and her robot doubles—as versions of Calypso in the myth. But there is no analog for Odysseus in the video: no male figure to whom this spectacle is addressed, and for whose privileged gaze it might unfold. There is no place in the video for a hierarchy of this sort. Rather, the flow of images emulates the music's pulsing insistence and jagged, modular logic. "Calypso" is what Manuel DeLanda might call an audiovisual *assemblage* (DeLanda 2016). The video juxtaposes, and cuts among, multiple, unreconciled image sources: live capture, digital animation, data feeds, and cyborg constructions. Through all this heterogeneous footage, we remain "waiting so long" in Ogygia, caught in the immanent circuits of the electronic network that the video both participates in and portrays.

Richard is at the center of "Calypso," but our connection to her is indirect and highly mediated. Throughout the video, we only see Richard *on video*. Sometimes, her image appears on a video monitor located within the frame. More often, her face, or entire body, fills the screen; but her image is then always presented as if it were still in process of being recorded by some video device. Frame lines wrap in a rectangle around the edges of the screen. Target crosshairs are centered somewhere on Richard's figure. A red "now recording" light flashes in a corner. And visible scan lines run across the screen. There are often small graphics on the left and right sides of the screen as well: rotating wire frame models of a human body, spiraling double helix DNA strands, and continually refreshing alphanumeric codes (see Figure 3.1).

Richard dances throughout the video, but in a curiously restrained and stylized way—slightly reminiscent of earlier hip-hop dancing styles, like that of Missy Elliott in her "Get Ur Freak On" video (Missy Elliott 2001). At one point, Richard flaps her arms as if they were made of rubber; at others, she moves them in discontinuous gestures. She bends backward, shakes her long braids, and moves her hands in abrupt patterns around her face. Some of these gestures are repeated as she lies on the ground, her upside-down head filling the frame, her braids spread, Medusa-like, all around her. It is in this curious position—eyes at the bottom, mouth at the top—that she lip-syncs for the first time in the video: it's the single line, about waiting so long, that she sings *in propria voce*. Richard's dancing isn't robotic, exactly—her gestures are still fluid, even though they are

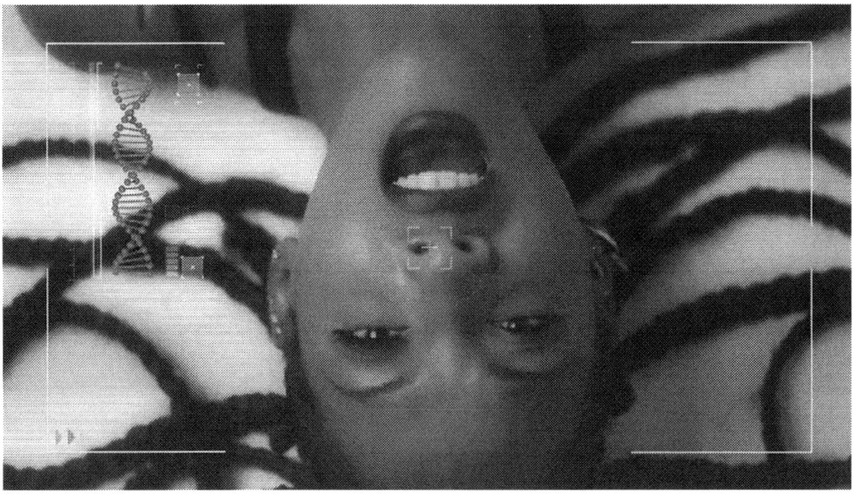

Figure 3.1 Dawn Richard, "Calypso." Dir. Kyttenjanae, 2015.

broken up or modularized—but her movements tend to undercut the distinction between living fluidity and mechanistic rigidity that Henri Bergson saw as the basis of comedy, and that is customarily carried over into our depictions of the differences between organic living beings and artificially constructed ones (Bergson 2014).

The video also toys with our notions of space and place. Even when we see Richard's full body in motion, she is never actually present within a concrete, three-dimensional physical location. We always see her placed against a blank background—presumably the result of filming her in front of a green screen—regardless of whether she is standing or lying on the ground. As she dances, sparks and flashes seem to emanate from her body. When we are presented with Richard's full figure, it is often flanked, and partly covered over, by computer animations. These animations sometimes appear in sync with changes to the music. They take the form of cartoonishly stylized palm trees and other vegetation, brightly colored floating bubbles, sparkles and gleamings, and abstract graphic renderings of wavy liquid. These animations fit well with the idea of Ogygia as an alluring tropical island; but they are never naturalistic in appearance. They are overtly presented as two-dimensional, computer-generated forms. They occupy a different graphic layer from that of Richard's own figure. There is no effort to combine these layers seamlessly, or to create the illusion that they share a common three-dimensional space.

As for Richard's cyborg avatars, they appear (unlike Richard herself) within a fully rendered three-dimensional space, with gradations of lighting and a sense of depth. The first of these scenes starts at 0:11. It is a long shot of a deep room, dark in front but lighter toward the back. Stacked video monitors display images of Richard's head. There are also gleaming piles of unidentifiable electronics, and inert plastic dummies of female figures. One of the dummies is seated on the floor, with a video monitor weirdly replacing her head. This image recurs later, in the video, even more surrealistically, when the head/monitor shows Richard lying on the ground, upside-down, as if the mannequin's own head were inverted.

In any case, the (virtual) camera moves forward, into this computer-rendered three-dimensional scene. The shot is interrupted by glitchy feedback, and then at 0:18 the screen goes entirely black. A second or two later, the image returns, and the camera moves backward from a three-dimensional cyborg figure roughly based on Richard's features (including braids and nose ring) but clearly artificial. As we look at her, she awakens: she raises her head, and her eyes open and fill with gleams of red (see Figure 3.2). Of course, this image conventionally signifies the moment when a cyborg comes alive, or at least comes online. But it is also suggestive because the female cyborg seems to be actively looking out *at us*, at the same time that the video as a whole refuses any power to our external, spectatorial gaze.

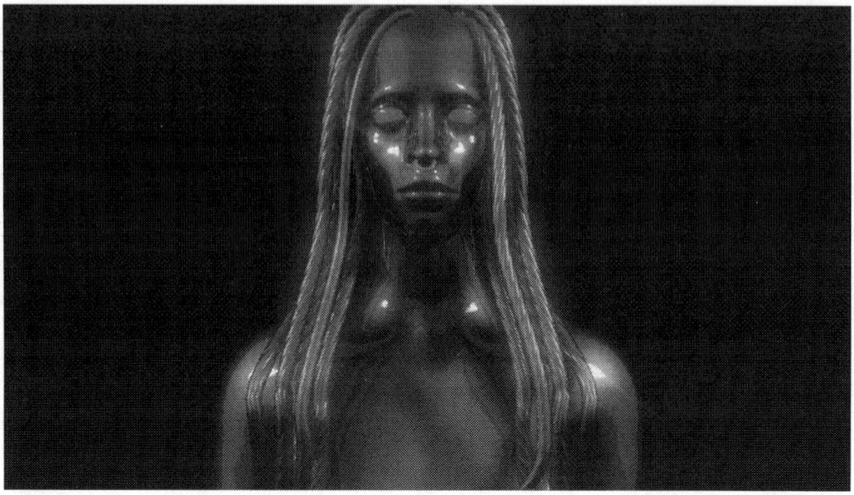

Figure 3.2 Dawn Richard, "Calypso." Dir. Kyttenjanae, 2015.

Richard's cybernetic double reappears a number of times in the course of the video. She sits casually on a throne limned by a circle of reddish lights. Her legs are crossed, and her figure flexes up and down in slight, barely perceptible waves. The throne is centered in the frame, and flanked on both sides by slender pillars, wound from top to bottom in glowing coils. The lighting is purplish-reddish on the left and bluish on the right. The overall design suggests a sleek digital updating of Art Deco; it emphasizes forms that are geometrically reductive, and yet at the same time almost decadently decorative. This look is at once retrofuturist—reminding us of decades of science fictional set design that now looks dated and "advanced" at the same time—and yet attuned to the way that our current science-fictional imaginary conceives machines that (in Haraway's words) "are all light and clean because they are nothing but signals, electromagnetic waves, a section of a spectrum" (Haraway 1991, 153).

On both sides of the throne, and somewhat closer to the (virtual) camera, two additional female cyborg figures are dancing. Unlike the central Richard cyborg, they are smooth, shiny, and bald, with no red gleam in their eyes. However, a colored sheen or aura seems to emanate from their bodies. Their dance movements are more limited and repetitious than Richard's, but also smoother and more continuous. They seem to fluctuate and flow. This impression is reinforced at 2:38–2:46, when one of these smaller cyborg figures bobs gracefully and minutely up and down, as if she were immersed in water, facing an enormous curved screen divided by a rectangular grid, and as a whole conveying Richard's upside-down face (see Figure 3.3). The cyborg's reflection or shadow also appears on the screen, bisecting Richard's forehead. The video doesn't entirely efface our conventional distinctions between the real and the artificial, or between the living being and the robot; but it blurs the differences a bit, by exchanging some of their characteristics.

All these images are highly unstable. They flicker in and out of existence, frequently interrupted by artifacts of noise like glitchy, pixelated interference lines and staticky color bars. It is as if we were not watching a completed playback, but looking through a viewfinder, and observing pixels of raw information. When Richard herself appears, we get the impression that video recording is still going on. When we see the cyborg figures, the implication is that these are momentary, incomplete results of the scanning and rendering process—which in fact they are, since, as the director tells us, the cyborg figures were generated from "a series of 3D scans and measurements of Richard" (Mufson 2015).

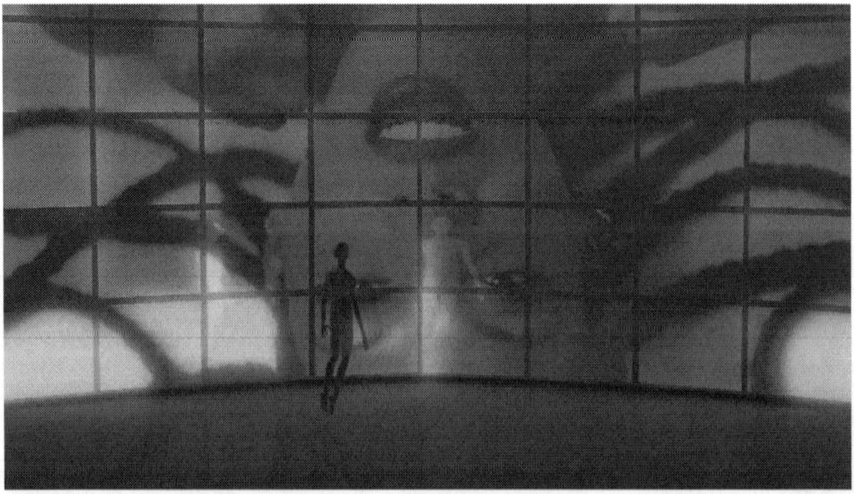

Figure 3.3 Dawn Richard, "Calypso." Dir. Kyttenjanae, 2015.

In other words, throughout the video Richard is continually in process of being captured, sampled, and compiled into multiple datasets. At the very start of the video—and at several later times as well—the screen is filled with a series of extreme close-ups. These show only small fragments of Richard's face or body: her mouth and one cheek, her eye, her ear, her profile. The close-up shots only last a second or two each; they imply that Richard's image is being divided into small slices, the better to be sampled and mined for data. All in all, the video asks us to understand its images as *renderings* rather than full-fledged *representations*. That is to say, the video's images enact a provisional, mutable mapping of incoming information, rather than claiming to give us a full and accurate reproduction of appearances. Richard herself is caught up in the immanent process of becoming a cyborg.

It is for this reason, too, that the video denies us any position of voyeuristic mastery. By seeing Richard only through a viewfinder, we are reminded that we have no direct access to her figure; we can only grasp her by means of a complex technological apparatus. Even if these images of Richard beguile us, we remain aware that they are not *for us*. The implied viewer is neither an embodied person nor a normative subject position; it can only be the video/computational apparatus itself. We are wrong to think of sampling and data-gathering as methods of panoptical surveillance; they are better understood as a cyborg processes, or self-referring and self-reinforcing feedback mechanisms.

When these loops become dense enough and recursive enough, they might well become autonomously alive, aware, or conscious. At least, such is the suggestion of Integrated Information Theory, currently popular among neuroscientists and philosophers of mind (Tononi 2008, 2012).

There is, of course, a political dimension to all this. Neoliberal society, as Robin James reminds us, is powered by a multiplicity of positive "feedback loops [which] literally re-cycle outputs and plug them back in as inputs—like investing profits back in a business rather than paying them out as dividends" (James 2015, 46). Under our current financial system, such feedback loops serve the purpose of expropriation: the seizure, and endless accumulation, of both data and capital. And this is precisely the point of capitalism as a cyborg mechanism (Mirowski 2001). The accumulation of data and images, and beyond them of capital, serves no purpose besides its own continuing increase.

But "Calypso" offers us an alternative to any such recuperation. The song and video provide us with a utopian, science-fictional extrapolation of the whole self-reflexive, accumulative mechanism. Richard repeats and amplifies cyborg replication, even to the point where it implodes. Cyborgs are figured in the video on all levels. The singer herself is in process of becoming cyborg; her cyborg doubles weave their Calypsonian magic; and the video as a whole is best understood as a cyborg process. An artificial intelligence arises from all these feedback loops, and can indeed be equated with the loops' continued functioning. The video envisions a situation in which this fractally multiplying cyborg process declares its independence from all purposes—and even (or especially) from the purposeless purpose of capital accumulation itself. This means that the cyborg mechanism no longer functions for the sake of capitalization and appropriation, but instead indulges in its feedback loops simply as its own continually renewed enjoyment. In looping back upon themselves, these cyborgian data-compiling processes repeatedly (and repetitively, following the syncopated dance rhythm) consume their own productions. Such a process at once involves, absorbs, and exceeds Richard: it is immanent, autoerotic, machinic, and asubjective.

Richard lives and moves in the video in a state of continual cyborg self-enjoyment. Her figure is therefore not presented for the delectation of a male gaze. At most, the voyeur may secondarily enjoy Richard's (or the Richard-bot's) enjoyment of herself. The dancing figure is always in process, as it actively samples and transforms itself—or better, as it is *transduced*, continually converting itself from one form of energy to another. The video is both quick and dense; its images, no less than the sounds they accompany, are always being transmuted and modulated. The multiple data streams indicate that the video apparatus is recording much more information—and indeed, much more sensation—than any viewer is able to retain and comprehend. In this way, the video models an open, dissipative structure (Prigogine and Stengers 1984)—rather than any system of recuperation and capital accumulation.

The video alternates, as I have already noted, between sequences that featuring the ongoing video capture of Richard herself, and those that unfold within a space that is fully rendered in three-dimensional, and occupied by her cyborg doubles. But the most fascinating passage in the video is the one in which singer and cyborg (or process and product) meet. It takes place at approximately 0:34 to 0:40. Richard, in head-and-shoulders profile on the right half of the screen, faces a similarly framed female cyborg on the left. This cyborg is at once bland and creepy. She does not seem to have been modeled upon Richard. Rather, her figure is whitish and entirely bald, and her skin seems to be made from highly reflective plastic. Perhaps she is a generic model, without having yet received any specifically personalized traits. The video's director, kyttenjanae, remarks that she is

> really fascinated by all these online 3D resources that would offer a "generic base mesh" to download. I thought it was really interesting that these models always seemed slightly male, but lacked any genitalia, and were always very fit, bald, and eyeless. The idea that this represented the "generic" human really struck me. (Simoneau 2015)

The director slightly feminizes the generic cyborg; but she also leaves it white, since whiteness is the norm—or the unmarked term—in our racist society.

In any case, Richard and this cyborg have a moment's stare-off. But then the cyborg lowers her head in a mute acknowledgment of deference and defeat (or even, perhaps, of shame). Richard responds by closing her eyes and lifting her head upward, in a gesture implying ecstasy (see Figure 3.4). Once again—just as with the awakening red eyes of the cyborg Richard—vision is contained in the form of an immanent, self-affirming, female gaze. It cannot be recuperated in any form of spectatorship, and it does not even need to look outward, because it already grasps and includes itself. Richard reigns supreme over her simulacrum, even as the data capturing process continues.

Odysseus may well complain that he has been "waiting so long" in Ogygia. But for Calypso, this waiting is itself the rhythm of enchantment, the eternal renewal and refreshment of the dance. In Greek mythology, Calypso is a minor

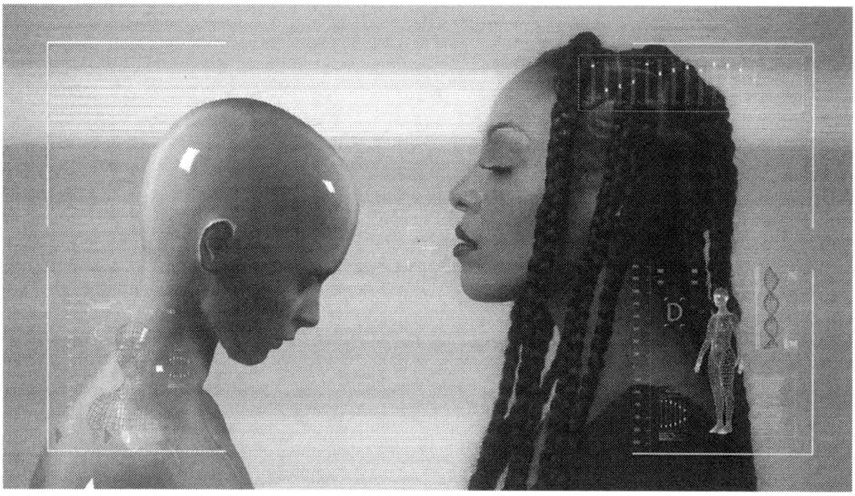

Figure 3.4 Dawn Richard, "Calypso." Dir. Kyttenjanae, 2015.

goddess, existing eternally. But in the syncretic myth-science of Afrofuturism, Calypso is not being but becoming: not eternal, but continually self-generating and self-subsisting. Her power and enchantment are carried in the pulsating rhythms of her dance, with its repetitions and its cuts. This is a cyborg process, involving the ongoing transduction of energy. And in this process, there is no contradiction between nature and technology, no tension between desire and satisfaction. Donna Haraway famously ends her "Cyborg Manifesto" with the declaration that "I would rather be a cyborg than a goddess." She notes, however, that this is not really an exclusive choice, since "both are bound in the spiral dance" (Haraway 1991, 181). And indeed, in the spiral dance of "Calypso," Richard manages to be both cyborg and goddess.

4

Pulses of Distraction (Tierra Whack)

Sound and Vision

Tierra Whack is a young rapper from Philadelphia. *Whack World*, her independently released first album—or, as she prefers to describe it, "audiovisual project" or "visual and auditory project"—came out at the end of May 2018, when she was twenty-two (Tierra Whack 2018). *Whack World* is fifteen minutes long, and consists of fifteen separate songs, each of them lasting exactly a minute. Each song is accompanied by a music video, directed by Thibaut Duverneix. Short songs have become more common in hip-hop over the past few years, especially among younger, independent rappers who, like Whack, post their music on Instagram, SoundCloud, Bandcamp, and other DIY sites. But few rappers have pushed brevity to the degree that Whack has. "What distinguishes Whack," Doreen St. Félix writes, "is how her concision avoids stasis, and transports us someplace new" (St. Félix 2018). Or as Briana Younger puts it, "where others stretch small ideas and repetition, thinning them out for easy absorption, Whack uses the time constraint to make her big ideas seem larger than the space they're allotted" (Younger 2018).

Whack World's fifteen videos were each posted individually on Instagram; indeed, their length is partly explained by the fact that, at the time, the platform limited videos to no more than a minute each (Maher 2018; St. Félix 2018). The songs are also available by themselves, without the visuals, on streaming music services like Spotify and Apple Music. But the entire suite was posted as a single long-form video on YouTube and Vimeo; *Whack World* is clearly designed as an audiovisual whole. Although its fifteen sections are entirely distinct from one another, the album has a cumulative power when heard in sequence (Christgau 2018), and all the more so when the songs are seen as well as heard (Breihan 2018a).

Audiovisual interchange is at the heart of contemporary media production in the age of Web 2.0, or of the rhythm image. We can no longer take for granted the existence of sounds and images in isolation, strictly separated from one another. Each seems to attract the other; they accrete together. Moving images require a soundtrack; sonic sequences cry out for visualization. Images and sounds are both transcribed and edited, after all, on the same computing devices, and rendered through the same underlying binary code. We encounter the online world in audiovisual streams (and in tactile and proprioceptive streams as well, at least to some extent, thanks to the development of haptic interfaces on phones, tablets, game controllers, and other devices). Tierra Whack herself, like most musicians, has of course often released songs without video accompaniment. Nonetheless, she says in an interview that "I have to have some type of visual in my head to finish a song. I can't finish a song if I can't see anything" (Horn 2018).

Indeed, media reception today, no less than media production, crucially involves audiovisual feedback and sensory crossings. The film theorist Vivan Sobchack insists upon the importance of *synaesthesia* ("cross-modal transfer among our senses") and *coenaesthesia* ("the potential and perception of one's whole sensorial being") not just when we watch movies, but in our perceptual experience generally (Sobchack 2004, 68–9). We feel sensations across different bodily systems, and ultimately with our entire bodies, even when we are overtly focused upon just a single sensory channel. We often think of digital or virtual media as dispersed and disembodied, as many media theorists (including Sobchack herself) have tended to argue. But this formulation ignores (or at least massively understates) the way that such media, with their simultaneous *immediacy* and *hypermediacy* (Bolter and Grusin 1999, 5 and passim), pull us in two directions at once: they both enthrall us and distract us. In our current digital environment, which claims not to show us representations so much as to provide us with actual experiences, multisensory crossings are intensified further than was ever the case before.

Music Video Technologies

How does all this work for music videos in particular? Cutting-edge digital technologies are probably deployed for military and surveillance purposes first of all, well before they show up anywhere else. On the internet, according to Mark B. N. Hansen, these new, computationally intensive technologies, with their "data-gathering and passive sensing capacities," are used by corporations and government agencies in order to "grasp the 'operational present' of sensibility at time frames from which conscious activity is excluded" (Hansen 2015, 25). Such media are too fast for us; they register changes beneath and beyond the human threshold of apprehension. This means that they work without our awareness, let alone our permission; and that they are able to influence our desires and feelings prior to our becoming aware of them (if we ever do). To the extent that such technologies eventually do leak out into publicly available forms of cultural expression and entertainment, they are found first of all in computer games and in pornography. Music videos tend to lag behind these genres when it comes to technological innovations; but videos are still usually ahead of the movies and television. This is the case both for economic reasons (it is a lot cheaper to use new technologies in a three- or four-minute video than in a feature-length blockbuster or an extended TV series) and for formal ones (music videos are not constrained by the demands for continuity that come up in extended narratives, so they are freer to experiment, and to go off in different directions even at the risk of incoherence).

Music videos are also difficult to account for, because they originate as adjuncts to previously existing sound recordings. The rock critic Robert Christgau begins his review of *Whack World* by playfully promulgating the basic Commandments of Orthodox Rock Criticism, one of which is: "Thou shalt not watch the video." Rather, Christgau says, the rock critic must strictly "stick to music music music." Christgau goes on to make some sharp observations about Whack's vocals and instrumentals. He notes the musical "fragments gain emotional weight as they accrue," and adds that "the most emotional moment of all is the 15 seconds of wordless, keyboard-brushed cymbal ticks that transition out of Whack's final line: 'I know that I am worth mo-o-o-ore.'" But once Christgau has gone through all this, he concedes that the video too is essential, and even that it might well give us a "reason for living . . . and we all need those these days" (Christgau 2018).

Despite Christgau's disclaimers, his insights are only amplified when we attend to the images of *Whack World* as well as the sounds. The "emotional moment" at the end of the album registers visually as well as aurally. Whack is nearly motionless for all of the minute-long video for "Waze," the final song on *Whack World*. She sits almost entirely still, aside from moving her lips to the words of the song, speaking about loss and recovery. She wears a multicolored shirt/dress; her hair is tied back in a straightened ponytail. She is seated on a chair by a table in a small and mostly featureless room. A teacup and teapot are on the table in front of her, but she ignores them. Thick wads of cotton, looking a bit like solidified smoke, tumble slowly out of the window of a house crudely depicted on the back wall. It's a picture of the house that we just saw in three dimensions in "Doctor Seuss," the song and video just previous.

"Waze" alternates between long shots of the entire room, and somewhat closer shots showing only the left half of the room, with Whack at the table. As the song continues, the cotton keeps oozing out from the picture on the wall, until it has almost entirely filled the room. And thus we reach the song's culminating moment. Whack goes silent, but the cotton still undulates toward her. The cymbals continue to play, punctuated by an occasional "brush" from the keyboards. A few seconds later, synchronized to the next keyboard stroke, the video cuts to a freeze frame of the longer shot. Cotton fills the center of the frame, obliterating everything except for face and torso of Whack herself (see Figure 4.1). As the music continues, the credits roll over this freeze frame. When the music ceases, the credits continue to run in silence; the freeze frame is held for another thirty seconds or so.

Such lingering muddies the question of just exactly when the album/video actually ends. In this way, the image track responds to the soundtrack—but without illustrating the lyrics in any straightforward or literal way, and also without directly mimicking the formal structure of the music. The sounds and the images respond to one another, but they still both go along their separate paths. And they both end in a sort of suspension or hesitation. The music continues after the vocals have cut off; and the freeze frame is held after the music ceases. Whack announces her self-recovery, and her refusal to settle for less than she wants, needs, or deserves; but there is no guarantee as to what will

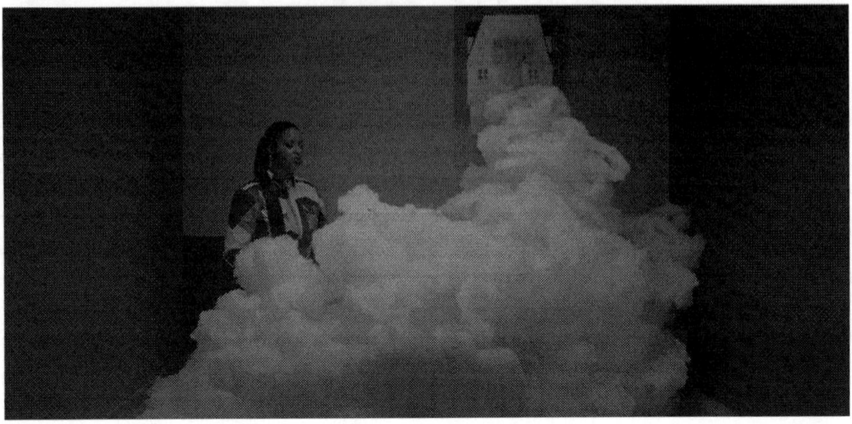

Figure 4.1 Tierra Whack, "Waze," from *Whack World*. Dir. Thibaut Duverneix, 2018.

happen to her next. Here, as throughout *Whack World*, sounds and images relay each other—or resonate with each other, to use a sonic metaphor—providing emotional punctuation and amplification.

Audiovisual Crossings

What can we make of such audiovisual crossings? Recent film theory has started to pay more attention to music and sound, as well as to "cross-modal transfers" of the sort discussed by Sobchack, than used to be the case. But film analysis still starts with the visual register. In the movies, we usually take it for granted that the images come first. However, we now realize that this does not mean that the visual dimension is somehow autonomous or self-sufficient. When Michel Chion points to the *added value* that sound provides to moving images (Chion 1994, 5), he is not far from the logic of deconstruction. Chion's *added value* may be compared to what Jacques Derrida calls the *supplement*. Derrida famously insists that the seeming plenitude and self-presence of the human voice, which we imagine to be primary and autonomous, is always already conditioned and compromised by—and indeed cannot exist without—the supposedly secondary activity of writing (Derrida 1977). Chion makes a similar argument in inverted form. He shows us that the seeming plenitude and presence of the cinematic image is an illusion. Sound in the movies is commonly dismissed as secondary and inessential (it "merely duplicates" a pre-given meaning); and yet, sound is necessary in order to produce (or "bring about") the very impression that cinematic images mean on their own and stand by themselves. This was already the case even in the era of so-called silent film, which nearly always relied on live musical accompaniment for its full emotional impact. The arrival of the "talkies" only expanded the range of ways in which sound was able to add value to what was seen. In particular, Chion notes that cinematic sound both *temporalizes* images that otherwise might appear relatively static, and gives linear definition to "rapid visual movement" that otherwise might seem blurry and indistinct (Chion 1994, 11–14).

Chion only discusses music videos briefly in his *Audio-Vision* (Chion 1994, 165–8). And indeed, in the second edition of his book, he omits the chapter on music videos altogether (Chion 2019). Nonetheless, Chion implicitly suggests that music videos also operate according to the logic of added value—only with yet another inversion. In music videos, contrary to the movies, sound comes first. Videos are made to accompany, to illustrate, and to advertise previously existing songs. Images are matched to music that has already been recorded, music that seems "sufficient to itself." Nonetheless—or precisely because they are ostensibly secondary and inessential—these visuals provide added value, often in the form of what Chion calls "a joyous rhetoric of images" (Chion 1994, 166). The video track spatializes the flow of the music, giving it body and location. This includes (but is not limited to) presenting the persona of the singer and the other musicians, interpreting the lyrics visually and narratively, and matching the music with dance.

In all these instances, the images are supplemental: they work to produce meanings and feelings that we then attribute to the music in and of itself. This added value was already crucial in the very first decade of music videos, the 1980s. Just think of the three preeminent musical artists of that decade, Michael Jackson, Madonna, and Prince. None of their careers could be imagined without the music videos that put their performing bodies on display (or in Prince's case, without his movies, especially the 1984 release *Purple Rain*). The meaning of Madonna's songs is crystallized in her ever-changing costumes and personas. The magic of Jackson's rhythmic and melodic inventions is expressed in his dancing no less than in his voice and in the instrumental backing. Prince puts his body on display in his movies in ways that were previously reserved only for female stars. All three performers absolutely needed to be seen as well as heard. We might say that the video image is the heretical supplement that haunts Christgau's church of stick-to-music Orthodox Rock Criticism.

Of course, music videos themselves have changed in major ways—formally, technologically, and contextually—in the years since MTV started broadcasting them in 1981. In the 1980s and early 1990s, music videos were only available on cable television channels. They were designed by videomakers, and understood by critics and viewers alike, to be part of what Raymond Williams famously calls televisual *flow*: "a *sequence* or set of alternative sequences" of programming, continuously available without beginning or end (Williams 1974, 87). Flow undermines any notion of discrete media events, each accessible on its own. It was only in extremely rare cases—such as Michael Jackson's "Thriller" video, directed by the Hollywood filmmaker John Landis (Jackson 1983)—that a music video stood out from the flow as a unique media event in its own right.

Today, in contrast, the discrete events have taken over. While streaming platforms like YouTube still propose indefinitely extendible autoplay sequences, they also offer us certain affordances that old-style television programming did not. We can watch any particular video on demand, rather than having to wait for it to come up in the course of the programming. We can play videos over and over, pause them when we like, and mix and match them at will. YouTube has arguably led to a second "golden age" of music videos, reversing their decline in the late 1990s and early 2000s (Unterberger 2018). It's not only that we don't need MTV to watch music videos anymore, but also that, as Tom Breihan puts it, "music videos are way more culturally relevant than anything that MTV actually *does* air" (Breihan 2018b). Videos that have a strong cultural impact—such as Rihanna's "Bitch Better Have My Money" (Rihanna 2015), Childish Gambino's "This Is America" (Childish Gambino 2018), and Lil Nas X's "Montero" (Lil Nas X 2021)—have done so almost entirely online, without ever appearing on broadcast or cable television.

Music videos are also produced in very different ways today than they were in the 1980s and 1990s, and are therefore able to present us with new and different sorts of moving images. The digital tools that we take for granted now were just starting to be developed back then. Many of the most interesting videos from recent years could not possibly have been made prior to 2000. It is not just that the necessary technology was lacking, but also that—in the absence of the requisite digital tools—nobody could even have *imagined* certain looks and appearances. I think here of some of the music videos that I have discussed in earlier writings, such as Grace Jones's "Corporate Cannibal" (Grace Jones 2008), with its dramatic morphing effects (Shaviro 2010, 11–34); or Rihanna's "Disturbia" (Rihanna 2008), with its superimposed images, and FKA twigs' "Papi Pacify" (FKA twigs 2013) with its GIF-like looping (Shaviro 2017a, 27–37, 59–67). Marshall McLuhan points out that every new media regime works to "alter the ratio among our senses and change mental processes" (McLuhan 1962). Today, digital production and online digital streaming articulate images and sounds in new, previously unanticipated ways. Radical technologies shatter old unities, and give birth to new ones.

Visionary Distractions

Whack World exemplifies many of these technological changes. It gives us some idea both of how disparate the contemporary mediascape is and also of how these disparate parts can hang together, without forming anything like a unified whole in the old sense. Whack says in an interview that, in her original conception for *Whack World*, she wanted to use "a crane machine, a claw machine," so that she would be “picked up from the actual claw and dropped into each set” (DeVille 2018). This turned out to be too expensive to do. But the idea remains relevant for the completed video sequence, because it suggests how separate the fifteen songs/videos are from one another. In their succession, they form a composite in which the discrete events, despite having a particular order, do not coalesce into a *flow* in Williams’s sense of the term. Sometimes we get tenuous visual transitions from one song to the next. For instance, “Hookers” is set in front of a trailer; Whack walks into the trailer at the end of the song. The camera follows her; as the next song, “Hungry Hippos,” begins, the image becomes blurry and unfocused. When it sharpens again a few seconds later, we naturally assume that we are inside the trailer. At other times, the shifts are more abrupt. An arbitrary wipe marks the transition from “Hungry Hippos” to the following video, “Pet Cemetery.” Even when the transitions suggest some sort of continuity, the sixty-second time limit for each individual song makes it impossible to build up anything like an overall, continuously developing mood. Rather, this structure almost requires radical changes of direction from one track to the next.

The fifteen sections of *Whack World* therefore differ wildly from one another, both musically and visually. No two of them are alike. Each one offers us a distinct tableau, creating a striking mini-environment for the expression of one of Whack’s very particular moods. Some of the songs are entirely closed and self-contained. Others are suspended and open: they seem to stop in the middle, with no final cadence, and no filling out of the verse-chorus structure. But even when the latter is the case, I always get the sense that any further expansion or repetition would be superfluous. The song has said what it has to say, so there is no real reason for it to go on. As for the images, each of the songs is set in a single room, with its own lighting and its own props. Most of these sets are lurid and cartoonish, with distinctive color schemes. And in each of them, Whack has a different appearance: she wears different clothes, sports different hairstyles, and makes different gestures and facial expressions.

And so, even if the maximum song length is initially determined by platform constraints, this brevity is positively expressive in its own right. Whack’s presentations of her various moods last no longer than the moods themselves do. As St. Félix puts it,

> Whack uses her brief songs to riff on those swooning states that young women enter intensely and fleetingly—infatuation, frustration, mania, grief, that sudden and intoxicating burst of self-confidence that mercilessly dissipates into self-loathing.
>
> (St. Félix 2018)

As *Whack World* passes through its many short-lived moods, and its many modes of expression, it does for contemporary hip-hop something like what, in the pre-internet early 1980s, the Minutemen did for rock, in such albums as *What Makes a Man Start Fires?* (1983) and *Double Nickels on the Dime* (1984). With the brutal concision of their songs, the Minutemen worked both to cut the crap (this is their version of punk's well-known disdain for long, self-indulgent guitar solos), and to expand the boundaries of musical and emotional expression (thanks to their odd rhythms and instrumental clashes). Similarly, *Whack World* multiplies the music's styles—with sounds that vary from trap to mumblecore to mournful r&b to slow organ chord progressions to carnivalesque circus riffs to what Christgau aptly describes as a "hooky hillbilly stomp" (Christgau 2018)—while at the same time reducing each particular instance to its expressive core.

Each song on *Whack World* thus suggests both a different mood and a different musical sub-genre. Some tracks are playful and silly; others are painful; still others are bitter or grudgingly resigned; and some are upbeat, even triumphant. Whack both sings and raps, and her vocals are often heavily processed. In "Fuck Off," singing in an exaggerated country twang, Whack exults that she feels "ten feet tall" as she hilariously tells off an obnoxious ex. In "Sore Loser," feeling lonely and lost after another breakup, she describes herself as a corpse; she lies motionless in an open casket, rapping in a near monotone over swirling, dissonant bass tones and a vicious drum riff, as the camera slowly tracks from her feet to her head, and then at the end back down to her feet, all in a single take (see Figure 4.2).

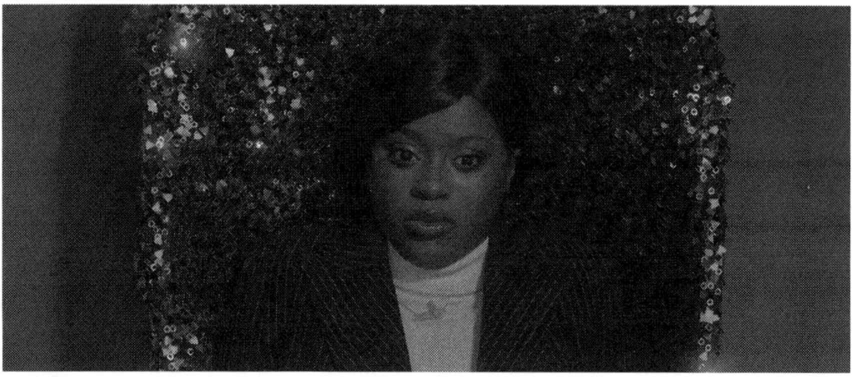

Figure 4.2 Tierra Whack, "Sore Loser," from *Whack World*. Dir. Thibaut Duverneix, 2018.

In an entirely different way, “Silly Sam” is a playfully lilting yet also sarcastic ditty about some guy entirely absorbed in literal and metaphorical games. I guess that means he’s a “player.” Whack looks bored at the start of the song, but soon enough she is smirking right at the camera. In “Pretty Ugly,” her intonation takes on a harsh edge as she boasts about her prowess as a rapper, and threatens to obliterate her rivals, all the while staring at the camera through an array of distorting lenses (see Figure 4.3). In “Doctor Seuss,” she is trapped in a toy house far too small to contain her, in a scenario reminiscent of *Alice in Wonderland*; her voice is pitch shifted, so that it descends, bar by bar, from a cartoonish treble all the way down to a slurred, barely intelligible bass.

In contrast, “Fruit Salad,” with Whack’s continual declarations about healthy eating, takes place in a room scattered with gym equipment. The back wall is a solid yellow. Whack wears a heavily padded gym outfit, with a bright yellow top that matches the wall. She moves through a series of exercises: riding a stationary bike, lifting a medicine ball, and so on. Her trainer, a white man with a ridiculous fake moustache, oscillates on some sort of exercise machine on the right side of the frame. He is identified by the lyrics as Luigi from *Super Mario*, and his green shirt adds another layer of color clash (see Figure 4.4). “Fruit Salad” has an internally discordant look, and it is hard to know how seriously we should take Whack’s proclamation of a health gospel; but its particular sensibility distinguishes it from any other sequence in *Whack World*.

All fifteen sections of *Whack World* deserve—and indeed stand up to—this sort of close and extended scrutiny. But as I repeatedly watch and listen to the video, I also find myself tripping out on particular, momentary details. In “Silly Sam,”

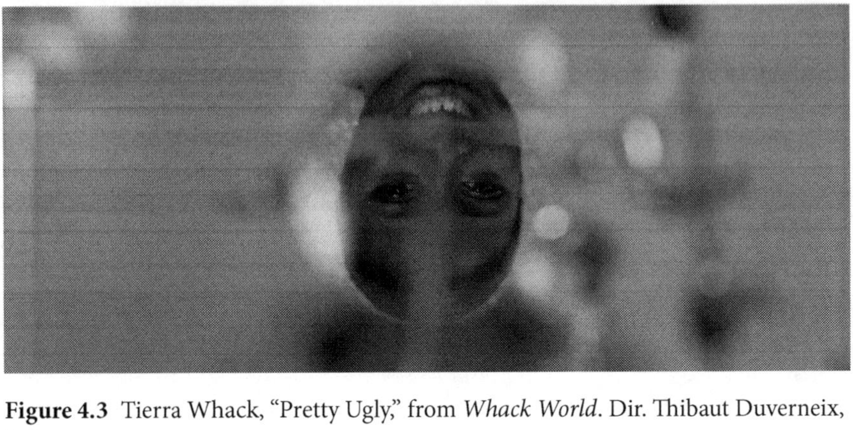

Figure 4.3 Tierra Whack, “Pretty Ugly,” from *Whack World*. Dir. Thibaut Duverneix, 2018.

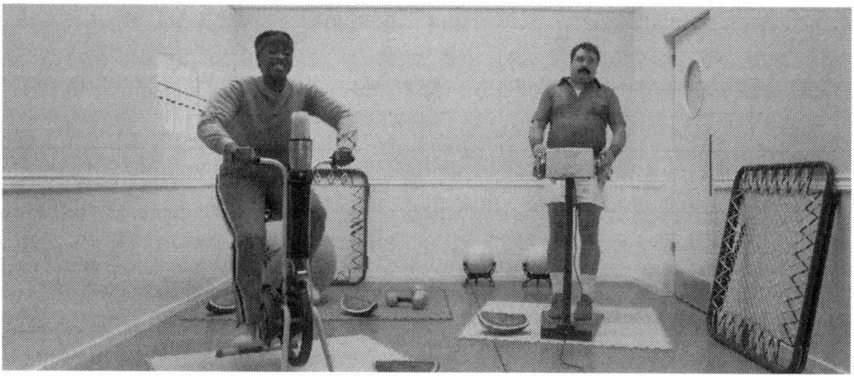

Figure 4.4 Tierra Whack, "Fruit Salad," from *Whack World*. Dir. Thibaut Duverneix, 2018.

there's a moment when Whack turns toward the camera and smirks, while she is playing patty cake with somebody we cannot see, except for his hands sticking out from the wall (9:53). In "Pet Cemetery," she mimes being pulled forward by a dog on a leash, as she laments how "they took my dog away" (7:28). In "Fuck Off," she is wearing black-and-white-checked bib overalls; she takes a pair of scissors out of a bib pocket, cuts the cords of a bunch of helium-filled red balloons, and then—once the balloons are all gone—carefully puts the scissors back into her little pocket (8:57—see Figure 4.5). Carol Vernallis writes of "peak experiences," or moments of "bliss," that overtake her at particular points in particular music videos, when, in conjunction with the images, "the song foregrounds its own

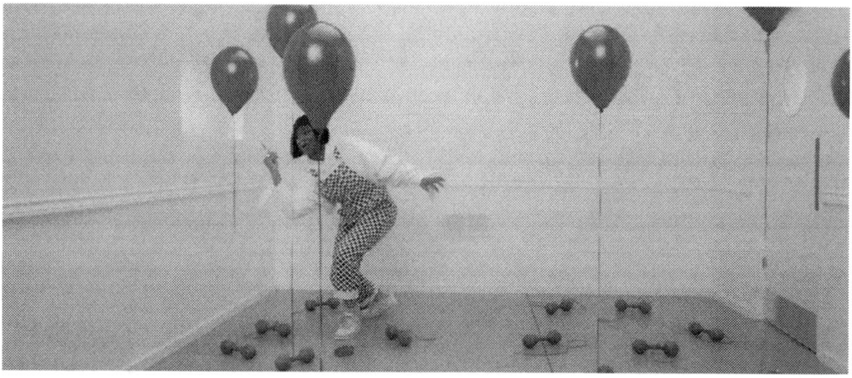

Figure 4.5 Tierra Whack, "Fuck Off," from *Whack World*. Dir. Thibaut Duverneix, 2018.

affordances, its own powers of levitation and drive" (Vernallis 2022a). I wonder if my responses to these particular moments in *Whack World* are something like this, even if in my case they arise out of disjunction and absurdity.

Whack World overwhelms us with its kaleidoscopic variety of ever-shifting feelings. Indeed, despite their short length, Whack's individual songs often go off in surprising, contradictory directions. The lyrics and visuals alike are filled with offhand remarks and seeming non-sequiturs. Heavy emotional states are mixed with silly jokes and everyday observations. "Cable Guy," which uses the boredom of repeated channel surfing as a metaphor for rejection and emotional disconnection, also turns network call signs into ridiculous acronyms: "ABC (all boys cry); MTV (men touch viginas); BET (bitches eat tacos)." The following song, "Four Wings," is mostly about Whack's love for "salt, pepper, ketchup, and hot sauce" on her fries; but it also touches on mourning for a friend who died, and gives us the heartfelt advice that, "if you love somebody I promise that you should tell 'em."

In interviews, Whack diagnoses herself as "being ADHD and getting easily bored" (DeVille 2018). She says that "my moods are like a roller coaster … It's hard for me to just feel one way all the time" (Horn 2018). And she insists that, when listening to other people's music, "the first 30 seconds" of a song are enough for her to tell "if I like it or not" (Horn 2018). *Whack World* fully embraces this condition; it is at once skittish and supersaturated. In "Sore Loser," Whack rapidly moves from dumping a boyfriend because he bores her to desperately offering herself to whomever will take her. In "Black Nails," the album's very first song, she resolves to "just be myself … listen to myself." In the accompanying video, however, we do not get to see Whack's face at all; it is covered by a hood adorned with a cartoon portrait. Whack enacts her lines instead with hand movements, and with her brightly painted and adorned fingernails. The line "listen to myself" is illustrated by a hand held to the side of the head, thumb and pinky outstretched, in the conventional gesture for talking on the phone. For Tierra Whack, listening to herself apparently involves distance and mediation. Indeed, there seems to be a change of direction, and a different message, in every line of the song. "Myself" is not necessarily a stable entity.

This oblique playfulness continues through all the fifteen minutes of *Whack World*. As Briana Younger rightly says, the album, with all its humor and imagination, creates "an opportunity for Whack to celebrate herself" (Younger 2018). But I want to add that, by the very act of being herself, without limit or reserve, Tierra Whack *also* gives voice to something that is more than—or other than—personal. For she contains multitudes. Taken cumulatively, her songs and videos express the perpetually shifting state of what Dominic Pettman calls "infinite distraction" (Pettman 2015) in which we all find ourselves in the world of social media and Web 2.0. Whack doesn't lament this condition, and she doesn't offer a cure for it. But in the act of claiming distraction for herself, she *does* transfigure it. With its manic intensity, and its unexpected twists and turns, *Whack World* holds out the prospect of something that Pettman theorizes and calls for: an "enabling form of distraction," one that might "open up the range of encounters" beyond our boringly habitual ones. The aim is not to return to older forms of rapt attention that were aligned with older media regimes, but rather "to rethink distraction as a potential ally" in our hypertrophied present (Pettman 2015, 134–5). Whack's short, ever-shifting attention span becomes the key to another experience of time. Nonlinear disturbances rupture the feedback cycle between repletion and boredom.

The video for "Hungry Hippo" (a title invoking a popular children's game) presents pearls and other jewels laid out on a nude body like sushi, and eaten by partygoers with chopsticks. Against a garish blue and pink background, Whack wears furs, sunglasses, thick lipstick, and a silly party hat; she gives us a sophisticated glance, with just the trace of a smile, as she proudly intones: "He likes my diamonds and my pearls; I said, thank you I designed it." This claim to authorship clearly applies to *Whack World* as a whole. We know that Tierra Whack designed it, even if we do not quite know who she really is—and even if she does not quite know who she really is either. Indeed, the more sides of herself she puts on display, the more uncertain her identity becomes; she reminds us that she is "not your average girl."

5

Living with Time-Space Compression (Bonobo)

Migration

The British electronic producer known as Bonobo (Simon Green) released his album *Migration* in 2017. The album's music is grounded in midtempo dance rhythms, but its sonic palette is diversified with touches of (so-called) "world music." With such a soundscape, Bonobo might well be accused of musical tourism or colonialism. But I am willing to accept at face value his claim that the album is not primarily engaged in appropriating cool sounds from the developing world. Rather, as its title indicates, *Migration* is concerned with *passages* from one place to another. Bonobo is more interested in shifting identities, and especially in the process of transit itself, than he is in identifying, or appropriating and laying claim to, fixed styles, and fixed points of origin and destination. He says that he is fascinated by "how one person will take an influence from one part of the world and move with that influence and affect another part of the world. Over time, the identities of places evolve" (Bandcamp 2017). Bonobo's music traces and enacts these fluctuating processes, rather than reveling in exoticism for its own sake. At a time when politicians in the United States, Britain, and Europe are cynically manipulating anti-immigrant hysteria, I can only welcome Bonobo's celebration of open borders.

Nonetheless, I cannot help feeling that the music in *Migration* is a bit bland. The problem is not so much that Bonobo appropriates from so many non-Western sources, as that he doesn't seem to *do* anything compelling or distinctive with these appropriations. The textures are varied, but the overall effect is still fairly indifferent. One pseudonymous reviewer cruelly—but not to my mind entirely wrongly—describes *Migration* as "a melodically pleasant electronica record that completely blends together towards the beginning and never really shows any unique musical characteristics" (Zabboo 2017).

This all changes, however, when we consider Bonobo's music videos. Four of the twelve tracks in *Migration* have been given video treatments; there are actually five videos overall, because one of the songs ("Break Apart") has been made into a video twice. All these videos are unique, provocative, and powerfully expressive—in a way that (to my mind at least) the music by itself is not. The five videos also resonate strongly with one another, even though they are all made by different directors. None of the videos feature Simon Green himself, or display any sort of musical performance. Rather, they are all more or less abstract; they either lack narratives altogether, or place their human figures into stories that are fragmented and enigmatic at best. Most of them feature understated, but still disturbing, visual anomalies. They are all edited in ways that not only call our attention to the rhythms and textures of the music, but also make these rhythms and textures stand out in higher and more explicitly varying profiles. Michel Chion tells us about how sound temporalizes and vectorizes the cinematic image (Chion 1994, 13–16); but in Bonobo's post-cinematic videos it is more the case that moving images temporalize and vectorize what would otherwise be a fairly static soundtrack.

It is in these videos, rather than through sound alone, that Bonobo reaches his full measure as an artist. This makes sense for a music that is more oriented toward blissing us out (synesthetic absorption and mental travel) than toward making our bodies writhe on the dance floor. We know that music resonates in time and space, and that perception is multimodal, or at least implicitly synesthetic. Digital production accentuates these tendencies, both because it encodes sounds and images alike in ones and zeroes and because it allows for the ready combination of contents that, as Bonobo says, "originally had nothing to do with each other" (Ableton 2016). Digital production allows for the ready migration of sonic and visual elements, their displacement from one setting or context to another. In this way, digital production provides an analog for—or better, it gives an idealized aesthetic form to—the migratory movement of bodies through space and time that Bonobo celebrates.

Bonobo's visual collaborators tease out the ways that music is an art of time and duration, which works by passing through and permeating volumes of space. In this way, the music videos follow the logic of the rhythm image. The videos unfold, and make fully explicit, the implicit multidimensionality of Bonobo's musical tracks. All five of the *Migration* videos do this to a greater or lesser extent. But in what follows, I will focus on the two most intense and perplexing of these videos: "Kerala" directed by Bison aka Dave Bullivant, and "No Reason" directed by Oscar Hudson. Bullivant and Hudson are both accomplished video directors of a decidedly experimental bent. In their work for Bonobo, they respectively explore the paradoxical formations of time ("Kerala") and space ("No Reason") in Bonobo's music.

In their different ways, Bullivant's and Hudson's visualizations of Bonobo's soundscapes tease out and complicate our sense of what is at stake in the processes of globe-spanning migration. In the twenty-first century, we do not experience time and space as being even and homogeneous. Time does not flow uniformly, but knots up, stutters and repeats and jumps irregularly. Space is not smooth and continuous, but lumpy and cluttered and folded and stretched out, densified at some places and rarefied at others. Migration, or the movement through space over the course of time, is therefore not an easy and open flow. It is continually being interrupted, impeded and redirected, or even pushed back against itself. Not all substances transport themselves in time and through space with the same degree of ease: financial capital passes quickly and seamlessly over the entire globe, while human bodies are all often boxed in, shut out, or even exterminated. As I write these lines, the British Home Secretary has just announced, with an air of jubilant self-congratulation, her intention "to end the free movement of people once and for all" (Daily News 2019). Where Bonobo's album expresses a utopian hope for free movement, Bullivant's and Hudson's videos offer us allegories for the vicious, actually-existing impediments to this hope.

"Kerala"

"Kerala" can best be described as midtempo electronica (125 bpm); it is in a minor key, but fairly bright and relaxed. It is an instrumental track, in 4/4 time, mostly strings and percussion, with wordless vocals (a repeated "hey yeah yeah yeah yeah yeah" sampled from the chorus of Brandy's 1994 song "Baby") added in the second half. "Kerala" starts out sparse, but becomes increasingly dense as instrumental layers are added, one at a time. These layers occasionally stutter or syncopate, but usually stay on the beat. The samples wash through the song in repeating loops, perhaps invoking the ebb and flow of (not very funky) dancing. At the same time, the piece's changing textures do suggest a limited degree of narrative progression. As the sounds thicken, a simple two-chord alternation is fleshed out into an almost-melody. Bonobo avoids the dramatic soars and drops of mainstream EDM;

but the song does build in intensity, with occasional lighter interludes. There's no climax, however; rather, the track ends with an extended coda, allowing its energy to slowly dissipate. All in all, "Kerala" walks a fine line between putting the listener into a hypnotic trance and sounding, well, cheerily chintzy.

Why does the track have this particular title? Kerala is a state in southwest India. It is best known, internationally, for the fact that it has been under Communist Party rule for most of the time since 1957, and that it has flourished economically and culturally as a result. Indeed, Kerala has the highest Human Development Index, the highest literacy rate, and the highest life expectancy of any state in India (Wikipedia 2016). Bonobo says in an interview, however, that he named the track not for political reasons, but because the state is an important stopping-place for birds from North Asia, migrating south for the winter (O'Connor 2017). Migration, as a global phenomenon, includes, but is not restricted to, human beings. It can be a response to climate change as well as to wars or economic crises—indeed, all these processes are intimately interrelated.

Bullivant's video for "Kerala" performs an additional act of migration or transfer, moving the track into an entirely new register. On the most obvious and literal level, the video is set in London, rather than Kerala. But Bullivant transforms the song in more complex ways as well, radically altering its mood and its import. The video for "Kerala" shows a woman (played by Gemma Arterton) in a state of absolute panic. She runs through a park, past some shops, down a street, and up to the roof of a high-rise building. The video begins pastorally, with a shot of the sky, seen through the crowns of some trees, accompanied by the background noise of birds and traffic. The camera descends through branches, and down the trunk of a tree. As the first layer of music fades in—a loop of two alternating, arpeggiated guitar chords—the camera circles around the tree and closes in on Arterton. She is squatting with her back against the trunk, shaking and panting in fear, with her eyes closed. A second instrumental loop begins: a short synthesized drum roll, one long beat and three short. At the very first beat, Arterton jerks herself upward and abruptly opens her eyes. She pulls herself to her feet and begins to run. The camera backs away from her, keeping her face in focus, while the background goes blurry.

From this point on, the video employs a remarkable visual stutter effect. There's a jump cut at every return of the opening beat of the drum roll, which is looped continually throughout the song. (The drum roll is sometimes syncopated or phased slightly, but it remains the track's most fundamental and steady pulse.) This means that there is a visual discontinuity roughly every second. But where most cinematic jump cuts tend to elide a few seconds of action, pulling us slightly forward in time, Bullivant instead uses these cuts to repeat action, jumping backward in time. The image track's repetitions answer to the repeating loops out of which the music is constructed. But these image repetitions, unlike the sound loops, are never total. At each strong beat, the cut brings us back to partway through the previous shot. For each second of elapsed time, we are pulled back something like half a second. Each new shot repeats the latter portion of the previous shot, and then extends a bit further—at which point it is interrupted and partly repeated by yet another shot.

The video's action is therefore cut into overlapping segments. Each gesture is broken into multiple iterations: Arterton spinning around, glancing back anxiously over her shoulder, running and stumbling and recovering and running on. She turns a little, then the frame jerks back, then she turns a little more. The rapid cuts produce an uneasy feeling of speed and agitation. At the same time, the reversions and repetitions stretch things out: actions unfold with a dreamlike slowness, and the simplest gesture seems to turn into a Sisyphean task. We never get a moment to relax, but we also never break free of the nightmarish sense that time has somehow congealed, and become an impediment that can only be overcome through titanic effort. This amounts to a violent reinterpretation of the relaxed back-and-forth dance rhythm of Bonobo's track. Instead of measuring repeated motion, time in Bullivant's video seems to hold back motion, preventing it from accomplishing itself. Zeno's arrow gets stuck at every point along its flight.

These jump cuts break up what would otherwise be three long takes with a highly mobile handheld camera (this is evidenced by several reconstructions on YouTube which remove the repetitions—Winsane 2017, AMathMonkey 2017). In the first of these implicit takes, Arterton stares toward the sky, as if looking at something beyond and behind the camera. She runs away from whatever it is she sees, while still fearfully glancing backward at it. She bumps into a businessman walking along a path, jostles him, stumbles back, grabs at him to avoid falling, and whirls around as the camera moves to keep her in frame. The businessman waves his arms in remonstration, but Arterton turns away from him and runs forward along the path. The camera pulls back as she heads in its direction; it keeps her in focus as the background once again devolves into a blur.

The second section of the video (corresponding to the second long take) starts at 1:35, when the choral vocal sample is heard on the track for the first time. We get a brief respite from the drum loop, and therefore also from the jump cuts. Arterton is hunched up against a wall, her eyes closed, with an anguished expression. For about ten seconds, we see her face in extreme close-up; the camera is jittery, but without a break. Starting at about 1:47, when the drum loop resumes, Arterton opens her eyes again and stands up; the camera pulls back from her, and the jump cuts resume. As Arterton runs, she shakes herself away from various people who try to grab her, whether in order to help and comfort her, or to restrain her. At one point, she bumps into a man holding a bag of chips; as she jostles him, the chips pop out of his hands and fly through the air (see Figure 5.1). At another point, she momentarily stares at a television in the window of a shop, which is playing footage of her running, from a slightly later section of the video. (The television appears between 2:21 and 2:30; it shows a sequence that itself appears between 2:50 and 3:00.) She eventually turns a corner, and runs down the street without any more interference. The jump cuts continue, but the camera ceases to follow her as she draws further and further away.

The final section of the video (corresponding to what would be, if not for the jump cuts, the third long take) coincides with what I have called the song's coda. The instrumentation becomes sparser and lighter; eventually, tones are held for longer intervals, until they gradually fade away. Arterton emerges onto the roof of a tall building; she runs to the edge, still frequently glancing backward in terror. She looks down at the ground, turns away, and collapses into a heap, her hands holding her head in despair. The camera then passes her by, and glides

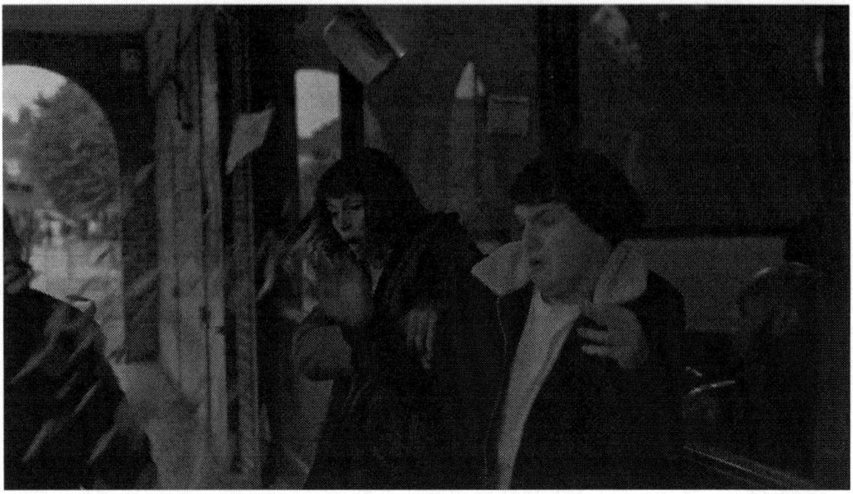

Figure 5.1 Bonobo, "Kerala." Dir. Dave Bullivant, 2016.

over the edge of the roof. It shows us, way down on the ground, a parking lot eerily filled with people standing motionlessly in rows, in an orderly grid, looking upward. The jump cuts finally cease. The video ends by reversing the movement with which it began. The camera pans upward from the parking lot, to take in the London skyline shortly before sunset. The music is replaced by traffic and other city noises; an enormous swarm of black dots (birds? or something more sinister?) swirls menacingly on the horizon.

Aside from this main action, there are many subtle, creepy background details scattered throughout the video. You can only notice them by paying close attention to the background; it took repeated viewings for me to find them. The director thinks of these additions as "easter eggs," like the ones hidden in DVDs or pieces of software (Brookman 2016). The glitches are rare at the beginning of the video, but they become more frequent as it proceeds. Online fans have obsessively scrutinized the video in order to pick out these anomalies (Reddit 2017). For instance, when Arterton is running through the park, a rock in the far distance appears to levitate (1:08–1:30). Later, a metal gate on the side of a building suddenly buckles inward as Arterton passes it (2:02–2:05). Still later, as Arterton is running down the block, a parked car changes color with each looped repetition (3:02–3:16). A man seems to be suspended in midair, arms stretched out (3:06–3:20—see Figure 5.2). A fire breaks out on an upper floor of a high rise council building (3:19–3:22).

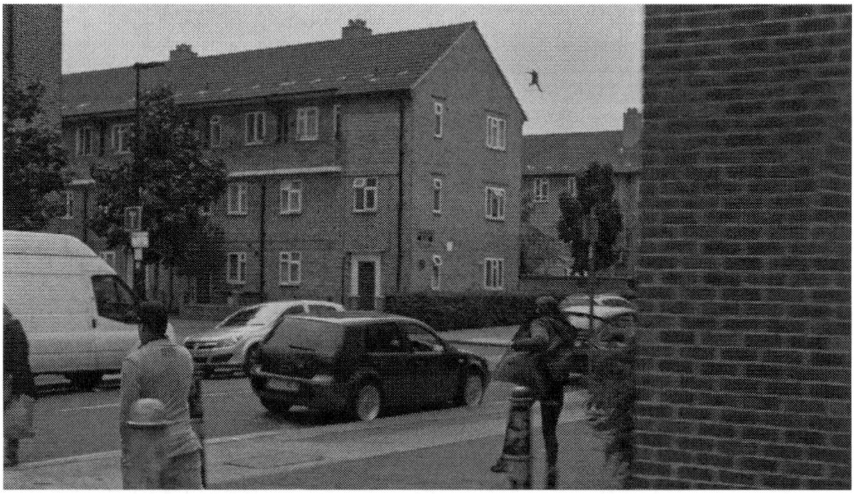

Figure 5.2 Bonobo, "Kerala." Dir. Dave Bullivant, 2016.

These signs and portents only last for a few seconds each, but together they help to account for Arterton's panic. For they suggest that something is seriously wrong, either with the world or with the way that we are perceiving of the world. Fan theories online are split between subjective explanations (Arterton's character is suffering from drug hallucinations, or from a schizophrenic breakdown) and objective ones (she is witnessing an alien invasion, or even *The Rapture*). In an interview, Bullivant says that he "like[s] everyone else's theories about it—I think they're really interesting." He does not endorse any particular interpretation as being definitively correct, but he says that the range of responses gave him "all the stuff that I wanted, really—I kept it purposefully open" (Brookman 2016).

It is crucial to note that the bystanders in the video do not notice any of these glitches; even Arterton's character doesn't necessarily see them, since she is usually looking in a different direction. In effect, the anomalies only exist *for us*, the viewers of the video. (This is even literally the case, since they were evidently added in postproduction.) The looping repetition of footage would also seem to be something that *we* experience, rather than a process that Arterton's character is going through. In addition, we never actually get to see just what it is that so terrifies Arterton's character. She is always staring (or in one case, pointing—2:35–2:38) out of frame. Even when she glances backward, more or less toward the camera, she is not looking toward its actual position, but rather beyond it (as it were, over its shoulder). In other words, Arterton is condemned to witness what she is unable to share with anyone else: visions that even the camera is unable to show us. It is only at the very end of the video, on the roof, when the camera abandons Arterton, that it pans down and shows us what she might have been looking at a moment before: the enigmatic sight of people lined up motionlessly in the parking lot.

We are therefore closed off from Arterton's character. We cannot really "identify" with her; we see her staring, but the reverse shot of whatever she is staring at is systematically withheld from us. Indeed, we only get near enough to see her face in close-up at the two moments when her eyes are closed. As soon as she opens her eyes again, the camera pulls away, even as the jump cuts resume. By closing her eyes, Arterton's character refuses the horrific vision with which she has been cursed. As Bullivant says, this is what makes her "the one fighting against [whatever she sees]—she did have power, she knew that if she shut her eyes she could have an element of control" (Brookman 2016). But in thus closing her eyes when the camera holds her in a close-up, Arterton also refuses any sort of reciprocity with the camera's own gaze, or beyond it with the gaze of the video's spectators. Even if we accept the hypothesis that the video depicts an alien intrusion, the experience of Arterton's character is much closer to that of a refugee or migrant—a person who does not fit in to the surroundings in which she finds herself—than to that of a homelander suffering from invasion.

With its form as well as its content suggesting migratory displacement, the video is neither purely objective (creating a consistent fictional world) nor purely subjective (giving us the perceptions of Arterton's character, or putting us in her position). Instead, it is something in between; it engages in a sort of *free indirect discourse*. Pier Paolo Pasolini introduced this literary term into the theorization of cinema. A novel engages in free indirect discourse when its omniscient, third-person narration takes on some of the linguistic and subjective characteristics of the character it is describing. We do not get all the way to a first-person voice or point of view, but the impersonal narration nonetheless seems to be tinged by the traces of that first person. The novel's creator takes on some of the characteristics of what they have created. According to Pasolini, something similar happens in movies when the director "looks at the world by immersing himself in his neurotic protagonist," to the point that the director "has substituted in toto for the worldview of [the protagonist] his own delirious view of aesthetics" (Pasolini 2005). We find ourselves in a strange position in between subjectivity and objectivity, in between the first person and the third person, and in between the existential suffering of the character and the expressive aestheticism of the director.

This situation is perhaps even more complicated in the case of "Kerala." For the ambiguity between Bullivant's point of view and that of Arterton's character is doubled by a similar ambiguity between Bullivant's perspective and Bonobo's. The video translates its implicit narrative into formal terms, by means of its glitches, its looping repetitions, and its refusal to align gazes. These strategies are tinged by the protagonist's experiences, but they do not work in any direct way to convey those experiences to us. Rather, they *alienate us* from those experiences, by refusing any possibility of representing them. On a meta-level, however, this process is itself analogous to the way that Arterton's character is radically self-alienated (or *out of place*, like an unwilling refugee). For her very experience is one of the failure of experience: that is to say, of being unable to bear, let alone to grasp, the events that are nonetheless being imposed upon her, and that she is forced to witness.

In a similar manner, the video closely follows the formal articulations of the music for which it provides an image track, giving visual equivalents for changes of rhythm and timbre. But at the same time, the video does not express the feelings conveyed by the music in any straightforward way. To the contrary, it denatures and uproots those feelings. Bonobo's "Kerala," heard by itself, is a bright and inviting track. It idealizes migration as a sort of open, equal exchange, as influences fluidly move from one place to another. But Bullivant's video insists instead upon the way that such exchanges are continually being impeded. It envisions the flow of influences from one place to another as a traumatic, irreversible process of irreparable loss.

"No Reason"

"No Reason," like "Kerala," is a midtempo (121 bpm) minor key track in 4/4 time, structured by overlapping layers of repeating musical figures, and ending with an instrumental coda and fade-out. Beyond these generic similarities, the biggest difference between the two cuts is that "No Reason"—unlike "Kerala"—features a singer (Nick Murphy) providing lead vocals. Also, the overall feel of "No Reason" is decidedly melancholic; this is already the case for the music on its own, even without the video. The song's main motif is a quick arpeggiated chord, repeated throughout in a treble register. This motif is accompanied, and grounded, by a steadily pulsing beat in the lower frequencies. Murphy's plaintive vocals seem to float above the instrumental background, adhering to its rhythm but never quite meshing with it. In the course of the song, other, more complicated percussive rhythm patterns are added and subtracted at intervals, thickening the sound and then thinning it out again. The most intense passages are driven by a full-on rhythm section: bass and drums erupt during the first chorus, then drop out, then return to power the second half of the song. Murphy's vocals conclude at 3:11. The remaining forty-five seconds of the song are an instrumental coda, which thins out and eventually fades away. (The video uses a shortened, four-minute version of the song: it clocks in at 7:28 on the album.)

Despite its patterns of rising and falling intensity, "No Reason" is even more static than "Kerala." There are no soars or drops, and there is no sense of narrative drive. The track just establishes a steady state, or perhaps a *plateau* (Deleuze and Guattari 1987, 22 and passim). Nick Murphy's singing is impassioned, but also oddly evasive; his voice fluctuates between resignation and despair. The lyrics are strategically vague. They ominously evoke spectacles of depression and hopelessness. But they also express a hope for survival: "we'll move or go on somehow." Even though everything is out of joint, Murphy sings, we are still living "the time of our lives now." This latter phrase isn't ironic, exactly; but as Murphy sings it in a quavering falsetto, it scarcely feels like anyone is actually having a good time. The mood is rather one of precarity: we are holding on for the moment, but there are no guarantees for the future. In terms of the album's overall theme of passage and transition, the song perhaps evokes a state of indefinite in-betweenness, with no memory of departure and no prospect of arrival. This is the negative underside of the transitional condition that Bonobo himself evokes in more upbeat, idealized terms. Oscar Hudson, the director of the music video, suggests that the track works to express "the senses of alienation and detachment" that Bonobo might have "experienced during his extensive time touring" (Knight 2017).

Hudson's video therefore inverts Bonobo's concern with "physical places and landscapes" (Knight 2017) into a vision of claustrophobic enclosure. If you are always on the move then you are always in the middle of things. You never arrive anywhere, never get a chance to relax, never achieve the state of feeling at home. But a similar sense of alienation might arise from the opposite situation: if you never leave home, then home is less a place of refuge than it is a trap. Once again you are in the middle of things, engaged in an indeterminate suspension of life. There is no prospect of release, no final term to your imprisonment, no sense of a future different from the present. Hudson says he conceived the scenario for the video when he learned about "the Japanese phenomenon of *hikikomori*, young people who become so overwhelmed by life that they retreat to their bedrooms and don't leave for years at a time" (Stone 2017).

The video for "No Reason," in accordance with the *hikikomori* theme, rings changes on the idea of a single human figure, stuck in a single, sparsely decorated room, with everything reduced to a bare minimum. The set is composed, as Hudson says, entirely of "minimalist furniture and straight graphic lines" (Stone 2017). The opening of the video gives us a fixed tableau. We see semi-opaque rice paper windows on the left, a wall made of particle board on the right, and a door in the back with a light fixture above it. The edges of two tatami mats covering the floor form a groove that runs down the middle of the room, front to back. The camera sits on the floor at one end of the room; it uses a wide angle lens, creating an effect of forced perspective. Nearby objects seem disproportionately large, and the mostly empty floor stretches back a good distance. Close to the camera, a food bowl with a pair of chopsticks sits on the floor to the left, next to what might be an abandoned restaurant menu. Halfway down the length of the room, an apple lies on the floor. At the same distance from the camera as the apple, but much closer to the windows, we seen the back of a large video monitor. It is connected to a game box and a controller. On the right side of the room, several other objects sit abandoned on the floor, including a pile of clothes and some magazines.

A futon occupies the far left corner of the room. A young man lies upon this futon, on his back, with his head against the room's far wall. Next to the futon, there is a sleek white wastepaper basket, filled to the brim with crumpled paper. Clothes hang from a line that runs from the window to the back wall, well above the futon. There is only one piece of raised furniture in the room: a small table in the back right corner. A teapot, a coffee machine, and an open magazine lie on the tabletop. There's a mirror on the right wall, and a blue jacket on a hanger; otherwise, this wall is completely blank. On the back wall, however, the door is flanked with posters, a calendar, a graduation picture, and a hanging bamboo scroll with Japanese calligraphy reading "this is my house." The framing is wide enough to include much of the ceiling as well. Despite the objects strewn randomly across the floor, the room as a whole seems to be meticulously arranged, and mostly empty. Even the mess is minimal and stripped down, as perhaps befits the *hikikomori* aesthetic (see Figure 5.3).

For the first half minute or so of the video, the camera is still. During the opening verse of the song, the young man slowly gets up from the mattress and slips sandals on his feet. He has short black hair. He is wearing a white t-shirt and red shorts. A white surgical mask covers his nose and mouth, suggesting that he is deeply concerned with avoiding germs or any other form of outside contamination. He walks toward the camera, and picks up the bowl on the floor.

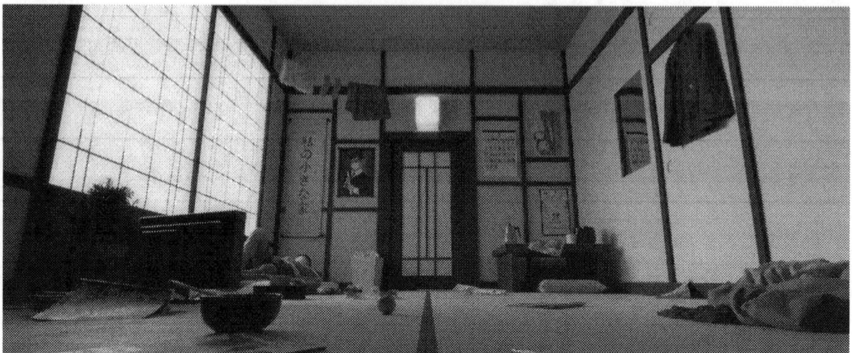

Figure 5.3 Bonobo, "No Reason." Dir. Oscar Hudson, 2017.

Next, he moves away from the camera, and sets the bowl back on the floor next to the tea table. Then, without removing the surgical mask, he scrutinizes his face in the mirror. He bows his head in weariness or frustration, until his forehead touches the mirror, right up against its reflection.

At 0:36, just as the song's pre-chorus begins, the camera starts moving forward along the central groove on the floor. At the same time, the door in the back wall opens outward. Centered in the doorframe we see a second room, and in the frame beyond that a further series of rooms, apparently stretching all the way back to the vanishing point. The young man seems puzzled or surprised by the opening door; he turns toward it and walks through. The camera, continuing to glide forward, follows him into the second room, which is a near-replica of the first. The furnishings are the same, except for a few minor details (the teapot is red in the first room, and blue in the second; all the crumpled paper is in the wastebasket in the first room, and some of it lies on the floor in the second). In the second room, just as in the first, an identical-looking and identically dressed young man scrutinizes his image in the mirror (see Figure 5.4).

The camera passes the two iterations of the young man, and continues to move forward at a steady pace. This goes on for approximately two and a half minutes, as the camera traverses one room after another. The rooms are all nearly identical, aside from still more minor variations. In the third room, for instance, the young man sits on the near edge of the futon, working the game controller and staring at the monitor. In the fourth room, the young man sits on the floor, holding the food bowl, and stirs noodles with his chopsticks; however, he keeps his surgical mask on, and the camera passes him by before we have the chance to see if he will lift the mask above his mouth, so that he can actually eat.

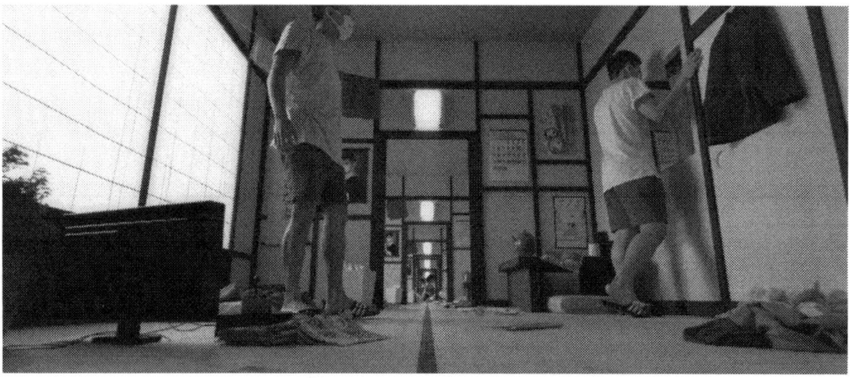

Figure 5.4 Bonobo, "No Reason." Dir. Oscar Hudson, 2017.

In the eighth room, the young man is wearing a black surgical mask instead of a white one.

The main difference between the rooms, however, is that, as we proceed, they get progressively smaller. Or rather, it would be more accurate to say that, as we progress from room to room, the young man seems to get slightly bigger each time, until the room is no longer able to contain him. This is once again an effect of forced perspective. The camera always remains on the ground, moving forward in its groove. The rooms are actually getting smaller, but for the camera each room takes on the same dimensions, filling the frame. Floor, walls, and overhanging ceiling remain in place on the screen. Many of the objects in the room are scaled down proportionately to the room's own size. But some objects retain their actual dimensions, just as the young man does.

By the time we reach the fifth room, the young man's body stretches out for the entire length of the room from back to front. In the sixth room, he sits and looks through books that have become so tiny that they fit in the palm of his hand. By the seventh room, he needs to crouch with his head down in order to avoid hitting the ceiling; the video monitor and futon seem tiny by comparison. By the eleventh room, as he stands straddling the entryway, we can only see the lower portion of his legs, which pass through holes in the ceiling just below knee level. In the twelfth room, an arm up to the wrist emerges from a hole in the wall; in the thirteenth, both arms hang down from holes in the ceiling. In the remaining rooms, the young man is absent, since his body can no longer fit; but the space is filled by enlarged physical objects—which is to say, strictly speaking, by objects that have retained their actual size even as the space containing them has shrunk. The fourteenth room features stacks of dirty dishes, and the seventeenth has piles of apples—both of which reach halfway up to the ceiling.

The camera stops moving at 3:01, once it has entered the eighteenth and final room. An enormous apple sits on the futon, which—like the teakettle, the posters on the back wall, and most of the other objects we can see—is a miniature, sized proportionately to the dimensions of the room. This final room, like the first one, and unlike all the others, has a closed door at the back. The door opens as the camera remains fixed. The young man looks through, but he is so big in relation to the room that we can only see about half of his face at once. From 3:09 to 3:11, he pulls down his surgical mask for a moment, so that we can see him lip sync the words "stay warm" (see Figure 5.5). These are the two final words of the song; they encourage us to stand firm against the catastrophe to come. Right after these words are sung, the door closes.

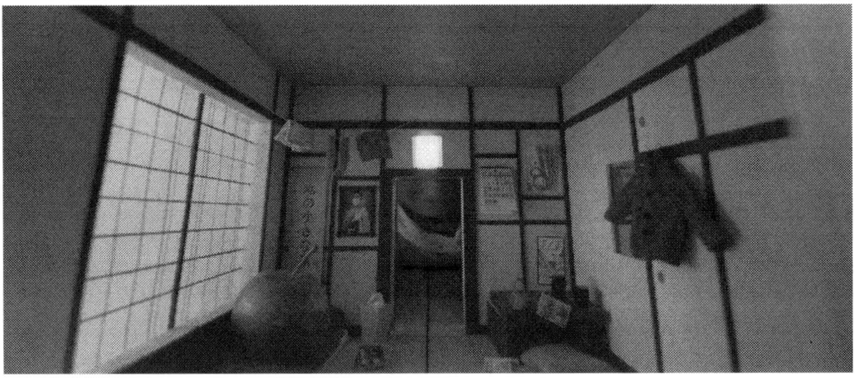

Figure 5.5 Bonobo, "No Reason." Dir. Oscar Hudson, 2017.

Murphy's singing is done, and all that remains of the song is the instrumental coda. At 3:14, the camera starts pulling back at a quick rate. Where the forward movement took two and a half minutes, the backward movement only takes forty-five seconds. As the camera withdraws, the lights above the open doorways in back of each room start flashing on and off. This combination of fast camera movement and strobe lighting creates a sense of urgency, which is further supported by the backbeat of bass and drums. Yet the absence of vocals also tells us that the song is winding down. As the camera withdraws, all the iterations of the young man reach after it, and eventually get up and try to follow it. But the camera is too fast for any of them. This also means, however, that their domain has only been invaded for a brief instant; the eventless stasis that they seemingly crave will soon be restored.

Once the camera has retreated all the way to the very first room, the door at the back closes, and the light above it remains steadily on instead of blinking. The camera continues to move backward until it has reached its original position from the start of the video. At this point, just as the music quiets down, the camera finally reverts to stillness. We find ourselves back precisely where we began. Once again, the young man lying on the futon sits up slowly, and slips on his sandals. At this point, just when the whole cycle seems on the verge of starting all over again, the song and the video end.

Oscar Hudson says in interviews that he is proud of the fact that "there's no post FX whatsoever" in this video. All the effects were achieved in-camera, and "the whole film is comprised of just two shots: the move forwards and the move backwards" (Knight 2017). For the director, "the whole appeal of the idea was trying to pull it off physically" (Stone 2017). By putting a physical camera in a constructed physical set, Hudson was able "to link psychological space and physical space directly," he says, in a way that could not have been achieved with CGI (Knight 2017). The entire set, with all the rooms and their (increasingly smaller) furnishings, was "made from scratch by hand" (Stone 2017); a tiny camera was mounted on a "flat base plate of wood," and pulled back and forth by a hidden wire (Knight 2017). Ten actors were used to portray the video's single human figure; the surgical masks hid enough of their features so as to make them plausibly seem identical (Knight 2017).

The materiality of Hudson's set creates a powerful sense of physical entrapment. This is only amplified by the camera's relentless movement. Motion in "No Reason" is intensive rather than extensive: usually we pass through space, but here we burrow into it instead. We may avoid the danger of shrinking all the way to the infinitesimal vanishing point, but we are unable to escape from the room either. Our vision feels fully embodied, thanks to the camera's exaggerated, forced perspective. The camera does not reveal itself to us, and its point of view is not a human one that we could "identify" with. But the camera does not offer us any sort of objective detachment either. Rather, it is fully embedded within the space it explores. We see this especially in the latter part of the video, when both the human figures and the flashing lights seem to respond to the camera's backward passage. Bonobo's track, on its own, is gently melancholy. It does not offer us any sort of release, but it gives the impression of a steady state that is at least livable and self-sustaining—even if not particularly joyous. Hudson's video transmogrifies this feeling, by giving the song a more troubling sense of imprisonment and implosion.

The figure of the *mise en abyme*—the image continually replicating itself within itself, on an ever-smaller scale—is a common one in recent theory and criticism, as well as in visual and audiovisual works. Mathias Bonde Korsgaard notes that several music videos make use of this device (Korsgaard 2017): most notably, Wild Beasts' "Brave Bulging Buoyant Clairvoyants," directed by OneInThree aka Ross Cooper (Wild Beasts 2008), and The Presets' "Are You the One?," directed by Chris Moyes (The Presets 2006). More generally, the *mise en abyme* illustrates, and indeed embodies, the paradoxes of recursivity and self-reference that tend to arise in many realms of modern thought and practice (set theory, cybernetics, aesthetics, and so on). Today, the networks within which we find ourselves contained are commonly said to exhibit fractal self-similarly across scales. The infinite regress of the *mise en abyme* is logically troubling: thinkers like Jacques Derrida invoke it in order to demonstrate that self-reflexivity is as incoherent as it is inescapable (Lee 2002, 94–9). Yet at the same time, figures of scale-free networks, of fractal self-similarities, and of holograms in which each part contains a full image of the whole, are all too frequently invoked in order to justify neoliberal fantasies of smooth spaces, frictionless markets, and unimpeded financial flows. The *mise en abyme* is also a handy alibi for the cynical flippancy that pervades so much of our media-drenched culture: it's all the same, it's all "fake news," endlessly replicating itself.

But Hudson's video undercuts these tendencies, by exhibiting a sort of material resistance. The *mise en abyme* is neither frictionless nor interminable. The messy physicality of all those objects at different scales gets in the way of an infinite regress. Most particularly, the presence of the young man, who stubbornly stays the same size across all of these iterated miniaturizations, becomes a sticking point. He no longer fits within his single room, even if he has nowhere else to go. This blockage is the underside, or the hidden actuality, of our society's vision of flexibility, mobility, and immediacy. "No Doubt" dramatizes the displacement and deprivation that drives the necessity for migration.

Blocked Connections

The videos for "Kerala" and "No Reason" reconfigure the songs that they bring to life. I have argued that their harsh, negative visions push against the otherwise more benign and hopeful sonic atmospheres of Bonobo's music. But perhaps I can phrase this more charitably, by suggesting that the videos unfold dimensions of perception and feeling that are already implicit within the soundscapes of *Migration*. Bonobo's eclectic cosmopolitanism operates on several registers at once; it links highly specific sounds and samples to much wider configurations that are global in scope. The two videos bring this out quite powerfully. Both Bullivant and Hudson project scenarios that are extremely condensed, confining, and specific, but that also directly express some basic conditions of twenty-first-century sensibility. Marshall McLuhan argued long ago, at the dawn of the computer age, that "the effects of technology ... alter sense ratios or patterns of perception" on the most fundamental level (McLuhan 1964, 18).

In the decades since McLuhan wrote, it has become ever more apparent that he was right. Space and time—those basic Kantian "pure forms of sensible intuition," underlying all of our particular experiences—are no longer what they used to be. They have mutated into strange new forms. David Harvey traces the violent "time-space compression" that structures the world of globalized financial capitalism (Harvey 1991, 260–83). And Manuel Castells, for his part, explores the "space of flows" and the "timeless time" that increasingly characterize our "network society" (Castells 2010, 407–99). We live in a world whose idealized dimensions are those of simultaneity and instantaneity. In theory, information travels across the globe at the speed of light; and any number of locations, anywhere in the world, can be put into immediate proximity via telepresence.

Of course, connections do not work as smoothly and seamlessly in actual practice as they are supposed to do in theory. We have all experienced delays, and problems of unequal access. But the ideal of frictionless and transparent networks is what lies behind the vision of global transit and exchange that animates Bonobo's music. The trouble is that omnipresence (the compression of space), and perpetual nowness (the compression of time), is tailored to the needs of capital accumulation, rather than to those of human flourishing. We experience these ideals in the form of imperious *demands* that we can neither evade nor satisfy. When time is drained of all prospects of futurity, when anticipation collapses into immediacy, then we may well feel that we are trapped in the stuttering, repetitive timescape of "Kerala." And when space implodes, so that everywhere is compressed into *right here*, as into the singularity of a black hole, then the isolation of the *hikikomori* in "No Reason"—a confinement that is also an incapacity to fit in, or to maintain proper and comfortable proportions—may well be our only fate. In their videos, Bullivant and Hudson bring into sharp relief the troubling underside of the utopia of incessant global circulation. This dystopian vision, too, is part of Bonobo's meaning: an intrinsic dimension of his rhizomatic music, with its "rolling flow of sounds" in "constant evolution" (Ableton 2016).

6

The Passion according to FKA Twigs

Secular Resonances

FKA twigs has made four music videos for songs from her 2019 album *Magdalene*. Here I will discuss two of them. The first, "cellophane" (FKA twigs 2019a), was directed by Andrew Thomas Huang, who has also made a number of videos for Björk. The second, "sad day" (FKA twigs 2020a), is directed by Hiro Murai, who is best known for his work with Childish Gambino (aka Donald Glover). The *Magdalene* album as a whole is largely about love and loss, or more broadly about pain, vulnerability, and loneliness. *Magdelene* has widely been taken as an expression of the hurt resulting from twigs' well-publicized breakup with Robert Pattinson, and perhaps also of the physical trauma she suffered due to uterine fibroid tumors. *Magdalene* certainly bears the weight of these physical and psychological scars.

But *Magdalene* pushes far beyond autobiography; nor does it ultimately focus on victimization and trauma. As its title indicates, the album is loosely organized around the New Testament figure of Mary Magdalene, one of the close companions and disciples of Jesus. In recent decades, feminist theologians have rehabilitated and championed the figure of Magdalene, seeing her as a counter to the patriarchal tendencies of the Church. FKA twigs does not seem to be particularly religious; in her album, she secularizes Mary Magdalene as an emblem of embattled, but ultimately self-redeeming, femininity. As Grace Chalmers puts it, in recent years "popular culture has been taking inspiration from the stories of religious figures, finding strength and healing through what they represent, rather than from religious doctrine." And so twigs uses the figure of Mary Magdelene to display her "understanding the burden it is to be a woman in a society where there are indoctrinated and subliminal expectations of their role within it" (Chalmers 2019). In this way, twigs generalizes beyond, and gives mythic resonance to, her personal experience.

This resonance is physical and visceral, as much as it is spiritual. Suffering must be enacted, traversed, and overcome in the flesh. FKA twigs is a dancer as well as a singer, and her music videos, no less than her live performances, are always rooted in her bodily presence, and in the intensities of movement and restraint. She has explored multiple dance styles, from ballet to voguing to krumping, as well as other bodily practices like Japanese shibaru. During the period leading up to the release of *Magdalene*, she added pole dancing and wushu sword fighting to her repertoire. These are both forms of movement performance that combine precise bodily control with extravagant display.

"cellophane"

Although twigs is well aware that "pole dancing and stripping" are conventionally "associated with the male gaze," she overtly seeks, as Clarissa Brooks puts it, "to shift that framing to something else entirely," in order to explore "healing as a practice" for "Black woman," and to "celebrate all different expressions of femininity and the female form" (Brooks 2019). It is in this spirit that the "cellophane" video focuses on pole dancing.

At the start of the video, twigs seems to be performing for an unseen audience. She emerges from behind yellow-brown curtains, and appears on a sumptuous stage. We hear loud applause as she strips off items of clothing. But we never see this presumptive audience; and in any case, the tapping of twigs' platform high heels as she walks is louder than the applause. We get an extreme close-up of twigs' heels as she walks across the floor. The floor over which twigs walks is so bright and polished as to be reflective (see Figure 6.1).

We no longer hear the audience once the song proper begins, and twigs starts dancing. She does splits, as if embracing the reflection beneath her. On the pole, she twists around vertiginously in a circle, as the camera circles the pole in the opposite direction. Eventually, twigs clings to the pole upside down; her hair cascades downward to touch the floor and meet its own reflection.

At this point, the image flips, so that the reflection is in the upper half of the screen instead of the lower. In the reflected image, the theater has no ceiling; we see white, open sky at the end of the pole (see Figure 6.2). Indeed, the pole itself now bends and twists as it pushes upward—as if it were a vegetal stem reaching for the light, rather than something made of rigid metal. The next shot gives us just a single image of twigs upside-down on the pole. We cannot tell whether

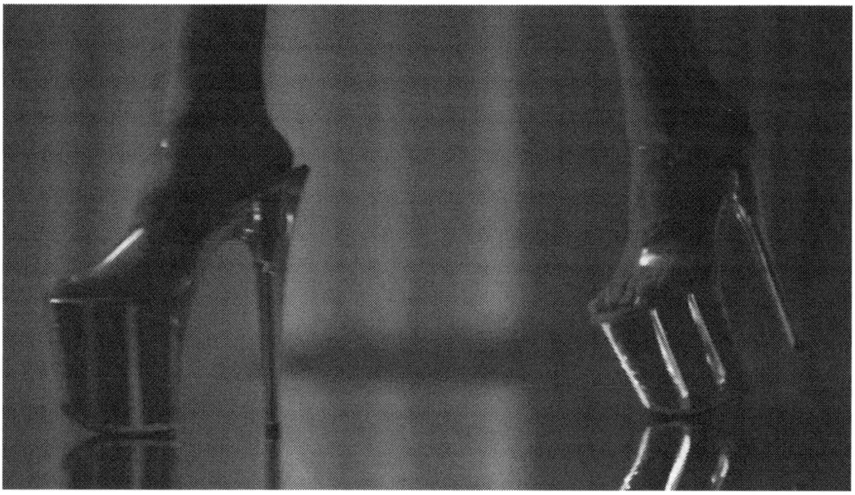

Figure 6.1 FKA twigs, "cellophane." Dir. Thomas Andrew Huang, 2019.

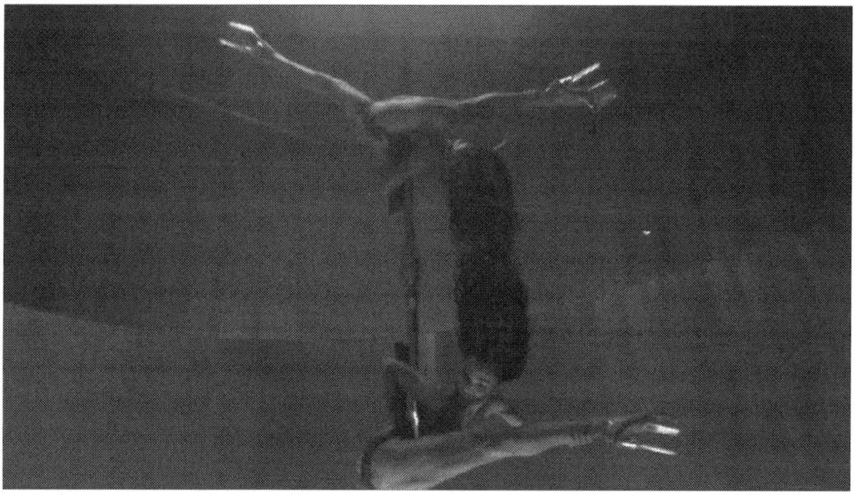

Figure 6.2 FKA twigs, "cellophane." Dir. Thomas Andrew Huang, 2019.

this is the original image, or the reflected one. But in any case, the camera pans upward, to give us a broader look at the celestial realm of blinding light.

The situation here is something like what Gilles Deleuze, in his second *Cinema* volume, calls a *crystal image*: that is to say, a visual situation in which

> the actual image itself has a virtual image which corresponds to it like a double or a reflection … It is as if an image in a mirror, a photo or a postcard came

> to life, assumed independence and passed into the actual … this point of indiscernibility is precisely constituted by … the coalescence of the actual image and the virtual image, the image with two sides, actual and virtual at the same time.
>
> (Deleuze 1989, 68–9)

This point of indiscernibility between body and reflection, or actual and virtual, is also the point at which twigs' intensely physical movements pass over into the realm of computer-generated morphing and special effects. She looks up from the curtained stage to the open sky, and ascends the pole to slip indiscernibly from one realm into the other.

The plaintive lyrics of "cellophane" suggest a wavering movement from bodily experience into unrequited yearning—which can also be regarded as a movement in which the actual is extended into, and covered over or replaced by, the virtual. twigs sings over sparse piano chords, eventually supplemented by a whispering synthesized beat. She yearns toward her lover, imploring him to respond to her. The lovers' reciprocity has broken down; the protestations of the *I* receive no answer from the *you*. "I just want to feel you're there," twigs sings. But the *you* is not there any longer. The relationship has volatilized; it may still exist as a potentiality, but it is no longer actual. This is again a point of indiscernibility, as twigs' overfullness of desire reverberates into emptiness.

Once in the sky, twigs encounters a monstrous winged creature. It is something like a cyborg pterodactyl, part organic and part metal. The organic part itself seems to combine aspects of animal and plant. The monster throws off several masks to reveal a casting of twigs' own face—yet another doubling of actual and virtual (see Figure 6.3). We hear the title line from the song: "all wrapped in cellophane," implying the public visibility of twigs' and Pattinson's relationship, and also suggesting that the relationship was artificial—plastic in the pejorative sense—rather than organic. At this very moment, twigs kicks out at the creature, but it engulfs her foot and high-heeled platform shoe. The encounter sets off a cascade of metallic fragments exploding out from the creature, as the simulated camera pulls away.

As the song's chorus resumes ("Didn't I do it for you?"), there seems to be a slight time glitch: we see twigs' kick all over again. This time, the result is that she immediately tumbles into the depths. What follows is an epic montage sequence, with varying degrees of lighting, and multiple overlapping shots at different distances. twigs' body descends through air and water, twisting on the pole, rotating end over end, and spiraling about as if caught in a whirlpool

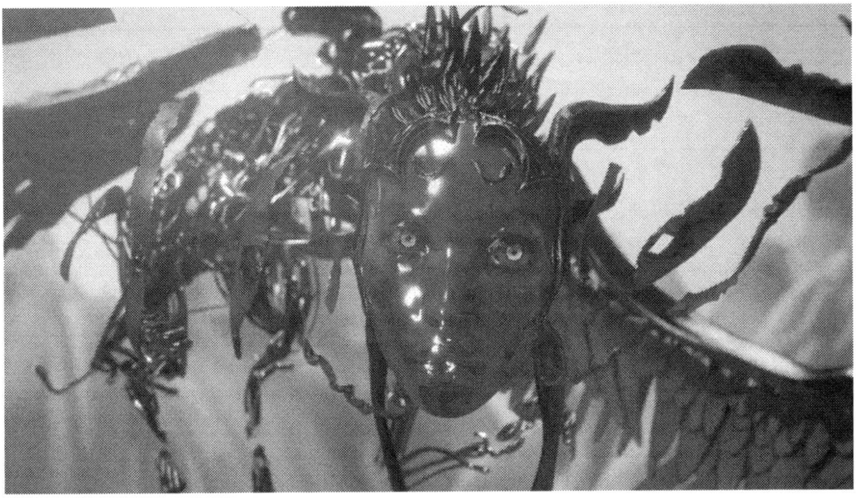

Figure 6.3 FKA twigs, "cellophane." Dir. Thomas Andrew Huang, 2019.

(see Figure 6.4). Cinematography and editing themselves circle down into the abyss, mimicking the very process that they are recording and representing. This doubling of what is shown to us in the process of showing it is yet another instance of Deleuze's crystalline indiscernibility. FKA twigs' passion—taking this word both in the sense of emotions suffered or undergone, and in the more specifically religious sense—is also a passion of the videographic apparatus itself.

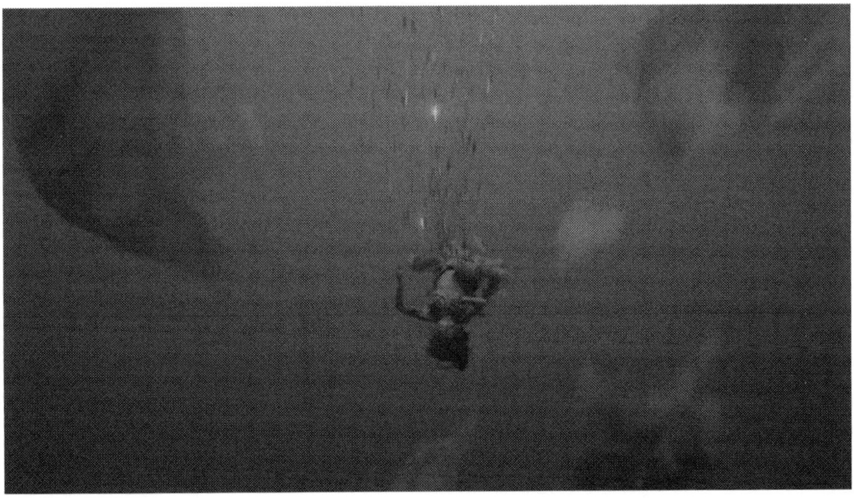

Figure 6.4 FKA twigs, "cellophane." Dir. Thomas Andrew Huang, 2019.

Finally, twigs lands in a crater of mud, panting, and coughing. This happens just as the soundtrack gives us the line "I try, but I get overwhelmed," with the word "tryyyyyy" melismatically extended. Whatever efforts twigs has made, her power to act seems finally to have been exhausted. The mud is rich and viscous. It is brownish-red in color, darker and denser than the curtains at the start of the video. A mysterious masked female figure appears at the rim of the crater; actually there are several of them, but they all seem to be iterations of the same woman. The woman or women approach, and smear mud all over twigs' body. On the soundtrack, we hear the song's Outro, in which twigs complains about the vicious media scrutiny she endured during the time of her relationship with Pattinson, with the media continually watching her, and expressing their hatred for her.

As the song ends, twigs sits up, covered in mud but alone. She rests her head on her knee, and stares toward the camera (see Figure 6.5). She is still panting from fatigue; after the music concludes, the last thing we hear is her breath. The mud might be thought, in line with the last words of the song, to symbolize the slanders flung at her by the press. But to me, this mud seems organic and potentially healing. twigs has said that she sees Mary Magdalene as a "healer" (Kent 2019), and many discussions of the album have seen healing—especially self-healing by Black women—as a central theme of the album (e.g., Brooks 2019; Kent 2019). The video depicts an ordeal that is both physical and spiritual, and indiscernibly both actual and virtual. It secularizes, and thereby reclaims, those old religious myths of the Fall and the Passion.

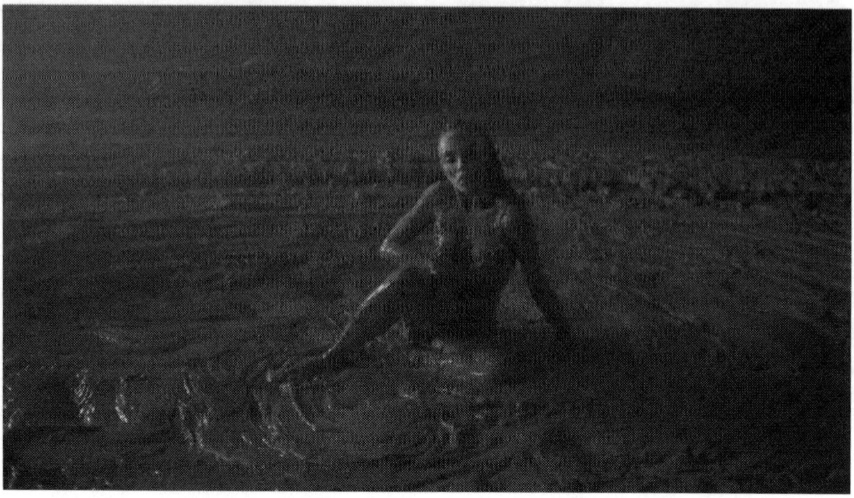

Figure 6.5 FKA twigs, "cellophane." Dir. Thomas Andrew Huang, 2019.

FKA twigs moves from self-exhibition, through self-consuming splendor, and on to exhaustion, purgation, and possible rebirth.

FKA twigs says on twitter that "when I wrote cellophane … a visual narrative came to me immediately, I knew I had to learn how to pole-dance to bring it to life" (FKA twigs 2019b). The song in itself is fragile and minimal: the instrumentation is quite light, never taking the focus away from twigs' voice. The "visual narrative" that twigs had in mind, and that Huang realizes in the video, opens up the song in significant ways. Most obviously, it gives the song a performative dimension, as twigs pole-dances for an unseen audience. But it also gives the song a broader temporal reach. The song itself seems to occupy a sharply delineated span of time, a particular present-tense moment of stress and disillusionment. But the video opens up this duration, extending it into both an immemorial past (the mythical cycle of ascent and descent) and an open future with its prospect of something new. This expanding past/future, resisting the harsh impositions of the present, is the realm of the rhythm image.

"sad day"

Just as the "cellophane" video focuses on pole dancing, so the "sad day" video features wushu sword fighting. FKA twigs fights a late-night duel with a Black man, played by wushu expert Teake. They cross swords first in a fast-food restaurant in London, then out in the streets, and finally in a rooftop apartment. The duel clearly expresses the tensions of a heterosexual relationship (see Figure 6.6). twigs explains in an interview that she named her sword Lilith, after Adam's first wife who "got banished to hell" because "she didn't want to be subservient to men" (Lowe 2019). In the course of the video, twigs waves Lilith above her head in impressive displays, as well as parrying Teake's thrusts. Both fighters also jump and fly through the air, in the style of Chinese wuxia films. This fantastical sort of move is probably most familiar to Western audiences from Ang Lee's *Crouching Tiger, Hidden Dragon* (2000), not to mention the Wachowskis *The Matrix* (1999); but it features in many Hong Kong movies from the 1970s onward.

The swordsmanship in "sad day," like the pole dancing in "cellophane," allows FKA twigs to demonstrate her physical virtuosity. But it also creates a situation in which twigs' physical presence can be transmuted by means of special effects.

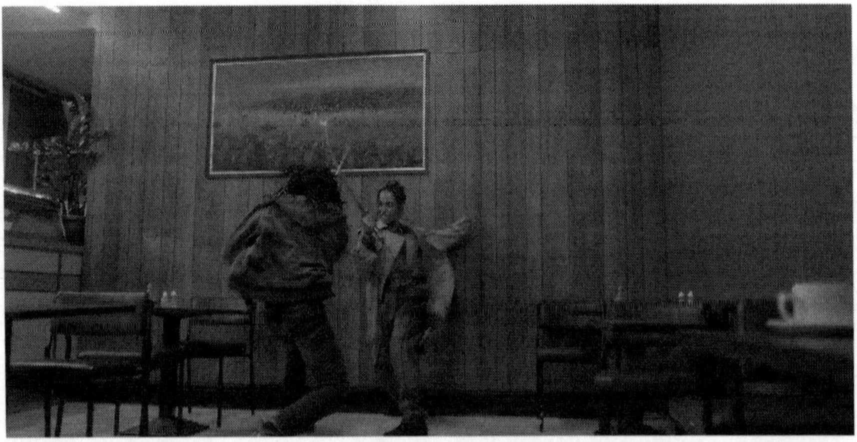

Figure 6.6 FKA twigs, "sad day." Dir. Hiro Murai, 2020.

In other words, twigs' insistent corporeality coexists with the virtualization of her body through cinematic and computational technologies. Physical intensity and virtual animation are often thought to be opposites, but in "sad day," as in "cellophane," they complement rather than contradict one another. The cinematic recording of bodily movement, and the computational rendering of bodily metamorphosis, exists on the same continuum, and cross over at a point of Deleuzian indiscernibility.

Multiple levels of bodily expression are therefore on display in the "sad day" video. FKA twigs pirouettes while flourishing her sword (choreography); she jumps into flight, soars through the air, and attains a rooftop (wire work); she is sundered as her opponent's *jian* sword penetrates her flesh (VFX). Through all of these renderings, FKA twigs also moves along a continuum of affective states. She slips back and forth between confidence and diffidence, between bluster and pain, and between dreamy musing and heightened alertness.

Something similar happens with twigs' singing voice in "sad day"—and indeed, throughout the *Magdalene* album. As Lucas Fagen puts it, twigs' "unencumbered soprano" is one of the most distinctive singing voices in contemporary pop music; its "high, lonesome sound" is breathy, quivering, and vulnerable. But in many of the songs in *Magdalene*, this voice "gets strained, squelched, and vacuumed through a series of queasy digital filters." At the same time that twigs' unvarnished voice is "presented as a token of intense feeling," its ostentatious digital alteration "comments on subjectivity and emotional representation" at a sort of ironic, critical remove (Fagen 2019).

In "sad day," as in most of the songs on *Magdelene*, twigs' voice is heavily foregrounded. On this album, twigs says in an interview, she finally "learned to write for her voice" (Lordi 2020). But this also means that, using her voice as an instrument. twigs modulates her voice throughout the album, treating it electronically in many different ways. In the three verses for "sad day," twigs' voice is on top of the mix; this creates a sense of isolation, heightened by the way that the voice is tinged with reverb. During the song's choruses, in contrast, twigs multitracks her voice, giving it a collective, choral quality as it addresses the "you" of her former lover. And in the song's bridge, twigs' voice is so heavily processed that it is difficult even to make out the words she sings.

The video for "sad day," unlike that for "cellophane," and indeed unlike most music videos, does not give us the entire album track. It strategically inserts sections of the song, as well as instrumental passages with the voice removed, into a soundtrack otherwise filled with ambient diegetic noises. We hear footsteps, traffic, and distant ambulance sirens, along with—in the restaurant—the entrance door's alert bell, the hum of overhead fluorescent lights, and the ticking of a clock. In addition, the latter part of the video, including the final credits, is accompanied by a different song from *Magdalene*: "mirrored heart."

The "sad day" video begins with FKA twigs walking down a sidewalk, flanked by trees. It is nighttime. First we see her from behind, wearing a Burberry trench coat (Burberry 2020), and desultorily shuffling along. A second shot shows her left side, from a low angle. Her profile is barely visible beyond its outline; it is backlit by a golden glow emanating from a streetlamp and filtered through the out-of-focus trees. The only sounds we hear are twigs' footsteps, crickets chirping in the trees, and some distant, barely discernible traffic noise. The mood is suspended and pensive.

Most of the outdoor shots in the video, like this one, use shallow focus. We get a blurry, washed-out sense of the city lights at night. Hiro Murai says in an interview that, though he usually shoots such scenes "in a pretty dry, matter-of-fact way," for "sad day" he was "nudging the dial towards something a little more sensual or misty. We pulled some cues from Wong Kar Wai movies" (Capper 2020). The poetry of romantic disillusion that suffuses Wong's Hong Kong is transferred to twigs' London.

After about twenty seconds, the crickets' chirping modulates into a mechanical, whooshing sound. There's a quick cut to a shot of something that looks like metallic rings or gears, or maybe the wire mesh of a fence. I cannot do better than the commentator dawndawndawn, who describes what we see here as “dark, congealed petal-like material” (dawndawndawn 2020). It is hard to tell more precisely, since the shot is dark and blurry; in any case, it is cut off after less than two seconds. The whooshing sound is quickly resolved into the click of a car door being opened; the video cuts to a shot of Teake emerging from the driver’s seat of his vehicle. We follow him from behind, in a continuing close-up shot. The back of his head, with its luxuriant Afro Locs, is framed by the flattened, out-of-focus blur of street lights in the distance. After a few steps, there is another cut as Teake opens a door, and enters a fairly well-lit late-night fish and chips joint. This is the New Ocean Bar, which Google informs me is located in the north London Borough of Barnet, close to the Grahame Park Estate, at 1 The Concourse, London, NW9 5XB. Murai says that he chose this location “because it was so unassuming and strange. It felt like the kind of place where you would see a drunk couple arguing late at night after leaving a bar” (Capper 2020). As we shall see, the video as a whole implicitly dramatizes a dispute of this sort.

Teake walks through the small restaurant, and tiredly sits down at a table in the back, against the rear wall. He looks out warily. These are the first shots in the video that are both brightly lit and fully in focus. If the blurry shots of the first forty-five seconds of the video suggest late-night fatigue, we now reach a moment of harsh clarity on the far side of fatigue: what William Burroughs famously describes, explaining the title of his novel *Naked Lunch*, as “a frozen moment when everyone sees what is at the end of every fork” (Burroughs 2013, 199). Teake just sits there, waiting. We hear the second-by-second ticking of a clock, along with all the other late-night ambient sounds. A close-up of an analog clock on the wall shows the time to be 1:59 am, with the second hand jumping, one second at a time, from 1:59:04 to 1:59:07. The time is drawn out, and all we can do is wait.

Finally, at just past the video’s one-minute mark, Teake hears the restaurant’s entrance chime and looks up. In a reverse shot from Teake’s point of view, FKA twigs enters the restaurant. We see her walk in slowly, stopping as she reaches a pillar. In a shot from behind twigs’ shoulder, Teake’s form is momentarily blurred, but it quickly snaps back into focus. Teake’s expression is both attentive and weary as twigs walks hesitantly toward him. Her expression seems to convey a flicker of doubt, covered over by grim determination. For the first time, music from “sad day” plays on the soundtrack. It’s not the beginning of the song, but rather the first chorus, with twigs asking her lover to “make a wish on my love.” While this plays, twigs walks unsteadily, step by step, toward Teake, in a kind of zombie shuffle, with her shoulders stooped forward. She mimes carrying an enormous weight on her back. After the last repetition of the chorus, the music stops for a second or two, and twigs pulls her sword out from behind her back (it wasn't there before).

Teake leaps up and pulls out his own sword (which also wasn't there before). The two of them quickly start sparring. It's like a dance: they both twirl around, waving their swords, in between raining blows. Wushu fighting is stylized action, and not actual warfare, as one expert tells us: "the practice of modern Wushu is a standardization of Chinese martial arts for sport and competitive purposes" (Jiayoowushu 2014). No words are exchanged between twigs and Teake, but the battle seems to express an emotional dynamic between them. As Murai says in an interview, he and twigs "sort of approached [the video] as an experiment to see how much story we can communicate just through movement" (Capper 2020).

In the video's narrative, twigs and Teake presumably have a history, as the expression goes. Their sword-fighting confrontation might be a metaphor for this history; or maybe it is a way to work through it, and find some resolution. "Would you make a wish on my love?," twigs plaintively sings. But if the answer were "yes," the question would not need to be asked in the first place. The lyrics express a yearning that remains unrequited.

On the soundtrack, as twigs and Teake fight, the diegetic sound of the clang of their clashing swords is accompanied, non-diegetically, by fast, dissonant electronic music. The fighters pause for a moment, swishing their swords through the air; then twigs gives out a yell and runs directly at Teake, smashing into him and propelling them both through a window and out onto the sidewalk. The music abruptly stops, replaced for a moment by the sounds of shattering glass (see Figure 6.7).

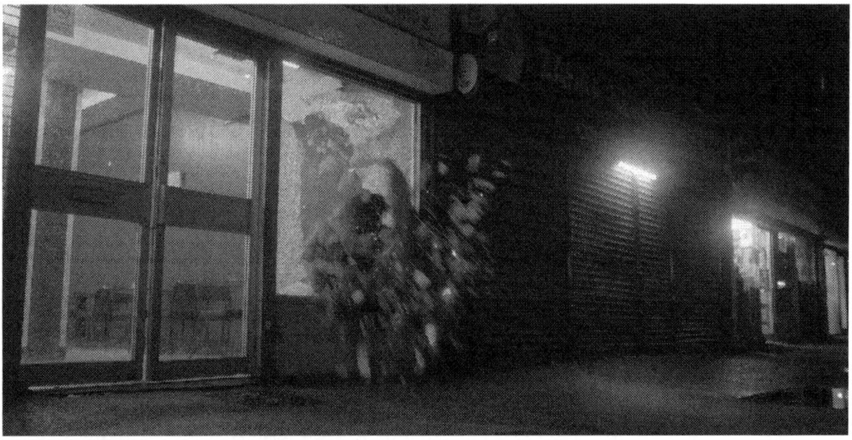

Figure 6.7 FKA twigs, "sad day." Dir. Hiro Murai, 2020.

The fighters take a moment to recover from their fall. Slowly, they both get back on their feet. twigs pants from the effort; she gives a questioning, perhaps imploring, look that turns into a slight smile. It's more an invitation than an expression of hostility; in this way, it reinforces the idea that the combatants are continuing to pursue an old, intimate quarrel. twigs brandishes her sword again; both fighters cut flourishes with their swords through the air. Finally, the actual fighting resumes. Slow piano music comes up on the soundtrack: this is the instrumental opening of the song, but without the vocals of the first verse.

Just as the music plays and pauses a number of times over the course of the video, so the swordfight too has a stuttering, start-and-stop rhythm. twigs and Teake attack one another, then pull back and separate for a moment, then attack again. At one point, twigs swipes her sword through a puddle in the sidewalk, lightly splashing Teake, as the opening of her sortie. At another point, twigs evades Teake's charge by flying backward through the air, and over a car. The fighters engage again, and soon they reach a standoff. They are directly facing one another, with enough distance between them so that each has their sword at the other's throat. I am slightly reminded of the scene in Jon Woo's *The Killer* (1989), where Chow Yun Fat and Danny Lee simultaneously have guns pointed at each other's heads. In a case, twigs and Teake remain in this position for a full twenty seconds—an eternity at the time-scale of the video. The slow introductory music of the song continues. Over the course of seven shots, twigs and Teake remain still as they stare at one another, then carefully circle around each other for a few steps, then both cautiously pull back. Teake maintains a look of grim but weary determination, while twigs displays a sort of careful and attentive hesitation.

At the end of this period of suspension, twigs finally pulls back her sword and disengages. The music dies out, making for another pause. Teake suddenly leaps or flies into the air, and speeds away, pumping his legs as if running in mid-air. twigs follows him up. There are several long shots, from ground level, of both bodies flying through the air. The song resumes, this time with the second chorus, where the same vocals as the first time—twigs begging her lover to "make a wish on my love?"—are now dramatically accompanied by a sharp repeating percussive figure.

Both twigs and Teake land with thuds on a rooftop, which is dark except for scattered red warning lights. They immediately resume fighting. A relatively long take (about 8 seconds) pans left, in order to follow twigs and Teake as she chases him across the rooftop and through a glassed-in corridor that we see from outside. We hear the instrumental transition from the second chorus of the song to the bridge. Exactly as the bridge proper begins, there is an abrupt cut to a shot of the inside of an apartment, just as Teake and twigs burst through the front door.

I will pause for a moment over the decor of this apartment, even though the action gives us little time to examine it. The ceiling is in tatters, with plaster peeling and falling off in many places. The walls are thick with mounted and tacked-up pictures, including anatomical diagrams, personal photographs, and maps. There is some discoloration where the back wall is bare, between the radiator and the windows. There are several standing lamps, whose full-spectrum incandescent light contrasts with the fluorescent light of the restaurant, as well as with the scattered streetlights outdoors. The video's color grader, Ricky Gausis, comments that the apartment was designed to look "warm," and "intimate and inviting," in contrast both to the "cyan/green tones" of the streets, and to the "sweaty" and "gritty" textures of the restaurant (Creative News 2020). The apartment's furniture is solid but not new: we can make out a dining table, a work desk, some plush chairs, a sofa, and a coffee table. All in all, the apartment looks lived-in, and fairly comfortable, but as yet ungentrified: the home, perhaps, of a semi-bohemian couple.

Inside the apartment, the fighting gets more ferocious and more extreme than it was before. There are none of the pauses that previously punctuated the action. We are reaching ground zero here; greater intimacy means more intense combat. The cinematography and editing are correspondingly more active and aggressive as well. The camera is continually in motion, just as the fighters are. The cuts are all matches on action; this sort of editing leaves us no breathing room. On the soundtrack, beneath the clangs of the clashing swords, we hear the most intense and cacophonous portion of the track: the bridge. Here (unlike anywhere else in "sad day") twigs' voice is almost drowned out by intense, synthesized percussion, and also distorted so that it sounds like it is issuing from a low-fi megaphone. In the barely discernible lyrics, twigs admits to her lover that "I made you sad before." In an interview, twigs says that she considers the bridge to "sad day" to be "the saddest part" of the entire *Magdalene* album; it even "makes me feel sad sometimes when I'm on stage" (Lowe 2019).

Exactly as the bridge ends, with a long held minor chord, the camera stops moving as well. There are a few moments of silence—a pause that is not in the recording. The video creates its own rhythms, which are superadded to those of the music. Teake holds still, after a downward thrust of his sword, and slowly looks up toward the camera. We cut to a reverse shot of twigs' face, which Teake has sliced in half, from top to bottom. After a brief additional moment of silence, the music returns with the third verse of the song. This musical passage—in sharp contrast to the immediately preceding high volume and dissonance of the bridge—is the clearest and quietest portion of the entire song. twigs' voice is nearly a cappella, accompanied only by the lightest of touches from piano and electronic percussion.

Both musically and visually, this is the still in the eye of the hurricane. Neither Teake nor twigs moves. Instead, we see a slow sequence of shots, roughly corresponding in duration to the lines of the lyrics. The first shot—corresponding to the sung line "I can imagine a world when my arms are embraced around you"—shows twigs' face, just as it starts to split apart. The camera slowly circles from a right profile to a frontal view. The second shot—along with the line "I lie naked and pure with intentions to cleanse you and take you"—is motionless, and shot from a bit further away. It shows Teake in a crouch, holding his sword in twigs' belly. The sword has sliced her whole upper body in half, through her head and her torso and all the way down to her belly. The cut to a third shot corresponds with the start of the third line of the verse: "The city howls with a cry to seduce you and claim you." The new shot is an extreme close-up of twig's sundered face, as the two halves draw further apart (see Figure 6.8).

This is the most visceral moment of the video. But of course it is also the most artificial moment of the video as well—since twigs' sundered face is so ostentatiously computer-generated and composited. The vision of twigs' sundering is vividly impressive, without being the least bit naturalistic. The

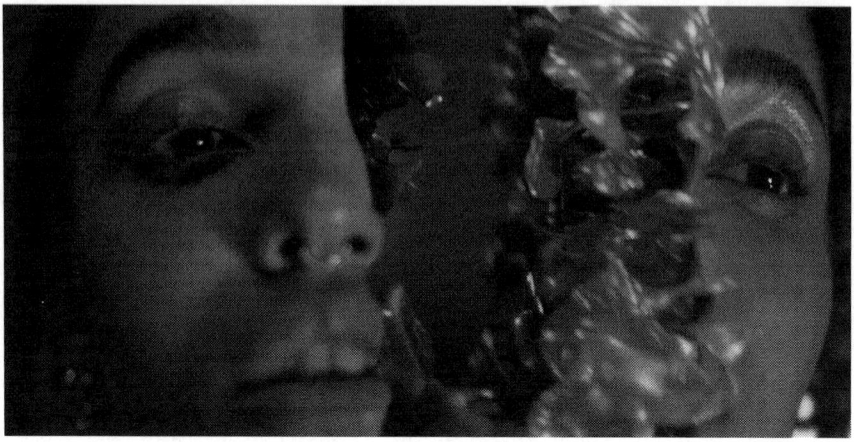

Figure 6.8 FKA twigs, "sad day." Dir. Hiro Murai, 2020.

complicated visual effects create a delicate balance. As Murai says of the scene, "we knew we wanted it to be sort of ethereal and otherworldly, not bloody, but it still needed to feel like 'flesh'" (Capper 2020). Although I just described the scene as *visceral*, we do not actually see twigs' viscera as she splits apart. No blood spurts out, either. Instead, each half of twigs' face and upper body seems like a solid container, within which we see a delicate network of reddish and transparent, almost plastic-like, little jagged fragments. The commentator dawndawndawn describes these pieces as "pearlescent pink clusters," and links them to the petals or gears we saw briefly toward the start of the video (dawndawndawn 2019). The effect, although narratively shocking, is finally more beautiful than gory. Indeed, the special effects house MPC released a "behind-the-scenes" breakdown of how the VFX were accomplished (Serra 2020); and FKA twigs herself released an Instagram filter of the special effect, allowing her followers to reproduce it in their own self-portrait photos (twigs 2020b; Yeung 2020).

What do we make of this moment in the video? Has Teake destroyed FKA twigs? Or has he, rather, reached a point where he can acknowledge, and respond to, her vulnerability and her need, displayed to him through the opening of her body? There is no unambiguous answer to this question. The special effect, in its hypervisibility, cannot be written off as merely a metaphor; but it also cannot be taken as a description of actual death. FKA twigs' wound is "ethereal and otherworldly," but these hyperbolic qualities are themselves insistently present. We might well say of FKA twigs here what Gilles Deleuze says of the French poet Joë Bousquet, who "apprehends the wound that he bears deep within his body in its eternal truth as a pure event ... my wound existed before me; I was born to embody it" (Deleuze 1990, 148). The wound is an *event*, around which everything else turns. It is more than simply personal. The wound, or the event, happens in a moment when time is oddly suspended: "an unlimited past-future rises up here reflected in an empty present which has no more thickness than the mirror" (Deleuze 1990, 150). In this moment of suspension, "the actor maintains himself [*sic*] in the instant in order to act out something perpetually anticipated and delayed, hoped for and recalled" (Deleuze 1990, 150). The wound, or the event, goes beyond my individual self, and "manifests in us the neutral splendor which it possesses in itself in its impersonal and pre-individual nature, beyond the general and the particular, the collective and the private" (Deleuze 1990, 148).

Such is the Passion according to FKA twigs. We might say that the Passion—as witnessed by the Mary Magdalene of the Bible—now returns, and is reincarnated, in a radically secularized and aestheticized form. FKA twigs is not destroyed by her wound; but she is forever marked and defined by it. She suffers this wound, but it also opens her to new potentialities. In the video, the affective heightening of this scene cannot be pacified; it cannot be explained away, or reduced to any one particular *meaning*. The lyrics suggest that twigs is "naked and pure," radically open to take and receive love; and indeed in this effect she has been *exposed*, to a point even beyond nakedness. It is hard to parse the expression on twigs' sundered face, but to me it seems to convey a sort of attentive anticipation.

Of course, even this radically open, suspended moment cannot actually stop time. As the video continues, beyond this moment of heightening and emptying, there is another cut, in the middle of the third line of the verse's lyrics. For the last few words of the line—"to seduce you and claim you"—twigs' voice is multitracked, creating an echo effect. Coinciding with these words, the fourth shot in the sequence is a medium close-up of Teake, still crouched on the floor. He looks pensive; or better, he seems musingly suspended in uncertainty, as if he cannot quite grasp what he has just done. We hear the two final lines of the verse, with twigs' voice still multitracked: "So it's time / And it's a sad day for sure." The camera tracks downward on Teake's body, and we see that the destruction is mutual: twigs' sword has also punctured Teake's chest.

As the final chord of the verse continues to reverberate, we see another special effect, less ostentatious but just as wondrous and dramatic. A small hand emerges from Teake's chest, and grasps the sword around its cutting edge. The hand then delicately pulls the sword deeper into Teake's body (see Figure 6.9). Is this Teake's

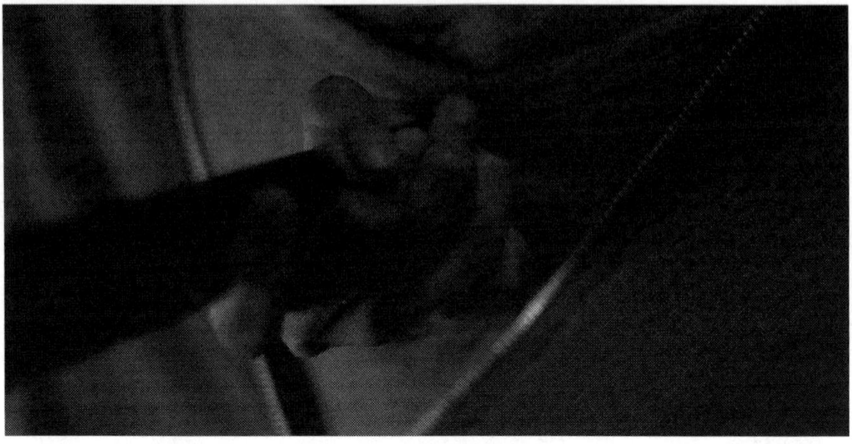

Figure 6.9 FKA twigs, "sad day." Dir. Hiro Murai, 2020.

response to twigs' opening up? Is the hand his own? Is the action voluntary? Can the hand really close around the blade without cutting itself? Once again, the special effect provides a striking image that suggests a number of possible interpretations, without allowing us to choose among them. The gesture seems both tender and painful. Its ambivalent affective charge cannot be reduced to a single, fixed meaning. During the fight, twigs and Teake seemed to challenge one another, suggesting enmity but also a kind of complicity. Now they have exposed one another, torn each other apart, forced each other to display their vulnerabilities. The two bodies are linked by their swords, but they also still remain at a distance from one another.

We hear no more of "sad day" in the rest of the video. A high whine as the hand pulls the sword further into Teake's chest is resolved into the buzz of the fluorescent lights in the restaurant from the early part of the video. This sound match coincides with a quick cut to a shot of twigs shaking herself awake from a doze. She sits in the same chair, at the same table, in the same restaurant, where we previously saw Teake. There's a cut to a close-up of the same clock that we saw before. It marks the seconds from 1:59:26 to 1:59:28. In other words, only about twenty seconds have passed in clock time, during more than four minutes of video time. In terms of narrative, this suggests that what we have seen up to now is all twigs' daydream.

FKA twigs sits at the table, musing and waiting. The song "mirrored heart" starts to play on the soundtrack. As the instrumental introduction to this song starts up, the video cuts from twigs in the restaurant to shots of Teake driving his car. Here once again Murai gives us the poetry of London at night, buildings and streetlights all in a blur due to shallow focus from within the car. The streetlights also reflect on wet splotches in the car's windows; presumably it was raining earlier. We only see Teake from the back seat, but then we see his eyes reflected in the rear-view mirror. This implies that we are still only seeing Teake indirectly, through twigs' anticipation of his arrival.

There is a cut back to twigs musing wearily at her table. She hears the tinkle of the restaurant's entrance chime, and looks up, eyes wide, with an air of expectation. This reminds us of the previous times that we heard the chime: first when Teake entered the restaurant, and then when he looked up to see twigs entering. But this time, there is no reverse shot. After a few more seconds of twigs staring in the direction of the door, there is a cut to black. It's over. The credits begin to roll, as "mirrored heart" continues playing.

I do not have much to say about the song "mirrored heart," because it is only used in the video as a sort of coda. We get a shortened version of the song, with the middle cut out; the opening verse segues directly to the concluding chorus. "mirrored heart," much like "sad day," is a melancholy, plaintive, medium-tempo song. But where "sad day" addresses a departing lover with at least some hope of salvaging the relationship, "mirrored heart" conveys a greater sense of finality. The song memorializes a later moment, when the relationship is definitively over. Other lovers, twigs sings, "just remind me I'm without you." There is no renewal, only the memory of loss. "It's all for the gain," twigs sings, "it's all for the lovers tryna chase the rush again." This implies, of course, that repetition is futile. With love, as with drugs, you will never be able to recover the rush that you felt the very first time.

Despite this melancholy sense of finality, the video as a whole still suggests that the future may be open. For we realize in retrospect that the video's time sequence is recursive. Teake driving to the restaurant, which comes near the end of the video, must happen before he parks and enters the restaurant, as he does early in the video. In other words, the video circles back on itself, only with the persons reversed. twigs now waits for Teake, and we infer that she imagined him waiting for her. The entire swordfight is therefore not actual, but virtual. It is a potentiality, something that *might* happen.

In addition to this recursive movement, the "sad day" video also reworks and enriches the song by expanding its temporal horizons. The video cuts up the song into discontinuous fragments, but it also employs its own diegetic sounds in order to produce new durations, new successions, and new continuities. The video thereby rearticulates the relations of present, past, and future. In the first place, the vivid action of the video's swordplay gives us a heightened, intensified sense of the present. But in the second place, all of twigs' and Teake's gestures are also imbued with a sense of their characters' mutual history: their long familiarity with one another. In this way, as a story told in movement, without dialogue, the video is anchored in the past, rather than the present. Every moment has a weight of deep recollections behind it. And finally, in the third place, the video stretches toward an open and uncertain future, by dramatizing twigs' as-yet-unfulfilled anticipation. Past time is compressed or contracted, as the long story of a relationship is played out in only a few minutes. But future time is expanded or dilated, as twenty seconds by the clock unfolds into a longer, indeterminate process.

Crystallizations of Time

Music and cinema are both arts of time. The videos for "cellophane" and for "sad day" alike rework the rhythms of their respective songs, stretching them into new, supplemental durations. Both videos do this by pushing toward a passage of what Deleuze calls indiscernibility between the virtual and the actual (Deleuze 1989, 69 and passim). In both videos, bodily presence and digital animation run into one another, and exchange places. And in both videos, FKA twigs suffers or experiences a Passion in which the blasting of her hopes, or the frustration of her desires, opens onto a new, as-yet-untapped potential. In my discussions of both videos, I have moved through a careful analysis of their audiovisual relations—what Michel Chion would call the "points of synchronization," as well as the divergences, between sound and image (Chion 1994, 15 and passim)—in order to arrive at a broader sense of how the videos multiply rhythms and durations, offering us new "crystallizations of time" (Lazzarato 2019, 1 and passim) as resources for new forms of affective expression. Though Deleuze describes indiscernibility in terms of the time image, FKA twigs multiplies and fractures these moments, opening them up to the pulsations and microperceptions of what I have been calling the rhythm image.

7

Vanishing Voices (Moses Sumney)

Aromanticism and Afropolitanism

Moses Sumney insists that love is not the answer; and he is not too keen on traditional formations of masculinity. Sumney seeks through his music both to redefine gender roles, and to question the all-too-often-taken-for-granted social norm of the romantic couple. The latter, even more than the former, is unusual in a popular music context, since so much of that music is focused on love, sex, and romance. In his early releases—the EP *Lamentations* (2016), and the full-length album *Aromanticism* (2017)—Sumney rejects the clichés about love that are so prevalent both in pop music and in American culture more generally. Sumney notes in an interview that romance "can't be separated from a patriarchal structure" that dominates and restricts our lives in so many respects. Indeed, "someone can love you and still be oppressing you, still not listen to your voice" (Cliff 2017). In these early works, Sumney both mourns, and yet finds comfort and strength in, a fundamental condition of existential loneliness.

Sumney continues and expands his gender-revisionist project in his second full-length album, *grae* (2020). The album's title is homonymous with the achromatic color "gray," which is both the absence of color and the result of mixing together all colors. Sumney seeks to explore an "in-between" space for himself ("neither/nor"), which has no single definition, and cannot be contained within our society's "edifice of boxes to put people in" ("boxes"), but where his "inherent multiplicity" ("also also also and and and") can flourish. This means that Sumney, much like the Black radical theorist and poet Fred Moten, asks us to "consent not to be a single being" (Moten 2017, 2018a, 2018b).

Sumney resists the formations of gender normativity; and he also rejects other identity markers as well. Like The Weeknd (Abel Tesfaye) and Tkay Maidza, about whom I write in the next two chapters of this book, Sumney is a first-generation citizen of an Anglophone settler-colonialist country, as a result of his parents' emigration from Africa. Moses Sumney was born in California to Ghanaian parents who initially entered the United States illegally (Sumney 2020b, 213ff). He grew up first in the United States, then lived in Ghana between the ages of ten and sixteen, and then returned to the United States (Kameir 2020). As a result, Sumney writes,

> I've never lived anywhere and not been the odd one out. I'm the African in America, the American in Africa, the African American among white Americans, the American African among black Americans.
>
> (Sumney 2020b, 222)

Sumney, like Tesfaye and Maidza, has experienced displacement and disorientation in the form of the contrast between his parents' homeland and his own. These artists are best understood in terms of what Achille Mbembe calls *Afropolitanism*, which he defines as "a way—the many ways—in which Africans, or people of African origin, understand themselves as being part of the world rather than being apart" (Balakrishnan 2016, 29). Afropolitanism works "in terms of movement, mobility, circulation," as African experiences are intertwined with those of other parts of the world (Balakrishnan 2016, 35). Such experiences undermine the "Hegelian paradigm," long upheld in Europe, that defined Africa "as out of history, as not belonging to the world" (Balakrishnan 2016, 29). Where the old cosmopolitanism was myopically Eurocentric (Mignolo 2000, 733ff), and the new Euro-American cosmopolitanism seems mostly to be an alibi for neoliberal globalization and corporate dominance (Gowan 2001, 79ff), Afropolitanism provides a broader vision: "a cultural, historical, and aesthetic sensibility," Mbembe writes, that involves "the awareness of the imbrication of here and elsewhere, the presence of elsewhere here and vice versa, this relativization of roots and primary belongings and this manner of embracing, with full knowledge of the facts, the foreign, the foreigner, and the far-off" (Mbembe 2021, 215). Moses Sumney is an Afropolitan artist, crossing among multiple musical and conceptual worlds.

Voice and Vision

Sumney's musical style, like his persona, is intrinsically difficult to pin down. His sound is sufficiently idiosyncratic that it is not likely to be confused with anyone else's. But for that very reason, it cannot easily be slotted into any particular musical genre. Simply because he is Black, Sumney's music has often been characterized as a sort of r&b. But this is one attribution that he summarily rejects, saying that "it's very obviously racist when people call me an r&b act" (Pearce 2020). In positive terms, Sumney's songs range from the bare minimalism of "Worth It" (where his falsetto voice is set against nothing more than finger snaps and hand claps), through the folkie riffs of "Polly" (with its backing of solo acoustic guitar, occasionally supplemented by long-held synthesizer notes), all the way to the multi-instrumental, heavy rave-up of "Virile." Sumney's melodies tend to avoid strong profiles; instead, they have a floating, unresolved feel. Sumney's voice, often multitracked, and nearly always mixed upfront, is the most distinctive feature of his music. Sumney slips easily back and forth between his rich, modal vocal register and a quivering, vibrant falsetto. His words are always clear, but he also often draws them out in ways that could not happen in ordinary speech. The intonations of Sumney's voice express both yearning and resolution.

Sumney's music always has an intense corporeal focus, despite his heavy use of synthesizers and filters. Some electronic dance music sounds and feels disembodied, as if it were made for robots; but this is never the case with Sumney's songs. His insistence on full embodiment is crucial. Maeve Sterbenz notes how the role of embodiment in musical experience has been ignored by critics until recently; it is only in "feminist interventions in music theory research since the 1990s" that this dimension of musical expression has really gotten its due. Sterbenz goes on to analyze how Tyler The Creator's body language in his music video for his song "Yonkers" (Tyler 2011) undermines the normative formations of masculinity that Tyler sometimes elsewhere projects, and instead expresses a "politically queer narrative" of disillusionment and refusal (Sterbenz 2016, 11).

Sumney's rejection of normative masculinity parallels Tyler's though it is far more explicit and wide-ranging. And as we will see, a lot of the work of this rejection is carried by his bodily postures in his music videos. But I also want to emphasize that a lot of the densely physical feel of Sumney's music is due to the power and weight of his voice. In both its modal and falsetto registers, and despite being so heavily processed electronically, Sumney's vocalizations never float free, but always remind us of their embedded origin in the chest, larynx, and lungs. TERFs and other bigots often blather on about supposedly fixed biological categories. But Sumney knows that doubts, hesitations, and fluctuations of identity are themselves most powerfully manifested and played out in the flesh.

In addition to his albums, Sumney has released a number of extraordinary music videos. And his self-presentation, in live performance as well as in videos, is a pointedly expressive one. He usually wears loose, all-black clothing: this sartorial style, together with his falsetto voice, suggests a flowing smoothness far from the hard-bodied masculine norm. His body is strong and impressively muscled, but also relaxed and graceful. It suggests an openness to touch and to affection, rather than any sort of self-enclosed masculine mastery. Thanks to his videos, as well as to his form of self-presentation, Sumney must be regarded as a fully audiovisual artist, rather than just a strictly musical one.

Sumney made lyric videos, with various collaborators, for nearly all of the songs on *grae*. These videos are usually fairly minimal in set-up. They invoke a low-fi aesthetic, recalling the look and feel of 1980s VHS tape recordings. For instance, in the lyric video for "Polly" (Sumney 2019a), Sumney simply sits in his room, staring at the camera, listening to the music without lip-syncing. The lyrics scroll by at the bottom of the screen, speaking of a polyamorous lover whose split affections make Sumney feel belittled and undervalued. Behind Sumney, we see two guitars hung on the wall to the left of the frame, and a piano on the right. Sunlight also streams in through a window way in the back left. Sumney simply sits there and softly cries for most of the video. Tears stream down his face, and his mouth occasionally convulses in sobs. But all these reactions are fairly restrained, as if Sumney were willfully holding himself back. Several times, he wipes his hands over his face, and back through his hair. At one point, he momentarily breaks into a winning smile. But by the end of the video, he is crying again. Throughout, Sumney continues to stare at the camera, never breaking eye contact. This music demands intimacy, even when it proclaims distance and solitude (see Figure 7.1).

The lyric video for "Me in 20 Years" (Sumney 2020a) is similarly held back and haunting. The camera seems to be set in a car, which drives over a country road at night, its headlights providing the only illumination. As the song reaches its first chorus, with Sumney singing in his "normal" chest voice, the car picks up Sumney in its headlights. He is sitting by the side of the road. As the chorus ends and Sumney returns to his falsetto, the car starts to move in reverse, back the way it came. Sumney springs up and runs after it. At the very end of the video, after the vocals have ended, there is a quick flash to a shot of Sumney running in the opposite direction, away from the car. This is followed by a shot of Sumney lying on the road, curled up in fetal position, as the car continues to move backward and away. During all this, the lyrics are printed on the screen

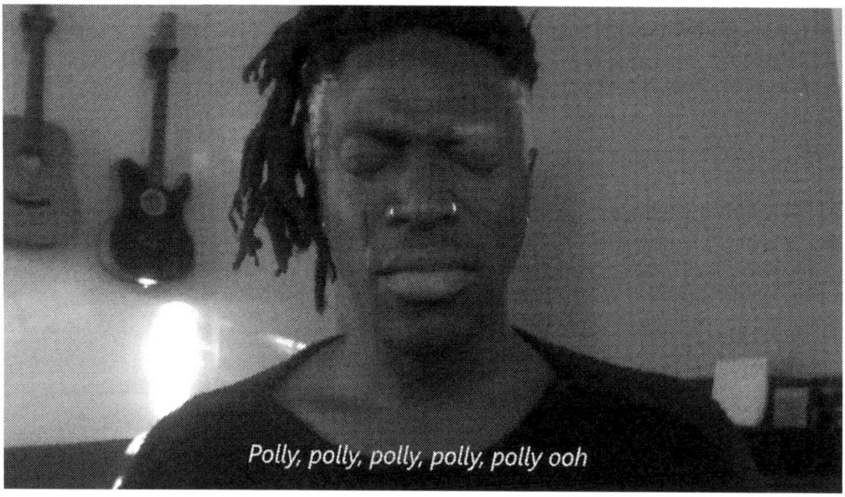

Figure 7.1 Moses Sumney, "Polly." Dir. Moses Sumney and Sam Cannon, 2019.

in an old-style monospaced computer font. This lyric video doesn't illustrate the song in any direct way. But it gives off a slightly creepy vibe, both in its form (the VHS look of the footage) and in its content (the headlights slashing through the darkness). It reminds me a bit of low-budget 1980s slasher films.

Alongside these low-fi lyric videos, Sumney has also made a number of full-fledged music videos, with higher production values and more intricate scenarios. To date, these have all been directed either by Allie Avital or by Sumney himself (in one case, "Quarrel," they are both listed as co-directors). In what follows, I will discuss three of these more ambitious videos: "Worth It," "Virile," and "Me in 20 Years."

"Worth It"

Sumney's very first music video, for the song "Worth It" from the *Lamentations* EP, is directed by Allie Avital (Sumney 2016). The video sets stark, minimal visuals against Sumney's brooding, multitracked falsetto voice and sparse instrumentation (consisting here only of hand claps and finger snaps). The lyrics are depressive: Sumney tells a prospective lover that he isn't good enough for them, and they should look elsewhere. The video has no setting; it is only a dark nonspace, giving us figures without ground.

Sumney, clothed in black, emerges out of the darkness. A series of wavering cuts brings him closer, until his face fills the screen. In alternate shots, his hand reaches out toward the camera. Finally we get a reverse shot, more tactile than visual: the naked back of another human body (the dancer Martha Nichols). Sumney's index finger hesitantly taps and traces a line down between her shoulders. In response, Nichols writhes back and forth; we see her muscles undulate. At this point, the video is almost an abstract study of the beauty of Black people's skin tones.

Gradually Nichols's movements modulate into a full-fledged dance. She keeps her back to the camera, but twists around in wider arcs, and bends her head and torso ever further back. We find that, disturbingly, she has no eyes: just smooth flesh sealed over where they should be. All this is conveyed discontinuously, with cuts between close-ups and even more extreme close-ups. Nichols's motion contrasts with Sumney's near-immobility, as the video cuts rapidly between them. Eventually, Sumney cradles Nichols's body in his arms, in a kind of inverse Pieta (see Figure 7.2).

After a few more jump cuts, during which Nichols continues to writhe and twitch, her body softens into passive immobility. The camera now tracks smoothly back, away from the two of them. This continues for a while even after the music ends, until a final fade to black. The song/video is intense, immersive, and intimate; yet also implosive and claustrophobic. Human contact

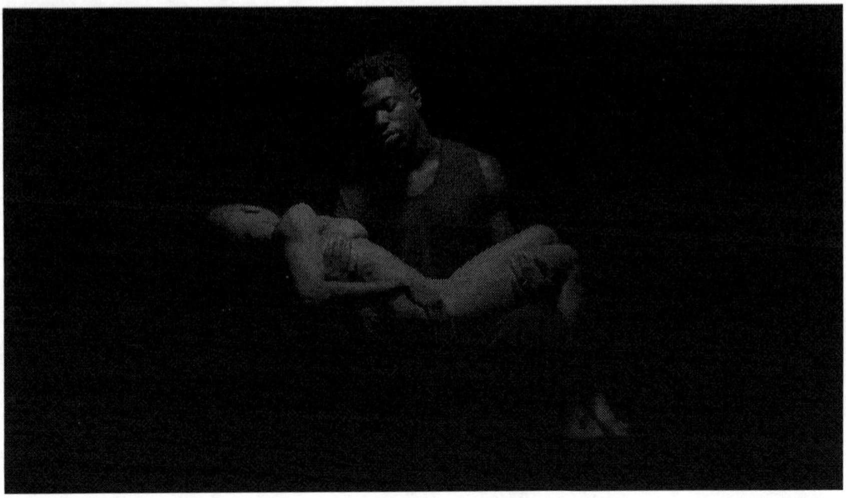

Figure 7.2 Moses Sumney, "Worth It." Dir. Allie Avital, 2016.

is inescapable and overwhelming, yet also nonreciprocal and uncommunicative. This is a truth about bodies and feelings, but also about the media environment that both sustains and isolates them.

"Virile"

"Virile" overtly rejects the mainstream social conception of masculinity: "You wanna slip right in / Amp up the masculine / You've got the wrong idea, son." It was the first song from *grae* to be released, and it was also the first full-fledged music video that Sumney directed himself (Sumney 2019b). Sumney says that the video "takes place in a post-human world; the last remaining man is caught between Beauty and Brutality's battle to dominate the earth and his body" (Aku 2019). The overall *look* of the video isn't as science fictional as this description might imply; but it is definitely strange and alienating, with its outdoor sequences in a barren landscape, and its indoor ones in the oddly lit decor of what seems to be a meat locker. "Virile" is mostly a dance video, with the dancing choreographed by Sumney in collaboration with Chris Emile, whose work in general is also concerned with redefining the Black male body (Emile 2021).

The opening shot shows Sumney lying on the ground, amidst dried grass. His shirt is open, and his chest exposed. The camera is way up in the sky, and the sound is indeterminate ambient noise; then the camera lowers itself, moving in on Sumney. The song proper begins with Sumney's a cappella voice, crying out wordlessly: "Ah, ah, ah, ah, ah, ah, ah … " Then we hear a series of shimmering runs on the harp. The video cuts to a new indoor location, the meat locker, just as a piano joins the harp, and Sumney starts singing the first verse of the song. In this verse, he comments on his awareness of mortality and bodily decay, which make "virile" masculine postures ridiculous and futile.

The lighting in the meat locker is bluish and indirect; it mostly seems to come from way back. Fumes of dry ice swirl around, close to the floor. Enormous slabs of dead meat hang from hooks. Some of the meat slabs are entirely still, while others cross the space, suspended on horizontal poles that slide back and forth. Sumney enters the scene from in between the moving slabs, also hanging down from a horizontal bar; his hands grip a small trapeze. Soon, he lets go of the bar, and jumps down to the floor. His chest and torso are bare; below them he wears loose, flared black pants. His dark skin glistens, and his muscles stand out in clear definition.

The sound thickens as the song proceeds. Flutes screech, and vigorous treble percussive rhythms cut across the melody and the singing. In the pre-chorus, guitar and drums join in, and Sumney's voice battles to stand out against the wall of sound, as he belts out some of his most sarcastic lines, about "patriarchs" and the monuments they build to themselves. When the song reaches the chorus, the mix gets even denser, with harsh skittering beats and bombastic emphasis at the beginning of each bar. This is where Sumney most overtly states his scorn for normative ideals of masculinity and virility. He almost screams, drawing out syllables as his voice fluctuates back and forth between modal and falsetto registers.

As we hear all this, Sumney engages in a furious dance. The camera moves forward toward him, and then pulls back again. For the most part, it remains far enough away to show either his whole body, or his body from the waist up. Sumney's dance adopts a start-and-stop rhythm. At times his body ripples and flows, while at other times it freezes momentarily into tight, contorted poses (see Figure 7.3). Occasionally, his back is to the camera; we see his shoulder muscles vibrating with tension, in a way that is reminiscent of Martha Nichols in the earlier video for "Worth It." All in all, it seems as if Sumney were both trying to free some energy trapped inside himself, and yet also trying to bottle that energy up and prevent it from escaping. Everything is taut and tensely would up. It is as if Sumney were taking the patriarchal, virile postures that he has been

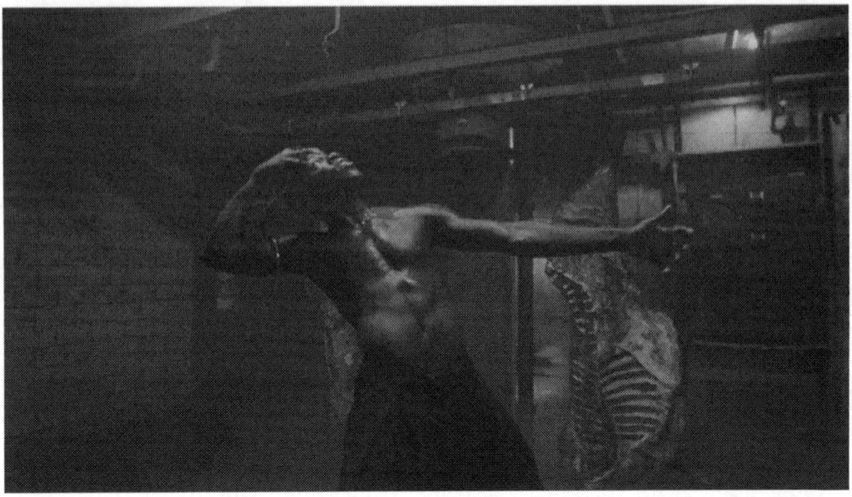

Figure 7.3 Moses Sumney, "Virile." Dir. Moses Sumney, 2019.

socially conditioned to adopt, and shaking them out, twisting them into harsh and bizarre shapes, in order to exorcise them once and for all.

When the song reaches the second verse—in which Sumney sarcastically sings of the normative masculine striving for "dominion" over everything, the video moves into another room. This room is reddish in tone, and it is set up like a religious chapel. There are rows of pews on both sides of a central aisle that leads to a kind of altar. Candles are burning on the altar, and to both sides of it there are giant slabs of meat hanging. Is this a site for the worship of virility, in the form of meat-eating and masculine violence? The camera moves down the aisle toward the altar, as Sumney writhes in front of it. His motions are a bit less frantic than before; he almost seems to be doing some sort of exercise routine, alternately stretching his arms up high and having them touch fixed points on his shoulders and face. As the song moves to the intensified beat of the second pre-chorus, Sumney writhes and gesticulates before the altar, in a parody of prayer.

Then the camera moves back and away from the altar. This is followed by a sudden cut to a metallic wall lit in cool blue, against which Sumney is now dancing. We get extremely brief jump cuts back to the red room, though mostly we see Sumney writhing against the wall in blue. These violent disjunctions of the image correspond to the musical ferocity of the second chorus, with its raving power chords and heavy percussion.

Finally we get a shot of the entire blue room. It contains still more giant slabs of meat. Some of the slabs are hanging from hooks as before, while one slab lies on a long work table, as if it has been prepared for dissection. As the chorus continues—grimly warning us that "too much is not enough"—Sumney skips across the room in boxer's pose. His fists are nearly clenched, as if he is going to punch out the meat, and he skips backward across the room, almost like Muhammad Ali when he would "float like a butterfly." But then—after a shot that pans across the ceiling of the blue room—Sumney crouches before one of the slabs of meat, seeming to caress it. When he pulls himself back upright, his right hand arm, all the way up to the elbow, is covered with some blue, glittery substance. As the chorus continues, we are reminded that "you pick your own prison."

The camera backs out of the room, and as it does so, the room lighting changes from blue back to red (recalling the light of the "chapel"). The room has no door, but it is separated from the rest of the space by hanging plastic strips (such as are often used at the edge of a refrigerated area). The camera, looking through these strips, shows us Sumney in silhouette, dancing just behind the strips, still in the (now red) room. Sumney's dancing is considerably gentler and more fluid than it was before; he waves his arms upward in alternation. All this takes place during the song's bridge, with a somewhat gentler sound than the chorus. The lyrics are once again sarcastic, with their accusation against masculine imperialism. Sumney repeats the word "are" many times, as if he were testing it out on his tongue. The instrumentals are still quite thick and loud, but now they play in unison with Sumney's voice.

While the stream of "are"s continues, the video cuts from the meat locker to a long shot in which the camera rapidly moves over a landscape, mostly dry grass with a sparse scattering of trees. The instruments suddenly drop out, so that for a moment we just hear Sumney's voice once more reciting wordless "ah"s. The video then cuts to an extreme close-up of meat, with ladybugs crawling over it. This is slightly reminiscent of the close-up of maggots on meat in Eisenstein's *Battleship Potemkin* (though ladybugs are far less disgusting than maggots). Then full instrumentation resumes, for the last reprise of the chorus; and we cut back to the outdoors. We see Sumney running along a path; from high up in the sky, we see that the path on which he runs is really a closed loop. Then the camera, from somewhat closer in, and closer to ground level, circles around Sumney as he dances in place. The sky behind him is filled with an ominous, spiraling swarm of insects or birds (it is hard to tell which; evidently this is a CGI construct).

There are a number of quick jump cuts as Sumney dances ever more energetically, waving his arms toward the sky, and with an expression of ecstasy. At the same time, the swarm fills more and more of the sky. Just as the singing ends, and the music fades out, we cut to a shot of Sumney lying on the ground, panting heavily as if exhausted. In the absence of music, his breathing is quite loud on the soundtrack. An enormous mass of ladybugs (like the ones on the meat earlier) crawl all over his face and torso (see Figure 7.4). The camera slowly moves closer and closer to Sumney's face, with the bugs in disturbing profusion. Finally, the video cuts to black, though the heavy panting continues on the soundtrack for a few more seconds.

The emotional power of the "Virile" music video comes from its accretion of details, both in the music and in the visuals. Though the song is a rave-up, meant to overwhelm, its instrumentation is finely articulated, and continually varies over the four minutes or so of the song. At times, staccato beats and ferocious treble riffs cut across the melody, while at other times the instrumentation

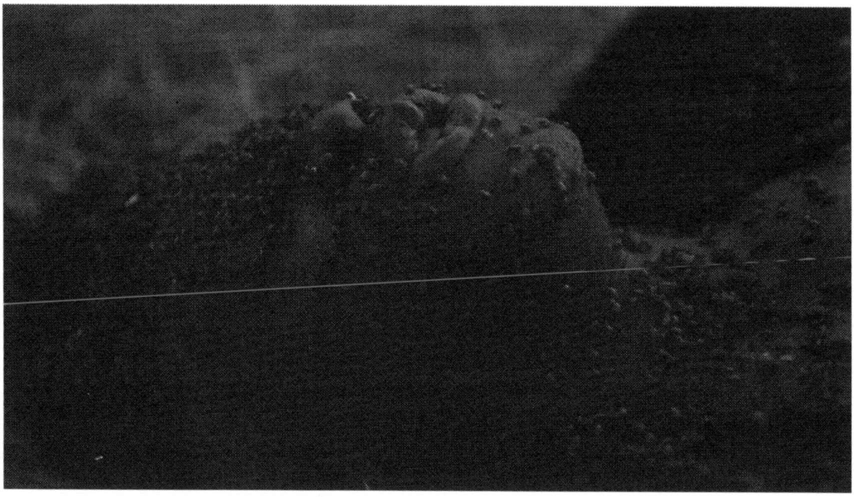

Figure 7.4 Moses Sumney, "Virile." Dir. Moses Sumney, 2019.

closely follows the melodic line. Meanwhile, Sumney's singing repeatedly shifts its register, as its mood varies between longing, anger and sarcasm, on the one hand, and resignation, on the other. Throughout the swirl of the music, our attention always comes back to Sumney's singing—which is to say, his embodied breathing.

Visually, the "Virile" music video is stylized in ways that open up the message of the lyrics, but without literalizing them, or forming them into a narrative. The subdued lighting of the meat locker, alternately reddish and bluish, sets off, in contrast, the sheen of Sumney's dark skin. Indeed, it has only been in recent years that cinematographers have learned to overcome the built-in white bias of the cinematic apparatus, in order to light Black peoples' skin properly (Latif 2017). Sumney's dancing in the video moves through a variety of gestures and postures; it is highly energetic and dynamic, as it both enacts what we might call the character armor of normative masculinity and pushes to break free of it. If Sumney's dancing expresses a conflict between Beauty and Brutality, it demonstrates the difficulty—no less than the necessity—of escaping from the latter. The video continually reminds us of death and carnivorous predation: we have taken life from the animals now reduced to slabs of meat, and this violence is very nearly our implicit religion.

We might see Sumney's dancing, and the video as a whole, as expressing the struggle of life against death—and in particular, against the violent putting-to-death that characterizes hegemonic masculinity and virility. But Sumney also reminds us that life itself is finite. Indeed, this is part of what makes normative masculinity's pretensions of mastery so absurd. The slabs of meat, no less than the ladybugs and the CGI swarms, remind us how life always gives way to other life. The music video is a living demonstration—as Sumney sings in the chorus—of how "the virility fades," and how all efforts to "amp up the masculine" are futile.

"Me in 20 Years"

In "Me in 20 Years," Sumney evokes the memory of a departed lover, whose gender is unspecified. "I'm still here," he sings, but the lover (addressed as "you") is gone. The singer is left with the lover's "imprint in my bed": a trace of departure, in the form of a "pit" or a "cavity." You have left me, he seems to be telling the former lover, but you have also left a trace of yourself behind. Your very absence remains with me; it is palpable, emotionally and even materially. I cannot touch you, but I also cannot escape your touch.

In this way, Sumney defines a mode of being that is different from our consensus conception of interpersonal relations, as well as from the usual gender binary. He describes this mode of being in other songs as the "in-between," or the "neither/nor." Using a philosophical language that Sumney himself eschews, we might call this mode of being the virtual. "It's the void. It's nothingness," Sumney says in an interview; but he quickly adds that "nothingness, to me, is not just an absence; it's its own presence" (Pearce 2020). The relation between self and other is uneven, dissymmetrical. It splits the difference, not only between male and female, but also between being and nonbeing.

"Me in 20 Years" explores this subtle persistence of nothingness and non-connection: this sense of loneliness and unrequited loss, this "endless January," this emptiness that is somehow also "its own presence." I am reminded of Wittgenstein's strange cry, when speaking of pain: "It's not a Something, but not a Nothing either!" (Wittgenstein 2009, 109, section 304). This sense of lingering, of the strange persistence of that which is no longer, comes through not just in the song's lyrics, but even more in its means of expression: its vocals, instrumentals, and rhythms.

Sumney sings most of the song (all but the first chorus and the concluding outro) in his gorgeous falsetto. His voice is foregrounded over a lavish, romantic backing track of piano chords and washes of synthesizer. The melody hovers, unresolved, with lots of minor chords; it never quite settles into, or returns back to, the stability of the tonic. Melodic uncertainty goes together with gender indeterminacy. In pop music, male falsetto singing has long worked to unsettle fixed gender identities—which is one of the central goals of Sumney's entire *grae* album. According to Anwyn Crawford,

> the male falsetto is transgressive. His voice can go to places that his body cannot, or rather, his body produces a voice that makes "his" a slippery assignation.
>
> (Crawford 2010)

In "Me in 20 Years," Sumney's falsetto resists stereotypes of masculinity, even as it doesn't sound conventionally feminine either. It has an ethereal quality, but it also testifies to deep embodiment. It primarily expresses an unquenched longing and sorrow; and yet somehow, at the same time, it also conveys a kind of acceptance of loss. Sumney mourns the lover's absence, but he also refuses to be overwhelmed by regret. He is not asking the lover to return; he seeks, rather, to persist in the lover's absence. We might even call this a kind of Spinozian *conatus*: "the endeavor by which each thing endeavors to persevere in its own being" (Spinoza 2018, 102, III.7). Sumney's falsetto quivers and soars; its unrest expresses a continuing will to go on, or to "hold out for more time," as the lyrics put it. But of course, you need to expend energy continually, even just to persist, or to stay alive. Over the course of the song, Sumney's falsetto seems to be pushing toward some absolute limit of embodied vocal expression, both ecstatic and painful. Beyond this limit, it would either cease to exist, or else have to transmute itself into some other, scarcely imaginable form.

Sumney himself recounts in an interview that, when he first played an early version of "Me in 20 Years" for his collaborator and co-producer Daniel Lopatin (aka Oneohtrix Point Never), Lopatin

> said that it sounded like an old lady screaming to herself in the middle of a Whole Foods. And I realized then and there that that is my brand … It's just such an exaggeration.
>
> (Breihan 2020)

Though Sumney's comment is humorous in a way that the song itself is not, it nonetheless points to an important quality of his performance. Sumney has no compunctions about using his falsetto *in extremis*. He remarks that millennials, the age group to which he belongs—he was born in 1991—are a "really melodramatic generation" (Breihan 2020). For Sumney, this melodramatic extravagance goes along with the way that millennials are "more open about sexuality, less ashamed, more open to acknowledging the spectrum" of gender positions than their parents were (Brown 2020b). Sumney's falsetto refuses to be reined in. It tells us, as the lyrics to many of the songs in *grae* also indicate, that he is open to bodily transformation, as well as to experimentation with gender positions, and with other aspects of his identity.

Allie Avital's video for "Me in 20 Years" both literalizes and hyperbolizes the song's overt meanings. Avital herself describes the video as "a literal illustration of the lyrics," made this way because "the feeling and the imagery was already there in [Sumney's] words" (Promonews 2020). Most notably, the video shows Sumney as an elderly man (see Figure 7.5). Furthermore, it overtly depicts what Avital calls "a pulsing crater" (Promonews 2020): the imprint, pit, or cavity described in the lyrics is visibly right there, in the middle of Sumney's bed.

But this literalism also means that the video—with its *noir*esque cinematography, and its combination of naturalistic details, prosthetic body enhancements, and CGI constructions—also pushes the song to its most extreme consequences. The video is dense, filled with telling details; as Avital says, recounting the process of making it, "everything was quite intentional every step of the way" (Promonews 2020). For instance, at the moment when, in the song, Sumney asks his future self, "does your milk still turn to rot too soon?," the video shows us the elderly Sumney opening the refrigerator and taking out a bottle of milk. The milk sits in between piles of rotten avocados and lemons; the refrigerator is otherwise empty. Everything seems on the verge of decay. Sumney

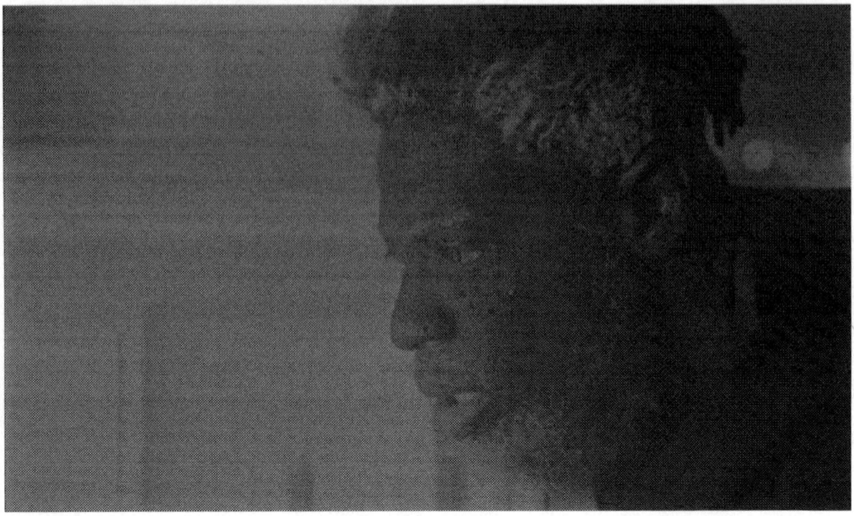

Figure 7.5 Moses Sumney, "Me in 20 Years." Dir. Allie Avital, 2020.

pours some of the milk into a glass, and leaves both the glass and the bottle on the kitchen table.

Moreover, although in the lyrics the 29-year-old Sumney interrogates his future self in twenty years' time, the video shows us, instead, a much older Sumney, who seems to be in his seventies or eighties. That is to say, the video projects something like fifty years into the future, rather than the twenty specified by the lyrics. Avital remarks, of this portrayal, that "I suppose it's accurate in terms of young people's projection of themselves when they age" (Promonews 2020). Sumney's prosthetics and makeup give him a grayish beard, graying hair, and moles and creases all over his face.

At one moment in the video, just as the vocals present Sumney musing about a future when "I'll burn alone / Like a star," the aged Sumney stares closely at his reflection in the mirror, and then removes something from his mouth—it seems to be a loose or broken tooth. He puts it down with others in a glass on the edge of the sink. The next shot just shows us Sumney's reflection; his virtual image, rather than his actual presence. The aged Sumney smiles, just for a moment. His remaining teeth look discolored in spots and worn down, but the smile is nonetheless warm and genuine. The elderly Sumney continues to shine like a star, even through the gloom of the video. He is still smoothly handsome, albeit in a decrepit sort of way.

The video shows the elderly Sumney living in a small, run-down apartment. At the start of the video, the camera is out of doors, and tracks across a series of high-rise buildings. This exterior is an actual location shot, taken with a drone, of a "Soviet apartment block" in Kiev, Ukraine; Avital says she chose this location because "we liked that often loneliness exists within close proximity to so many other people" (Promonews 2020). As the camera floats across these buildings, we hear a steady hum of what seems like background traffic noise. The song proper begins, with a piano chord followed by Sumney's falsetto. In an apparent continuation of the opening single shot—but which was actually stitched together from three separate shots in postproduction (Promonews 2020)—the camera pushes inside, through a window on a high floor, to show us Sumney sitting on his bed.

When we first see Sumney, he is sitting stolidly in place at the edge of the bed, with his hands on his knees. He is dressed in all black. He faces away from the cratered hole, which hollows out a considerable portion of the mattress. The apartment itself is poorly lit; there is soft light from the windows, together with a few lamps toward the back. Sumney's face is lit up at one point, when he opens the refrigerator. There is also a moment of bright illumination when Sumney passes in between the camera and a standing lamp. Aside from these two moments, the overall color palette of the video is extremely limited, washed out and tending toward grayscale. The footage also seems quite grainy; this was achieved, Avital says, by running the (digitally shot) footage "through a 16mm scan" (Promonews 2020). Though the video shows Sumney in the future, the Soviet-style apartment, with its old furnishings, pulls us back into the past.

The elderly Sumney hobbles around the apartment; we see extreme close-ups of his face, alternating with longer full-body or upper-body shots. After pouring the milk, and placing both glass and container on the kitchen table, Sumney goes across the room to a rack of clothes. He takes a long-sleeved shirt out from the rack, just as the lyrics voice a self-reproach, the singer asking his future self whether he still keeps sentimental souvenirs of the distant past. The shirt is evidently just such a sentimental souvenir. Perhaps it once belonged to the long-departed lover? In any case, Sumney avidly sniffs the shirt, then rubs it across his mouth as if he were trying to kiss it. Then he dances with the shirt as if it were his partner, twirling about in slow ecstasy. This is one of the most poignant sections of the video. The old man's dance is intercut with two shots—the only ones in the video—of the young, present-day Sumney, also dressed in black, caressing the shirt, and swaying with it in his arms; he also stares at the pulsing crater in the bed.

This sequence helps to delineate the intricately tangled temporality of the video. The song is slow and rhythmically subdued; it is not particularly danceable, and it doesn't produce the intensified sense of *nowness* that powerfully syncopated rhythms often do. But the falsetto vocals are insistent enough, and continuous enough, to create the sense of a single thick duration, an extended specious present that lasts for the entire 3 minutes 41 seconds of the song (or even for the entire 4 minutes and 14 seconds of the video, with its stretches that come before and after the song proper). On top of this, the video's visuals both project into the far future of the elderly Sumney and remind us of a long-distant past. This past precedes, and recedes from, not just the future of the aged Sumney, but also the present moment of the younger Sumney who wrote the song, and who is actually performing it as we listen and watch. The shirt is evidently a Proustian memory trigger that recalls the long-departed past; and that past is itself materialized—negatively, as it were—in the cavity in the bed, to which the camera keeps on returning.

I am thinking here of Gilles Deleuze's rejection of the cliché that "the cinematographic image is in the present, necessarily in the present." Deleuze refuses this common assumption, because "there is no present which is not haunted by a past and a future," so that "it is characteristic of cinema to seize this past and this future that coexist with the present image. To film what is *before* and what is *after*" (Deleuze 1989, 37–8). Deleuze associates this temporal overflow with what he calls the time-image. But I would suggest that here it rather exemplifies what I am calling the rhythm image. Here, time is no more revealed in its "pure state" than it is measured by movement. Rather, time becomes apparent as a pulsation, or a force. Time emerges in the video's presentation of the discorrelation (Denson 2020) between the elderly Sumney and the present-day young Sumney, and of both of them with regard to the past situation whose loss they both are mourning.

As he continues to dance with the shirt, the elderly Sumney inadvertently knocks over the not-entirely-empty bottle of milk sitting on the kitchen table. In slow motion, the milk spills out onto the floor, and the elderly Sumney throws himself down to the floor next to it (see Figure 7.6). This action coincides with

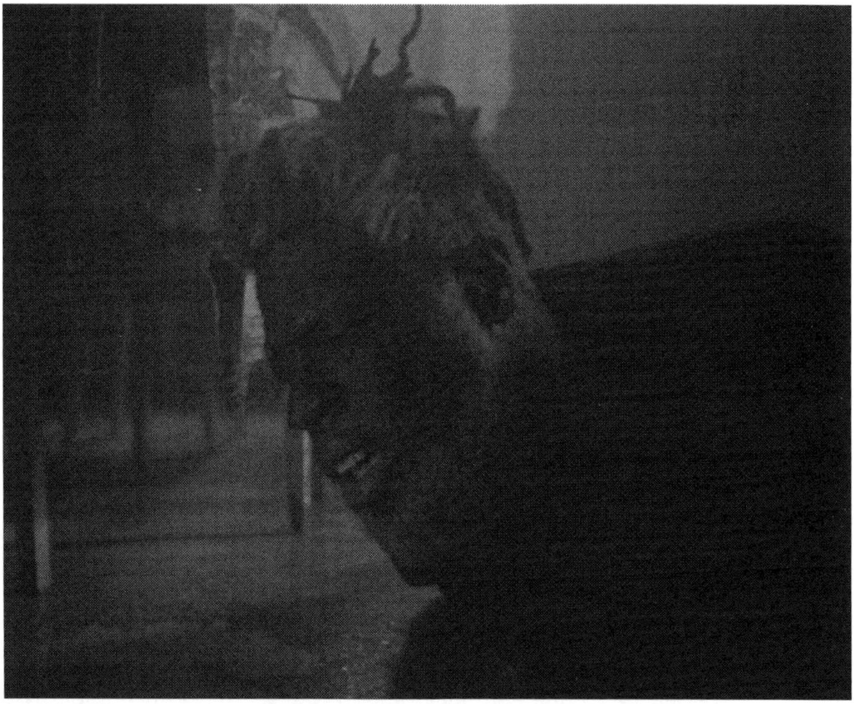

Figure 7.6 Moses Sumney, "Me in 20 Years." Dir. Allie Avital, 2020.

the vocal climax of the song, during the bridge. The music swells to orchestral levels, and Sumney's falsetto voice booms out, as he repeatedly exhorts himself to "hold out … A little bit longer, just a little bit more." The extended present moment, suspended as it is between a lost past and a future of deprivation, is tenuous and uncertain, stretched to the breaking point, just barely able to maintain itself.

Sumney continues singing in falsetto, now with what sounds like wordless choral backing, as the song moves to its shattering, and nearly ecstatic, final chorus. Sumney wonders how he can co-exist with the "cavity." As the music reaches its most hyperbolic, screaming-in-Whole-Foods pitch, we see the aged Sumney painfully crawling toward the bed, stumbling, but finally pulling himself on to it. During this climactic sequence, the video's frame gets progressively narrower: the aspect ratio shrinks from the standard 1.7:1 (with which it began) to something like 1.1:1. This straitening works to focus and intensify our attention, giving the video an almost claustrophobic feel. It's an effect I don't think I have ever seen before. It is also powerfully subliminal in its workings; although I felt a sense of emotional desolation, I didn't consciously notice this straitening until I had watched the video many times.

As the chorus ends and the song reaches its outro, the music finally calms down. Sumney sings the last lines of the song in his "normal" chest-voice range. He asks his final questions, about whether he is fated to be bound to this emptiness, this "endless January." The weather of spring—the time, supposedly, of youth and of falling in love—has given way to the winter of old age. The elderly Sumney carefully moves his hand toward, and then along the edge of, the cavity in the bed. It seems as if he is trying to caress it. In the next few shots, he seems to be dragged downward, or even to willfully evert himself into the hole. The last we see of him is one ringed hand, clutching the bedspread, but then letting go and sinking down into the abyss. Sumney sings the last line of the song, not answering his own self-questions, but instead telling us to "ask me in twenty years." The video's extended final shot tracks outwards from the hole in the bed, pulls outside the apartment, and finally moves in reverse across the same rows of buildings that we traversed at the beginning, accompanied by the same background traffic noise.

The crater in the bed, created by CGI in postproduction, is the video's center of gravity, the phantasmatic point around which all its naturalistic details rotate. No wonder the figure of Sumney himself is inexorably pulled into it. We see a number of shots of it in close-up, as well as in tracking shots that move inexorably toward it, following the line of the elderly Sumney's gaze. The hole is of indeterminate outline, roughly body-shaped. It seems to be filled with some sort of swirling but viscous liquid, dark, and highly reflective. The pit has no bottom, as far as we can tell. The material within it slowly pulses in and out, in and out. It is almost as if the hole were breathing, with its own alien metabolism (see Figure 7.7).

In an interview about the video, Avital says that this hole in the bed is

> about absence and negative space. One could interpret it as an absence of someone who was once there, or absence of an "other" to begin with. It's also the ever-present pulsing pit of your own mortality waiting to engulf you.
>
> (Promonews 2020)

Avital's allegorical suggestions roughly correspond to Sumney's own evocation of a nonexistence that nonetheless "is its own presence." Both of these descriptions

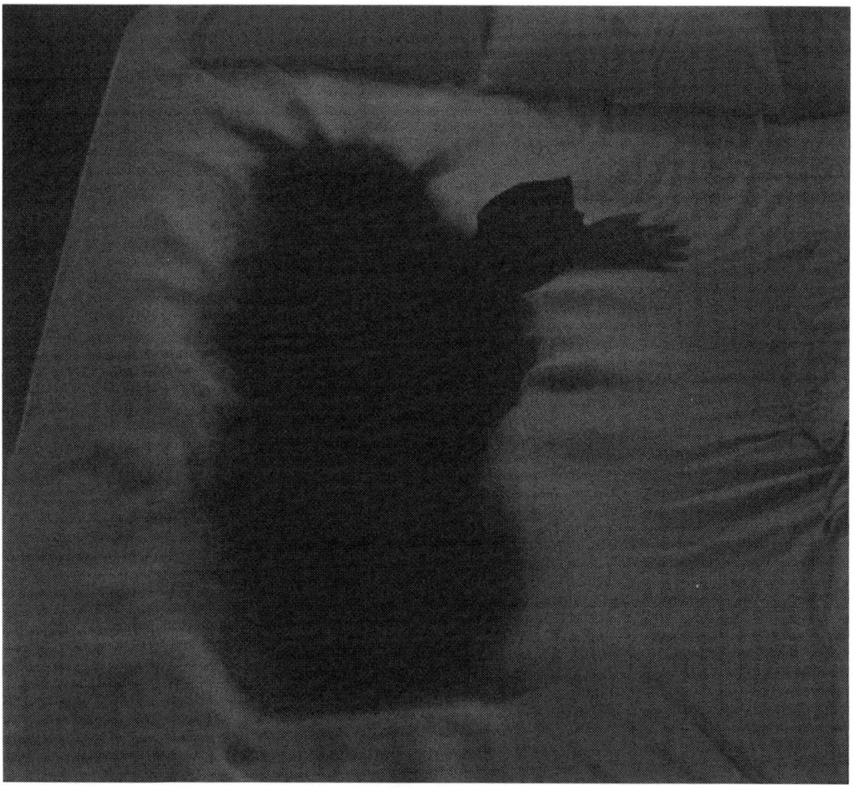

Figure 7.7 Moses Sumney, "Me in 20 Years." Dir. Allie Avital, 2020.

point to something that is not actual, not part of the here and now—but that nonetheless exists in its own strange way.

The cavity in the bed—a CGI construction animated by Erik Ferguson, and then composited into the digital footage by the visual effects studio B. Art (Promonews 2020)—might be thought of as *virtual reality* in its usual appellation. But I think that it can also be understood as *virtual* in a stricter, more philosophical sense. For Deleuze, the virtual is a sort of potential, but one that can neither be described as an Aristotelian positivity (a capacity for realization, as the acorn contains the oak tree *in potentia*) nor as a Hegelian negativity (an impulse toward change, through undermining the limits of whatever seems fixed). Rather than either of these, Deleuze's virtual is "endowed with an inefficacious, impassive, and sterile splendor" (Deleuze 1990, 20). It is an odd sort of in-between; Deleuze, citing Proust, describes it as "real without being actual, ideal without being abstract, and symbolic without being fictional" (Deleuze 1994, 208). The virtual is a kind of "quasi-being" or "extra-being," something that "insists or subsists" within things as they are (Deleuze 1994, 156). The virtual is never manifested within the actual situation, but it also cannot be eliminated from that situation. We might think of it as something like a black hole in physics. It is not directly present, as it cannot be seen or grasped. But it is also not entirely absent, since it warps its surroundings by exerting a sort of gravitational pull on them, attracting the aged Sumney into its abyss.

The hole in Moses Sumney's bed is non-actual; yet it is entirely concrete, as well as symbolically telling, in the heightened reality of the song and video themselves. This reality is at once experiential and abstract; or, it is at once deeply subjective, and yet irreducible to subjective experience. Sumney cannot grasp or recover the body—which is to say, the person—who left an "imprint" on his bed; but he also cannot escape the terrible pull of that imprint. And similarly, as listeners and viewers, we cannot *take ahold* of the "pit" or "cavity" that Sumney and Avital evoke for us through digital special effects; but we cannot think it away, or doubt its existence, either. We might also say, more generally, that digital sound and image constructions do not detract from indexical reality, so much as they plumb it and reveal its additional dimensions, its extension beyond the here and now and into a past that we can never recover, and a future that we will never be able to catch up with.

8

Metamorphoses of a Severed Head (The Weeknd)

Existential Loneliness and "Sonic ADD"

The Weeknd (Abel Tesfaye), like Moses Sumney, is a first-generation North American, whose immigrant parents came from Africa. Tesfaye is Canadian; his parents emigrated from Ethiopia, and he was born and grew up in Toronto. Both Sumney and Tesfaye can be credited with an Afropolitan sensibility: they are equally at home everywhere—or better, they feel equally foreign, equally alienated, equally uprooted, everywhere. But here uprootedness is a positive state, not just a negation. Afropolitans are able to claim a certain degree of freedom and mobility, and an ability to negotiate the most disparate situations. Afropolitanism, Achille Mbembe says, arises out of the "circulation of worlds," with movements of both *dispersion* and *immersion*; it involves "mixtures, amalgamations, superpositions—an *aesthetics of intertwining [entrelacement]*" (Mbembe 2021, 214).

Tesfaye and Sumney alike espouse this sort of aesthetic; they both reject the phobic opposition between the near and the far, the homely and the foreign. They both also sing of existential loneliness: most overtly, Sumney in his song and music video "Lonely World," and The Weeknd in his song (for which there is no video) "A Lonely Night." Both artists build upon an eclectic range of musical styles; and both extend their voices into the falsetto register in order to express their feelings of apartness and of yearning. For Sumney and Tesfaye alike, despite the vast differences between them, a primary feeling of "extraterrestriality ... becomes a point of transvaluation"—a movement that, as Kodwo Eshun observes, is vital to the Afrofuturist imaginary (Eshun 2003, 299).

But these two artists differ greatly, both in terms of their sounds, and in their treatment of gender and sexuality. Sumney, as we have seen, rejects and deconstructs normative masculinity; his music is eclectic, but it leans toward folk and indie rock. But Tesfaye uneasily inhabits and enacts a normative heterosexual masculinity, which he negotiates mostly through r&b-based sounds. He gives us a bleakly nihilistic view of masculinity, but without ever implying that any departure from it is possible. Performing as The Weeknd, and presenting varied facets of masculine willfulness and despair, Tesfaye adopts an avowedly fictional persona (as pop artists so frequently do). But the relation of this persona to the artist's biographical self remains teasingly uncertain. Asked in an interview why he sometimes appears in character and sometimes not, he replies that he likes to "play with the character and the artist and let those lines blur and move around"; to the follow-up question of whether he is in character for the interview itself, he responds: "I don't know, I'd have to ask him" (Aswad 2021).

The Weeknd dramatically presents himself as a heartless hedonist, who uses women for his pleasure without ever truly committing to them. This is highlighted in "Heartless," from the *After Hours* album, the first song and video that I discuss in detail below (The Weeknd 2019). But already, in an earlier song and video, "The Hills," The Weeknd warns the woman who is the current object of his lust not to expect too much, since "I just fucked two bitches 'fore I saw you." The video, directed by Grant Singer, shows The Weeknd walking away from a car crash on a Beverly Hills street, entirely ignoring the two women who were in the car with him—even as one of them, wearing elbow-length blue gloves, repeatedly shoves him and screams at him. The entire video conveys a mood of dreamlike estrangement (The Weeknd 2015a).

The Weeknd's songs evoke frantic sexual activity in much the same way that they evoke excessive drug use. Indeed, the two cravings often seem indistinguishable, as in "Can't Feel My Face," a love song that seems to be addressed to cocaine, rather than to a woman. In the video for this song, The Weeknd displays his best Michael Jackson dance moves (McDermot 2015), but the audience only responds after he concretizes a common metaphor for success by literally catching fire, his whole body consumed by flames (The Weeknd 2015b). Sex, drugs, and performance seem to be interchangeable means for filling up the emptiness of everyday life, and averting despair. The Weeknd indulges in all of these means, to the point where escape seems indistinguishable from self-destruction.

The Weeknd's songs and videos often take us through an infinite repeating loop, by implying that drug addiction and sexual obsession are themselves the very cycles of repetition from which (as well as by means of which) he is trying to escape. Contrary to Romantic myth, a Rimbaudian derangement of all the senses does not allow the poet to transcend himself. Rather, this derangement only serves to reinforce the very identity from which he is trying to escape. As The Weeknd sings in "The Hills," "when I'm fucked up, that's the real me" (The Weeknd 2015a). There is no release from the grind of masculine heterosexual desire and performance—except, perhaps, through visions of self-abasement and self-annihilation. In Director X's breathtaking video for Rosalía, "La fama," The Weeknd is murdered on stage by Rosalia's *femme fatale*, who is identified with Fame itself (Rosalía 2021). And in Amber Grace Johnson's music video for FKA twigs, "Tears in the Club"—which seems to be about a relationship that is broken and failed, but which the man and woman are unable to escape from—we first see The Weeknd motionless in a chair, tears streaming down his face as he sings, intercut with shots of a tiny twigs pole dancing in a flask of water. Then the sizes are reversed, so that we glimpse a tiny figure of The Weeknd running with a look of fear, then climbing up twig's legs and standing on the back of her hand, perhaps imploring her to take him back (FKA twigs 2021).

The Weeknd's music also displays an essential hybridity. Tesfaye himself says that "I feel like I have sonic ADD and I can't just stick to one sound. I feel like it irritates a lot of listeners but it's just how my mind works" (Cabooter 2020). Sometimes, he says, he will include "EDM, hip-hop and three other types of sounds in one song." Though he tries to maintain "a cohesive sound" for each album, he says, he "can't really stick to one style" (Skinner 2021). Despite this variety, many commentators have noted, and Tesfaye himself acknowledges, that his music especially emulates the 1980s r&b sound of artists like Hall & Oates and Michael Jackson—music he first heard, he says, when playing the *Grand Theft Auto: Vice City* videogame (Mamo 2021b; Skinner 2021). Tesfaye says, in particular, that he derives his falsetto, as well as his dance moves, from Michael Jackson (Gracie 2021). More generally, The Weeknd's silky vocals call back to the tradition of r&b crooners, men wooing the women of their dreams through song. At the same time, however, the harsh contents of the lyrics—alternately expressing self-aggrandizement and self-loathing—have much more in common with the taunts and boasts of male rappers, than they do with the heterosexual love songs common among male r&b singers.

The *After Hours* Project

Many of the songs in The Weeknd's 2020 album *After Hours* stand out individually; the album spawned three Number One singles. At the same time, the album as a whole does more or less exhibit "a cohesive sound," with its music starting out as big beat dance music, and gradually transitioning toward a "new wave/dream pop sound" (Chinapen 2021). When all its songs are heard in sequence, *After Hours* suggests a loose narrative, involving a breakup, and various unsuccessful attempts by The Weeknd to woo his departed partner back, to find a substitute for his disappointed love in drugs and other forms of escape, and to recover from the pain of loss, with the result being either final acceptance (Beaver 2020) or—more ominously—recurrence, as "the cycle will repeat again, and again, and again" (Chinapen 2021). Fans have speculated that the album is autobiographical, reflecting Tesfaye's on-again-off-again relationship with the model Bella Hadid (Brow and Boren 2020). However, Tesfaye has repeatedly insisted in interviews that the protagonist of the album is a persona, or a fictional character (Aswad 2020, 2021).

The fictionality of the Weeknd's persona throughout *After Hours* is especially evident in the music videos for songs from the album, as well as in Tesfaye's television performances during the period that the album was being publicized. For over a year—from December 2019 through February 2021 (Curto 2021)—and in the course of ten music videos (including animations, and lyric videos for song remixes), and eight live performances on television or online, The Weeknd always appeared publicly wearing the same red blazer, and usually with dried blood or bandages on his face (Mamo 2021a). The first four music videos in the series, which seem to depict a continuous narrative taking place over the course of a single night, are directed by Anton Tammi (Lyons 2020). A fifth video, apparently also directed by Tammi, serves as a sort of coda. The two most important subsequent videos, directed by Cliqua (the team of Pasqual Guttierez and Raul "RJ" Sanchez—Rindner 2020), pick up the story at a later point, and send it in new directions. Meanwhile, The Weeknd's television and online appearances during the period, all designed by Alex Lill, take place at moments within the narrative, even though they do not directly advance it (Strauss 2021). The Weeknd didn't appear in public in other garb until the entire broadcast sequence was completed; at that point, he said: "I'd like to thank God that I don't have to wear that red suit anymore" (Strauss 2021).

In this chapter, I will focus on the first four music videos directed by Anton Tammi. Taken in sequence, they recount a single narrative. The story is cinematic in scope; but the four videos together clock in at about nineteen minutes—and even including the other three, the total time is less than thirty-two minutes. This means that the story is tightly compressed, to a degree exceeding nearly all cinematic narratives. Tesfaye and his directors are working simultaneously at a macro-level and a micro-level. The story these videos tell is quite different from the one that is loosely suggested by the album. For one thing, the songs are arranged in a different order than they are on the album. For another thing, the third of the videos, "After Hours," does not even contain the song with that title; instead, it includes snippets from several other songs, together with ambient sound and non-diegetic music. It is described, not as a music video, but as a "short film." The narrative through-line of the videos does not match the lyrics of the particular songs, let alone the sequence of the album as a whole. The *After Hours* album does not have any single fixed meaning; the music video series is just one of several pathways through this material.

When asked about the way that the videos rearrange the album, Tesfaye concedes that "sometimes it feels like the music is more the soundtrack for it, the [musical] score" (Aswad 2020). The Weeknd does not lip-sync, or pretend to perform any of the songs; instead, they provide a background for the misadventures of the character or persona that he creates. In addition, the videos are filled with cinematic allusions. Tesfaye says that he "went full-on film geek" with these videos; he lists seven movies that are explicitly alluded to in the third video alone (Aswad 2020). Reviewers have noted other movie references as well (Gates 2021). These include Tesfaye's red blazer itself, which seems to be modeled on ones worn by Robert De Niro's characters in two Martin Scorsese movies: *The King of Comedy* (1982) and *Casino* (1995). Indeed, *After Hours* is itself the title of yet another movie by Scorsese (1985).

"Heartless"

"Heartless" is the first video of the sequence. It is also one of The Weeknd's many songs whose lyrics describe his difficulties with romantic and sexual relationships. The Weeknd is self-avowedly "heartless"; after trying for a while to be faithful to one particular woman, he always ends up going back to his old unfaithful ways. The song combines a ballad melody with heavy beats. The video starts with a blast of electronic distortion, against a black background with the title of the song in red. The letters of the title melt into pulsing shards: the first of many psychedelic visual effects. The video shows The Weeknd in Las Vegas, together with his associate, played by the producer Metro Boomin (who is the co-author of the track). The video emphasizes the garish lights of Las Vegas, gleaming from the ceiling and all about. The Weeknd wears sunglasses and his red blazer—his get-up matches the garishness of his surroundings. A typical recurring shot shows his face in close-up, as he gazes upward in bemused and stoned astonishment, his mouth open wide in a broad smile, and the ceiling's thousand points of light reflecting on his sunglasses (see Figure 8.1). We see vignettes of The Weeknd shooting craps, smoking, drinking so avidly that he spills half the glass, and making out with some anonymous woman. Sometimes we see the silhouettes of The Weeknd and Metro Boomin walking through the casino in slow motion. Other times the camera is at a tilt, or rotates upside down. The Weeknd's overall hedonistic stupefaction harmonizes with the ridiculous ornateness of the hotel. The video revels in the tacky grandiosity of Las Vegas, rather than criticizing it.

When the song reaches the bridge—the music slows down and seems less frenetically rhythmic, while The Weeknd's falsetto floats, as if suspended above the sonic murk—the camera moves in a slow tracking shot toward The Weeknd, who is seated at the edge of a fountain. Then, in a series of close-ups, we see The Weeknd holding a toad in his hand, staring at it, and then slowly and lusciously licking it (a gross slurping sound effect is layered over the music at this point)

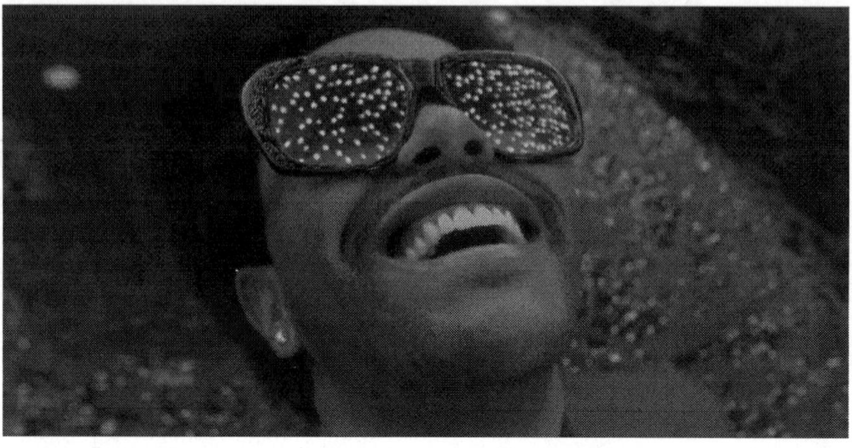

Figure 8.1 The Weeknd, "Heartless." Dir. Anton Tammi, 2019.

(see Figure 8.2). Tesfaye and Tammi are alluding to the psychoactive substances secreted by certain species of toad (though I don't think licking their skin is actually how to get high from them). From this point on, the video becomes even more deranged than it was before. Abstract CGI hallucination patterns pulse across the screen, while the music oozes into a fractally dissonant sludge (this is not heard on the regular recording of the song, but is only added for the video). These short sequences alternate with quick, askew shots of The Weeknd looking confused and disoriented, while the surroundings turn liquid and blurry. At one point, we even see, from The Weeknd's point of view, toad-like warts blossoming on his hands.

When we finally get back to the song's regular chorus, we see a long single take of The Weeknd running down a Las Vegas street. The camera first follows him from behind, then catches up, passes him, and looks back at him, still running. It seems as if The Weeknd is somehow trying to outdistance a nonexistent pursuer; finally he stops in the middle of the street, and pukes. All this while, the sky changes colors behind him, first morphing from night to day, and then turning into an enclosed roof, and flashing different colors as if in a sequence programmed by James Turrell. The Weeknd seems to have reached the end of his tether, in an exhausted moment of ecstasy tinged with paranoia. The last shot of the video, after the music has ended and we only hear the same industrial noise as at the beginning, shows The Weeknd smiling, in extreme close-up, as his face morphs through a series of wavy distortions. The camera moves closer and closer, until the image itself devolves into pixel noise. However horrible the experience has been, The Weeknd still evidently revels in it.

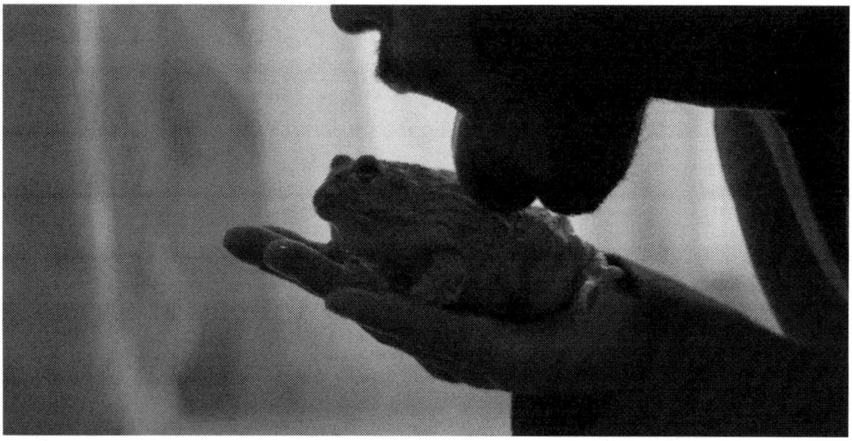

Figure 8.2 The Weeknd, "Heartless." Dir. Anton Tammi, 2019.

The "Heartless" video is evidently channeling *Fear and Loathing in Las Vegas*—both the 1971 book by Hunter S. Thompson, and the 1998 film adaptation by Terry Gilliam. Both book and film link the over-the-top garishness of Las Vegas with psychedelic drug distortions, implying that the latter is more a recapitulation and intensification of the former than some sort of countercultural rebellion against it. Las Vegas and LSD alike are grotesque expressions of the American Dream. The movie uses special effects to reproduce the bizarre hallucinations recounted in Thompson's prose, and the video follows along with this line of expression. Abel Tesfaye himself is Canadian; but The Weeknd's heartless pursuit of excess—as well as his mood of simultaneous self-loathing and self-congratulation with which he presents it to us—is American to the core.

"Blinding Lights"

"Blinding Lights" is The Weeknd's most commercially successful song to date; indeed, *Billboard* has crowned it "the No. 1 song of all time," due to its record-breaking ninety consecutive weeks on the Hot 100 chart (Mamo 2021b). "Blinding Lights" is a much more uptempo and dance-oriented track than "Heartless"; it is closer to a conventional love song, with lyrics that express sexual yearning, rather than satiety, and an ecstatic, booming chorus. But the lyrics are not directly illustrated in the music video; instead, we witness the further adventures of the red-suited character we first encountered in "Heartless."

The music video opens with a 17-second extreme close-up of The Weeknd's face; he is smiling and laughing, and nodding his head up and down, with mouth wide open, despite the blood encrusted around his nose and dribbling through his mouth and across his teeth (see Figure 8.3). He seems to enjoy being so messed up. The camera moves fractionally closer, and the image starts to break up, as a swelling dissonant roar resolves itself into the sound of helicopters overhead. Then, blackout and silence. A title card reading THE WEEKND, in red letters, appears against the dark screen. When the visuals and roaring sounds resume, the video picks up just at the point where the one for "Heartless" ended; The Weeknd stands on a Las Vegas street, with his face still unbloodied. Dissonant electronic hums slowly give way to the opening chords of the song. The Weeknd staggers down the street, and lunges drunkenly at a pigeon; the handheld camera following him is also shaky. Then The Weeknd stops—as does

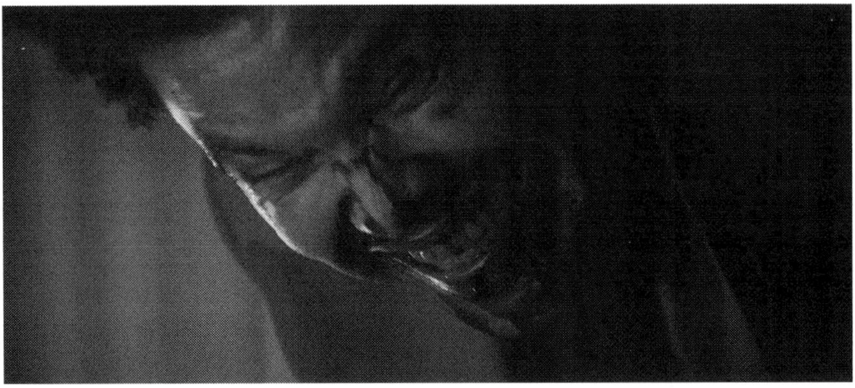

Figure 8.3 The Weeknd, "Blinding Lights." Dir. Anton Tammi, 2020.

the camera—and carefully puts on his black gloves. As the song's beat kicks in, he walks to a parked Mercedes-AMG GT convertible (Blanco 2020), gets in, and starts driving. The song title, BLINDING LIGHTS appears in red over the image.

The "Blinding Lights" music video is disjunctively edited, with rapid cuts among shots in scrambled temporal order. These shots are alternately bathed in reddish and greenish light. One series of shots shows The Weeknd driving, fast and recklessly. We see the car coming toward the camera, or rushing away from it. The car skids as it changes direction without slowing down. Sometimes we are on elevated city streets, and other times inside a tunnel. We also see rapid close-ups of the car's tachometer, as the dial rotates toward the maximum, and of The Weeknd's foot pushing down on the accelerator. The Weeknd lights a cigarette, and throws the butt out of the car's window. He screams as he accelerates. Many of these shots are tilted, or streaked by motion blur. The city's buildings and neon lights loom, or streak by, out of focus in the background.

There are several other series of shots interspersed with this one. We keep on returning to shots of The Weeknd dancing ecstatically in the middle of the street, either on an overpass or in the tunnel. His face is bloodied, but he smiles broadly as he turns and turns about. The camera gives us this spectacle in slightly jerky shots, taken from various angles and at various distances. The only traffic is blurry, in the distance. A number of critics have compared The Weeknd's dancing here, as well as his red suit, to those of Joaquin Phoenix's Joker in Todd Philips's eponymous 2019 movie (Alston 2020; Cuby 2020).

Yet another series of shots takes us inside Las Vegas hotels. The Weeknd walks through an empty banquet room. An Asian woman (Miki Hamano), in a sparkling evening gown, sings into a microphone, in front of red curtains. During the second verse of "Blinding Lights," a shot and reverse shot show The Weeknd and the woman looking at one another. In a series of wider shots, the woman points at Abel; and then, as she raises her arm, he magically rises several inches off the floor, and floats toward her (see Figure 8.4). In this series, the individual shots are longer in duration than in the other portions of the video, and they obey traditional continuity rules. Nonetheless, these shots continue to be intercut with ones from the other two series. The Weeknd lands back on the floor right in front of the singer; she touches his arm as he smiles at her. Next, we see a two-shot close-up of their faces, as they stare at one another in close proximity. But they do not kiss, because The Weeknd's cigarette, still in his mouth, creates a gap between them.

But then the second chorus kicks in, and immediately the video cuts back to shots of The Weeknd driving. For a couple of bars, the music slows down and plays, heavily distorted, over car-engine noise. We see psychedelic shots of the city through the windshield of the speeding car: the city lights on both sides of the road streak by, as in science fiction movies with warp-speed travel. We also see a close-up of The Weeknd, in the driver's seat, sticking out his tongue, in a way that recalls the toad-licking episode from the previous video. For the second half of the chorus, the music returns to its usual pitch and tempo.

The music is at its most upbeat and energetic in the latter part of the song, with the second chorus leading to the bridge, and then to a final reprise of the chorus. Visually, the montage is accelerated even more than before. The shots get shorter, and the camera gets more unstable. Yet this is also the portion of the

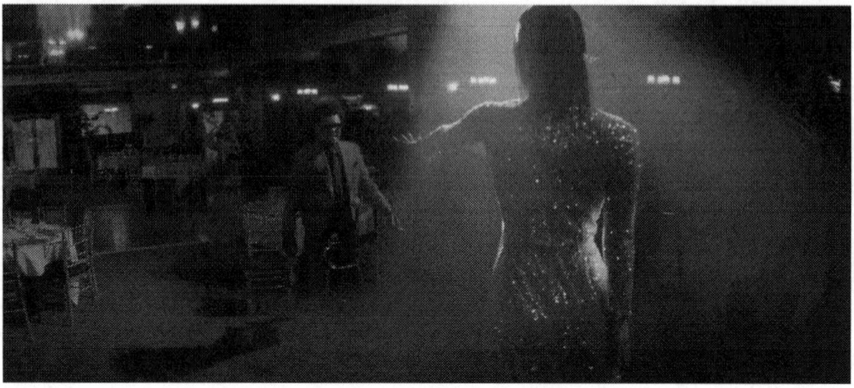

Figure 8.4 The Weeknd, "Blinding Lights." Dir. Anton Tammi, 2020.

video that gives us something like a narrative. We switch between flashes of The Weeknd's increasingly erratic driving, and quick shots from inside the hotel. We see two big, burly men walking, from behind. They grab The Weeknd, and they beat him up with professional efficiency: one holding him while the other lands punches. Are these men thugs, or are they bouncers working for the hotel? This is where The Weeknd gets blood all over his face, as we saw earlier in the video and as we will continue to see in the subsequent ones. Quick red-tinged strobe shots of The Weeknd's bloody face as he lies groaning on the floor give way to the shots speeding through the greenish tunnel that we have seen before. During an instrumental reprise of the chorus, we see shots of The Weeknd running out of the hotel and into the street, stumbling and getting up again, intercut with a few extremely rapid shots taken from earlier moments in the video. The run turns into a dance, as a shaky and unsteady handheld camera follows after The Weeknd.

Finally, as we get to the end of the song, the camera holds still, as vocals return for the last time in another reprise of the chorus, or perhaps what could be called an Outro. The Weeknd dances in the middle of the road, first in the tunnel, then on the overpass. There's a smile on his bloodied face. It seems as if we have finally reached the end of the narrative—though we have seen quicker shots of this action, in flashforward, throughout the video. The last line of the song, "I can't sleep until I feel your touch," is accompanied by a quick insert of the Asian woman singing into a microphone. Then, as the music fades out, the video ends with two relatively long-held shots of The Weeknd, face bloodied, but smiling triumphantly and dancing, standing on an overpass in the night, while out-of-focus traffic passes on the road beneath him, and out-of-focus skyscrapers loom in the distance.

The video allows us to discern a linear narrative sequence. The Weeknd, still woozy from the alcohol and drugs consumed in the previous video, gets into his car and drives wildly around town. At some point, he must have parked the car (though we do not see this), in order to wander into the hotel. There he encounters, and is bewitched by, the Asian singer. Then he gets beaten up. Then he runs out of the hotel, and dances in the street. But we are not given any causal connections between these events; we have no idea, for instance, whether or not the beating was punishment for his flirtation with the singer. In addition, though we can reconstruct this narrative sequence in retrospect, it does not correspond to the nonlinear way in which we actually experience the video. Each event in the story is chopped up into multiple shots, which loosely constitute a series, but which for the most part are not organized according to conventional continuity rules. The different series of shots are also so densely intercut with one another that it makes no sense even to describe the video in terms of flashbacks and flashforwards. Though the video does not illustrate the words of the song, editing patterns are established rhythmically, with reference to the flow of the music, rather than in accordance with any sort of narrative logic.

The "Blinding Lights" video, and indeed the whole sequence of videos for songs from the *After Hours* album, thus exemplifies what I have elsewhere called post-continuity (Shaviro 2016), and what I am here calling the rhythm image. Time is dense and multidimensional, rather than either being a straightforward linear progression, or being held all at once in suspension. Instead, the video gives us a dense assemblage of partially overlapping durations, that influence one another, and interfere with one another, in varying patterns across time. For Alfred North Whitehead, "the world we know is a continuous stream of occurrence which we can discriminate into finite events forming by their overlappings and containings of each other and separations a spatio-temporal structure" (Whitehead 1920, 110). In "Blinding Light" and other contemporary music videos, we experience the continuous stream of what Carol Vernallis calls the ubiquitous "media swirl" (Vernallis 2022b) in the form of microperceptions organized into fractal patterns of different resonances, through which we both perceive and are perceived. Abel Tesfaye's film noir and horror-film nightmares might be seen as the objective correlative of this overall media situation.

"After Hours" Short Film

The "After Hours" short film continues the storyline without being keyed to a particular song. The video starts with an atonal roar, and darkness. But the roar resolves into applause, and the camera zooms out, revealing that we have been looking into the dark pupil of The Weeknd's eye. He has just completed his live performance of "Blinding Lights" on Jimmy Kimmel's nighttime talk show (Jimmy Kimmel Live! 2020). The Weeknd shakes hands with Kimmel, and acknowledges the audience's applause with smiles, waves, and a bow. This was broadcast live on January 23, 2020, just two days after the release of the "Blinding Lights" music video (Mamo 2021a). To maintain continuity with the video sequence, The Weeknd appears on the show wearing the same loud red suit and black gloves, and with a bandage across his nose, and a streak of dried blood running down his right cheek.

The nose bandage is reminiscent of the one worn by Jack Nicholson's detective character J. J. Gittes, after he gets slashed, in Roman Polanski's *Chinatown* (1973). Since the sight of the face is our main point of connection with the actors in a movie, such a facial bandage is deeply disturbing. It is a disfigurement that disrupts our emotional identification with the character being portrayed. By linking his live broadcast appearance to his fictional persona, Tesfaye not only forwards the narrative of the music video sequence, but heightens the ambiguity between the singer himself, and the character he portrays in the videos.

In a single long-duration shot (nearly fifty seconds), the camera accompanies The Weeknd backstage, down a flight of stairs, and through a series of corridors. On the soundtrack, the audience applause dies away and is replaced by a rhythmic pounding, together with indistinctly murmuring voices. This swells into a menacing atonal roar. The corridors are poorly lit, with a dim reddish glow—continuing the reddish tint that appears in all the videos. Sometimes we can see The Weeknd's face, as his smile in response to the audience's applause slowly fades. At other times, we only discern his backlit silhouette. There is finally another cut as The Weeknd steps through a door and out into nighttime Los Angeles. The electronic roar is replaced by ambient musical fragments. The Weeknd winces, and raised his gloved left hand to feel the bandage on his nose. The video cuts to a visceral extreme close-up of the bandaged nose, as The Weeknd palpates it with his gloved fingers, revealing the raw bloody flesh between his nose and his upper lip. This is immediately followed by another extreme close-up of his left eye, just as at the very start of the video. This is followed, in turn, by distant shots of The Weeknd alone in the empty, nighttime streets of Los Angeles. He turns and looks back at the building from which he has emerged, as the title AFTER HOURS slowly appears in red, one letter at a time, on the screen.

The soundtrack mixes the noisy roar with melodic fragments from the album. The Weeknd walks through the streets, and then descends an escalator into the subway. He hears a sound and glances behind himself anxiously. We see a long-held close-up of The Weeknd's ravaged face, then shallow-focus shots of him walking through the subway station. He continues to walk, first at normal speed, and then in slow motion. At one point, a busker plays a few bars of "In Your Eyes" (the song that will provide the basis for the next video in the series) on the saxophone. The soundtrack otherwise remains dissonant and vaguely ominous. The Weeknd's changing facial expressions suggest greater and greater distress. A train pulls into the station. The Weeknd puts on his glasses and stares upward, as he did during the psychedelic portion of "Heartless." We once again get extremely rapid cuts, and strobing lights; a morphing pattern vaguely resembles a flower unfolding (see Figure 8.5). These shots are interrupted by equally quick ones displaying patterns of horizontal lines. But it all goes by too quickly for us to process.

All of a sudden, an insistent, repeated rhythmic figure begins to play on the soundtrack. The Weeknd immediately finds himself on the floor, being pulled all the way down the platform by some invisible force. This is conveyed through a series of brief shots. The Weeknd slides across the platform so quickly that his surroundings devolve into motion blur. This turns into a sort of strobe effect, as shots of The Weeknd being dragged along, waving his arms frantically and finally stumbling to his feet, alternate with the abstract horizontal patterns that we already saw when he looked up. Perhaps these latter patterns are the slats on the wall of the subway station, passing by too quickly for us to grasp. At one point, in close-up, The Weeknd opens his mouth into a scream. The camera rotates for added disorientation, showing us The Weeknd upside down, or as seen from the floor. Reddish tints continue to predominate throughout the sequence. Nevertheless, within this tonally defined block of duration, we are bombarded with glimpses that pass by too fast for us to follow. We process these images haptically and rhythmically, without distance and without recognition. There is no action for us to parse, but only a horribly pulsing undead vitality,

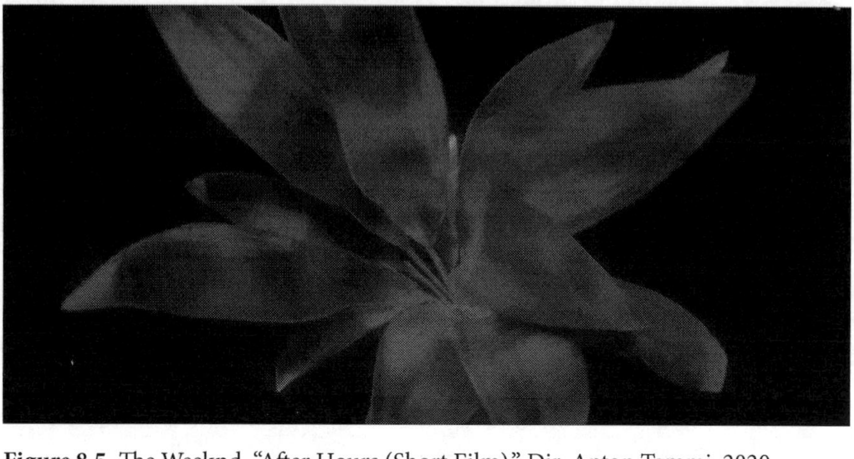

Figure 8.5 The Weeknd, "After Hours (Short Film)." Dir. Anton Tammi, 2020.

equally present in the camera itself and in the scene it views. The pulsation holds The Weeknd in its thrall; but it seems to capture us, emerging from somewhere and somewhen beneath the threshold of our attention.

Suddenly the pulsing rhythmic figure is replaced by an ambient wash of sound. The camera stays still, on a shot of an escalator leading up from the train platform. A young white man and a young Black woman come up the escalator from the subway. They seem to be arguing, though we cannot quite make out their words. The next shot shows them from behind, heading toward an elevator. The elevator door opens to reveal The Weeknd standing motionless. The couple, oblivious, get in. The elevator door closes. The camera stays still, peering at the closed elevator, as a red light begins to strobe ever more violently, until it is just an abstract pattern. Heavy electronic dissonance on the soundtrack increasingly blends with the sounds of a struggle and of screaming. Then the screen cuts to black, and we hear low bass sounds. The video teasingly ends on this horror-film cliffhanger.

"In Your Eyes"

The fourth video in the series accompanies the song "In Your Eyes." The song itself (like its predecessor "Blinding Lights") is co-authored by production maestro Max Martin. In consequence, it is relatively upbeat and dance-friendly, with a disco-ish beat, and a soaring saxophone solo. The song sounds overall celebratory to me, despite its melancholy lyrics, sung by The Weeknd in a plaintive tone of voice. The lyrics are confessional, telling us about lovers who deceive each other and cannot remain faithful. Tesfaye says in an interview that the song is "basically about two people who are in love with each other who are just f—ing each other over," with the two verses speaking from the two characters' differing perspectives (Aswad 2020). Once again, however, the video follows its own quite different narrative line.

The video for "In Your Eyes" picks up the narrative exactly where "After Hours" left off. We once again see elevator doors open, and the arguing young couple from the end of the previous video enter. As before, The Weeknd is already in the elevator, standing behind and between them in his red blazer and black gloves, with dried blood still running down his cheek, and the bandage over his nose. The video quickly cuts to a new shot, showing us the surveillance mirror in the elevator's back corner. We see, from the image in the mirror, that The Weeknd is holding a large knife, of the sort used in Hitchcock's *Psycho* (1961) and in numerous slasher films of the 1980s. We return to the shot from outside the elevator; then we cut to a closer shot of The Weeknd raising the knife just as the elevator doors close. There is a dissonant roaring noise as the doors shut. Then the video quickly cuts to a shot of downtown Los Angeles, with a street extending all the way back to the skyline at night. The title IN YOUR EYES appears over this shot in red letters.

The young woman from the elevator (Zaina Miuccia) enters the frame, blood strewn over her face and clothes, looking back toward the camera. She runs down the street, away from the camera and toward downtown. From here on, the video knowingly gives us a highly stylized take on 1980s slasher films, even as the bouncy song starts playing. We see shots of Miuccia desperately running away, often stopping to spin around and look anxiously back. These shots are intercut with shots of The Weeknd, who, in contrast to Miuccia, is either standing still, coldly surveying the scene, or walking slowly but implacably after her. There are also brief close-ups of the enormous knife.

Throughout these chase scenes, which continually reference 1980s slasher films, there is a lot of play with light and ambiance. The darkness of the nighttime streets is tinged with a yellowish glow from soft-focus streetlights. At one point, Miuccia runs down a street filled with billowing steam. At another point, a telephoto lens shows us Miuccia stumbling and falling in the middle of the street, as the Weeknd continues to walk, slowly and inexorably, toward her (and toward the camera). At still another point, a bluish tinge suffuses a series of shots in which Miuccia frantically tries to make a call on a pay phone. Despite this one series of bluish shots, however, "In Your Eyes" mostly sticks with alternating patterns of the complementary colors red and green. We see The Weeknd standing motionless, and raising his eyes toward the ceiling, repeating a motif from the previous videos; the camera pans upward toward his face, with the walls and ceiling behind him deliriously strobing in green. After running through the streets, Miuccia finally goes through a door, and enters what seems like an empty industrial warehouse, with violently strobing red light. She walks through a maze of indoor passages, and finally reaches a nightclub with lots of people dancing.

The nightclub is self-referentially called "After Hours." Overall, it is bathed in strobing red light, but there are also beams of green laser light crisscrossing the floor (see Figure 8.6). Miuccia, on the dance floor, looks back at The Weeknd standing in ominous stillness; we get a series of shots and reverse shots

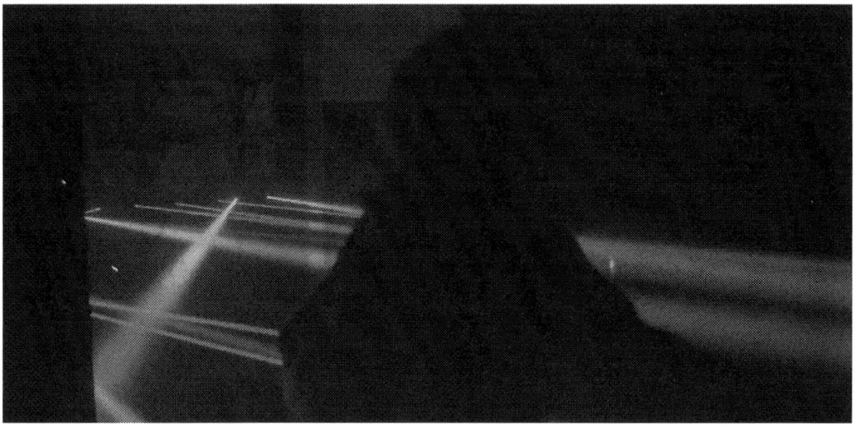

Figure 8.6 The Weeknd, "In Your Eyes." Dir. Anton Tammi, 2020.

alternating between them, the camera pushing closer into their faces each time. This series of shots follows the classical pattern of an eyeline match. It gives us the distinct impression that the two characters are looking directly at one another, even though we only see them in separate shots. And yet, in contrast to the continuity editing of traditional narrative cinema, here there is actually no indication as to whether Miuccia and The Weeknd are even in the same physical space. Miuccia is part of the dancing crowd; but The Weeknd stands motionless behind a railing, looking downward, with a diagonal bar of green light cutting in front of his body and through the frame.

Though the narrative of the video seems at odds with the emotions expressed in the song, its editing does respond to the song's musical and lyrical structure. Both times that the song reaches the chorus, and The Weeknd sings the title phrase "in your eyes," the video gives us a rapid-fire montage with extreme close-ups of both Miuccia's and The Weeknd's eyes, together with close-ups of the knife, of Miuccia's hands filled with blood, and of the lower half of Miuccia's face just as she starts to scream. Both times, these sequences resolve into images of Miuccia dancing in the club with the strobing lights.

At this point, we have heard most of the song, but we are still only about halfway through the video. During the song's instrumental break, in which a saxophone plays the melody of the chorus, Miuccia leaves the dance floor and runs down a corridor. She finds a do-not-break-except-in-case-of-fire cabinet, smashes the glass, and grabs an axe. Just as The Weeknd resumes singing, in a final reprise of the chorus, the music slows down and the voice gets deeper in tone—simulating the effect of decelerating an analog tape recorder. The music stops altogether, and we get about forty-five seconds of Miuccia and The Weeknd stalking each other through the corridors of the industrial space. Everything is lit with a reddish tinge, while the soundtrack gives us only ominous dissonant noises, and a vague musical tinkling in the background. Finally the music resumes; we are back to the final chorus. Miuccia keeps looking around cautiously, while holding the axe. She sees The Weeknd and screams. There's a quick cut, and the camera zooms into The Weeknd's face as he just stands there. There's another quick cut; Miuccia is still screaming, but she decapitates The Weeknd with one clean swing of the axe. The next shot shows blood spurting on the wall, and the shot after that shows The Weeknd's head falling to the floor. As the final chorus continues, Miuccia picks up the head and stares at it. We then get another shot/reverse shot sequence, again with an eyeline match, of Miuccia and The Weeknd's head looking at one another in extreme close-up.

All of this still clearly references 1980s slasher films. Miuccia is now the "final girl," who reverses the video's gender dynamics by becoming active instead of passive. She literally takes matters into her own hands, and kills the male slasher (Clover 1992, 35–41). In self-consciously following this pattern, the video shifts our attention from The Weeknd (who has been the center of attention throughout the whole sequence, as is typical for music videos) to Miuccia's character. Even though the song is almost over, the video continues for another minute and a half, with an extended instrumental outro. We see multiple shots of Miuccia dancing with The Weeknd's head. At first she still looks in shock; but as these shots go on, she becomes increasingly jubilant. We see her both in the corridor where she killed The Weeknd, and back in the club. She holds the head tenderly as she dances, and stares into its dead eyes. She nuzzles the head and almost kisses it, as she continues to dance. She even holds the head up like a trophy, just as in traditional depictions—in Renaissance and Baroque art—of Judith holding the head of Holofernes (Wikipedia 2021d). It has gotten so late that we have now transitioned from "after hours" to dawn; sunlight streams through the windows of the club, as people continue to dance, and as we see the saxophone player whose solo recapitulates the melody of the chorus one final time. After this, we see Miuccia dancing out of doors, on a rooftop, sometimes waving the axe around, at other times strutting back and forth with The Weeknd's head. She is backlit by the orange sky of dawn, and by the barely risen Sun, with the silhouettes of Los Angeles' palm trees on the horizon (see Figure 8.7).

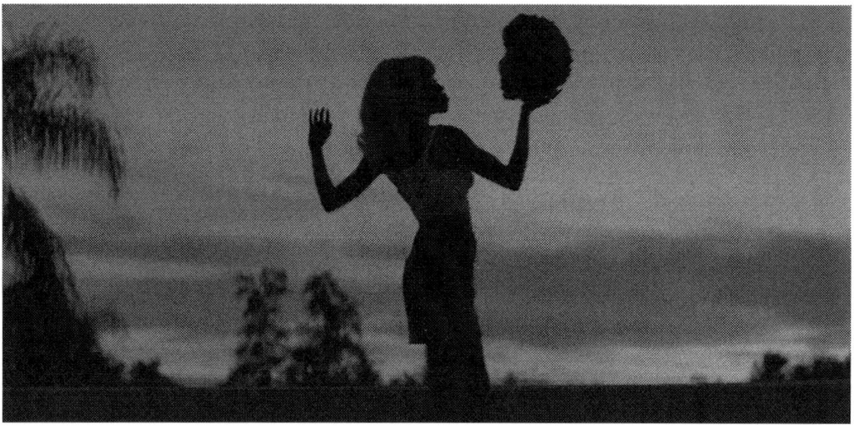

Figure 8.7 The Weeknd, "In Your Eyes." Dir. Anton Tammi, 2020.

It is hard for me to describe the emotions that I feel watching this video, and especially its final stretch. If we were to take the plotline literally, we would have to say that Miuccia's character has gone insane in the wake of killing her attacker. But there is something wonderfully exhilarating and triumphant about this final sequence. It is moving and uplifting. I could not have gotten these feelings just by hearing the song, nor from the slasher scenario of the first two thirds of the video. "In Your Eyes" works musically by a push and pull between how the music implores you to dance, and how the lyrics and The Weeknd's voice, express pain, vulnerability, and regret. The video ups the ante on this cognitive dissonance, transfiguring the song's lament for disconnection into some entirely different, undefinable dimension.

"Until I Bleed Out," "Too Late," and "Save Your Tears"

I will discuss the remaining *After Hours* music videos much more briefly. "Until I Bleed Out" is the final song on the *After Hours* album, and its short music video seems like a sort of coda to the preceding four (The Weeknd 2020d). The music is slow and sad, with only a weak beat—this is not dance music, but rather something like falling-into-a-stupor music. The Weeknd sings that "I keep telling myself I don't need it anymore"; it sounds like he is unsuccessfully trying to convince himself. The video has no director's credit (some of the web sites I have seen credit the video once again to Anton Tammi, but others just list the director as "XO," which is the name of Tesfaye's production company). A lot of the video consists in motion blur, as things rotate around the camera, or perhaps as the camera itself rotates, making the image nearly abstract (see Figure 8.8). When we are able to see clearly, the location seems to be a party in some sort of swanky mansion. There's a rotating platform, and the air is filled with confetti and balloons. The Weeknd's head is intact, with the bandage still over his nose. He seems pretty much out of it; his face expresses a look of agony. The Weeknd stumbles around in a daze, and he falls down several times. In several shots, the other partygoers seem to be mobbing him, grabbing his body from all sides. Toward the end of the video, shots in the mansion are intercut with shots in which The Weeknd seems to be stumbling around in a desolate outdoor area, at night, empty except for electric lamps at intervals. The Weeknd falls down again, and the camera circles around him from above, both in this wilderness and at the party. The video ends with a medium close-up of The Weeknd, standing up but looking ravaged; the indoor background seems to rotate behind him. This cuts to a brief shot of blinding white, tinged at the bottom of the frame with a brief flash of yellow (is that flame? or film disintegrating? I can't tell). The journey is over. If The Weeknd was killed in "In Your Eyes," then "Until I Bleed Out" might portray the actual moment of death, drawn out into an anticipation of the afterlife.

Two additional videos, directed by Cliqua, supplement the narrative by tracking The Weeknd's fate, post-decapitation. They are not as visually dense

Figure 8.8 The Weeknd, "Until I Bleed Out." Dir. Anton Tammi, 2020.

as the videos directed by Tammi, but the move the story in new directions. In "Too Late" (The Weeknd 2020e), two young white women in Los Angeles, their heads swathed in bandages from plastic surgery, find The Weeknd's head in the middle of the street. They take it home to their mansion, where they take turns kissing and caressing it. They hire a Black male stripper, slit his throat, mid-performance, with the same sort of slasher knife that we have seen before, and attach The Weeknd's head to this fresh body. The Weeknd awakens, and we see several shots of the girls' blood-spattered and bandage-swathed heads from his POV, as they dance with him and take him to bed as a sex toy.

After this video was released, The Weeknd himself appeared live on television wearing full-face plastic-surgery bandages, as he performed two songs at the 2020 American Music Awards ceremony (The Weeknd 2020f). A few weeks later, in Cliqua's video for "Save Your Tears," we see the results of this ostensible plastic surgery: The Weeknd performs the song without bandages, and without any traces of blood on his face, but with his cheeks, lips, and other features grotesquely swollen and remodeled. When asked in an interview about these transformations, Tesfaye said that "the significance of the entire head bandages is reflecting on the absurd culture of Hollywood celebrity and people manipulating themselves for superficial reasons to please and be validated." When further asked about why he had made his face "increasingly unattractive" over the course of all these videos and live performances, Tesfaye responded: "I suppose you could take that being attractive isn't important to me but a compelling narrative is" (Aswad 2021).

In the "Save Your Tears" video, The Weeknd sings the song in what seems to be a swanky nightclub. (This is the only video in the entire sequence where he lip-syncs.) Once again, he wears a red suit jacket; but this time it is a different one, adorned with spangles. Though his face is bare to display the plastic-surgery alterations, his backing band and the patrons seated at their various tables are all wearing ornate masks. Many of these masks are encrusted with jewels; others are blankly white, and still others are carnival masks. The audience members are all wearing expensive clothes, and they don't seem to react in any way to the performance. The Weeknd's red suit contrasts with the bluish light of the room. As The Weeknd sings the song, he moves among the tables where the audience is seated; he grabs and opens a bottle of champagne, letting it spurt all over the seated patrons before gulping from it himself. At one point, he grabs a gigantic trophy cup, then hurls it into the crowd. At another, he pulls a young woman (Bianca Rojas)—the only patron not wearing a mask—from a table and onto the stage to dance with him. Her delight turns to fear when he takes out a pistol and places it in her hand, pointing it directly at his forehead.

The club's lighting changes from blue to red, as The Weeknd resumes singing the song. He dances, exuberantly, holding the pistol and waving it around. At the end of the song, he steps back onto the stage, and puts the pistol to his temple. We see his face in close-up, and then cut to a shot of his head from behind. After a pause, he pulls the trigger—and confetti comes out of the pistol, instead of a bullet. After a moment of stunned silence, the audience breaks out in applause. The Weeknd smiles and nods in acknowledgment, his puffy face giving his smile a twisted and somewhat unnerving appearance. The applause continues after a cut to black, and the credits. The whole sequence of music videos ends with this rather ambiguous return to the act of performance.

Some Conclusions

The video sequence for songs from the *After Hours* album, directed by Anton Tammi and by Cliqua, does in fact give us a loose narrative. But it *also* pushes well beyond the bounds of narrative, in order to highlight a number of autonomous cinematic and musical elements. Even the formal structures that are traditionally used in order to further our sense of narrative continuity—like eyeline matches, parallel editing in chase sequences, and the articulation of complementary colors—work more or less independently of the narrative, highlighting other sorts of aesthetic values. These formal structures do in fact lead us to make connections among the bodies shown to us in disparate shots. But they no longer work to connote an underlying uniformity and continuity of space and time, in the way that classical continuity editing does in films of the movement image, or even in the more exacerbated way that modern "intensified continuity," as David Bordwell calls it (Bordwell 2002), does in films of the time image. Instead, all these devices form something like a new, emerging audiovisual network, with continually shifting, and continually renegotiated, nodes and connections.

In the regime of the rhythm image, traditional formal structures are atomized and decontextualized, the better to be recombined in new, multiple relational patterns. All the traditional modes of cinematography and editing are still widely used; however, now they dynamically construct new spacetime relations that do not preexist them, and also do not outlive them. These videos dazzle us with a mesh of crisscrossing shots, sounds, durations, and event-particles; although we experience them in succession rather than simultaneously, they do not quite coalesce into a single, unambiguous linear sequence. The videos' moving images do indeed tell us a story that has a "before" and an "after"; time is not reversible, so even when The Weeknd's head is reattached to a body, he is not quite the same character as he was before. And the videos' moving images continue to interact in complex ways with the music, even though they do not illustrate the songs' lyrics at all straightforwardly. But these videos *also* create their own rhythms and resonances, inflecting The Weeknd's persona in convoluted and sometimes contradictory ways. Even as normative masculinity implodes, we are caught up in the spirals of Mbembe's (and Deleuze's) "aesthetics of intertwining" (Mbembe 2021, 214).

9

Submerged (Tkay Maidza)

Floating Upside Down

Tkay Maidza is yet another Afropolitan artist. She was born in Zimbabwe, and came to Australia with her parents when she was only five years old. As an adult, she has moved from Adelaide to Los Angeles, in order to further her musical career. Her usual producer, Dan Farber, is Israeli (McArtney 2021). Maidza is accustomed to moving back and forth between worlds; she is also an eclectic shape-shifter in musical terms, both singing and rapping, while exploring the boundaries of r&b, hip-hop, and EDM (electronic dance music).

Maidza goes even further afield than usual in her song and video "Where Is My Mind?" (Tkay Maidza 2021). This is a cover of an indie rock classic by The Pixies; the song originally appeared on their 1988 album *Surfer Rosa*. The Pixies never released this song as a single, and never made a music video for it. But it became one of their most well-known songs after it was used in the final scene of David Fincher's 1999 film *Fight Club*. Since the movie, there have been many cover versions of the song, performed by a wide variety of musicians working in a wide range of styles. There is a bluegrass version (Trampled by Turtles), a solo piano rendition (Maxence Cyrin), a downtempo ambient take (The Coral Sea), and even a version that turns the song into a torch ballad (Storm Large).

Tkay Maidza's take on the song is (unlike the other versions I have just mentioned) at least as jagged and edgy as the original. The rock guitar, bass, and drums of the Pixies are replaced by synthesizers. The repeating drum motif of the original gives way to a more syncopated trap pattern. The synthesizers follow the same notes as the guitar and bass of the original; but they provide a more monolithic texture. Maidza's solo singing soars over the instrumentation; it is never buried in the mix in the way that Black Francis' lead vocals sometimes are in the original song. In addition, Kim Deal's spooky "oh-oh-oh" backing vocals in the Pixies track are mostly replaced in Maidza's version by overdubbed and insistent voices repeating "where is my … where is my … where is my …," over and over, through a thick buzz of distortion. These disturbing backing vocals, added to the pounding of the instrumentals, create what is nearly a wall of sound. But this background disappears when Maidza sings the verse and chorus proper. This gives us something like the loud/soft alternation of the original, but only in attenuated form.

"Where Is My Mind?" is a song about alienation and disorientation. In the lyrics, lead singer and songwriter Black Francis (aka Frank Black) recounts an anecdote about snorkeling in the Caribbean. He recalls that, immersed in the water, he was not sure which way was up. He also remembers being followed through the water by a little fish. These events lead to a sense of dislocation: the singer feels separated from himself, at a distance from his own mind. Metaphorically, the lyrics suggests schizophrenic displacement and paranoia—the singer worries that his head will collapse, and that the fish is trying to tell him something. But this self-alienation is expressed with a light and almost goofy touch. Frank Black in an interview says that the song is just "likeable," and refers to its "wacky cute little lyrics" (Carle 2009). Anna Kornbluh, considering the song's use at the end of *Fight Club*, describes it as "irrepressibly upbeat," as it propels the movie's quasi-apocalyptic ending: the emergence of the narrator-protagonist "as a new subject," along with "the establishment of a new, direct [heterosexual] relationship," and the demolition of the corporate headquarters of credit card companies (Kornbluh 2019, 171). Apparently losing your mind can be a positive experience of renewal, an enhancement of life, alongside the "creative destruction" of the capitalist order itself. It's all very rock 'n' roll.

The Waves

In Tkay Maidza's cover of "Where Is My Mind?," the tone of her singing is fairly clear and straightforward during the verses; it relaxes and becomes a bit plaintive and melancholy in the choruses. Maidza herself directed the music video that accompanies her rendition of the song. The video is a minimalist *tour de force*, consisting in a looped single take, evidently shot from a drone. Maidza, wearing a white dress with knee-high black boots, lies on her back on the top of a large rock. We are at the seashore; the sandy ground around the rock is periodically inundated by waves. At the start of the video, the camera is so high in the sky that we barely notice Maidza on her rock. But the camera steadily descends until it hovers just above her. Then the camera withdraws up into the sky again; then it

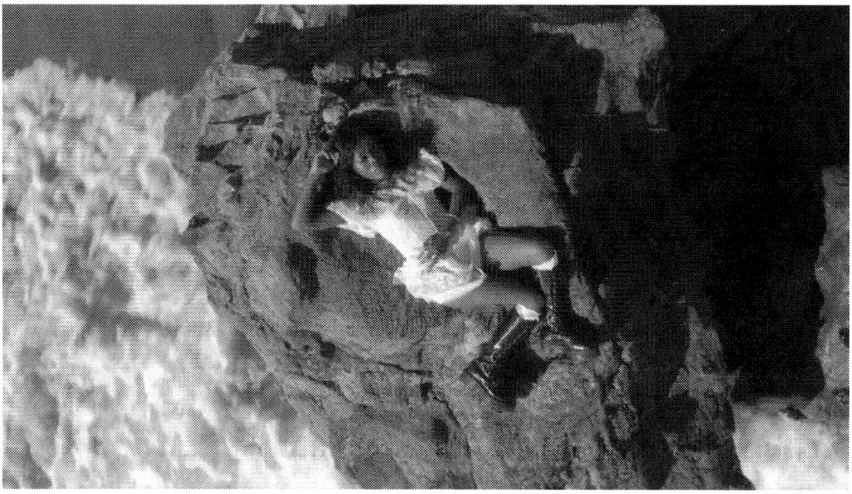

Figure 9.1 Tkay Maidza, "Where Is My Mind?" Dir. Tkay Maidza, 2021.

descends close to her once more; and then, finally, it rises back up to its starting point in the sky, just as the song ends (see Figure 9.1).

We soon realize, however, that there is only one camera movement in the whole video, rather than four. I noticed this by my second or third viewing. Each time the camera stops and reverses direction, the same footage is just repeated backward: down, up, down, up. You can tell this by the way the waves reverse direction as the camera does. Moreover, it seems that the descending sequences (the first and the third) are the ones that are being run backward, whereas the ascending sequences (the second and the fourth) are running forward. You can tell this by the action of the waves. In the ascending sequences, the waves run over the sand, and then slowly withdraw. In the descending sequences, in contrast, the water seems to be sucked back quickly from the sand—which only happens in reality just before a tsunami. When the video footage was actually shot, the drone must have started out poised just above Maidza, and then ascended into the sky.

This inverted motion works subliminally, even before you notice it consciously. Everything feels a bit counterintuitive and uncomfortable. For one thing, the camera's reversals disturb the continual onward thrust of the song. For another, it is discomfiting to see the reverse motion before we see the forward motion. This inversion perhaps resonates with the feeling of being upside down that is conveyed by the lyrics; but it still forces us to readjust over the course of the video, instead of just flowing along with the song's duration.

Also, the looped GIFs we are accustomed to online are usually much shorter than each of the four sections of this video. Most online GIFs either reverse back and forth in the course of just a few seconds, or else they never go backward, but simply replay from the beginning as soon as they have ended. The music video, in contrast, is nearly three minutes long, and the four sections are about forty-five seconds each. There's enough time to get mesmerized by the flowing water patterns, as well as by Maidza's unmoving figure, before we experience the reversal.

It also feels subtly wrong that the waves are moving backward while the camera is moving forward, toward Maidza; and conversely, that the waves are moving forward when the camera is moving backward, away from her. These associations may well be merely conventional; but somehow, in their misalignment, they interfere with what Scott Richmond calls the *proprioceptive aesthetics* that

> lies at the heart of the cinema as an aesthetic medium and as a technical system … *Proprioception* is the name for the set of perceptual processes whereby we orient ourselves in and coordinate ourselves with the world.
>
> (Richmond 2016, 6)

The video's camera movements, and the movements that the video camera observes and captures, seem out of sync with one another. We can add to this that the back-and-forth repetitions of the camera movement do not correspond very closely to the verse-chorus structure of the song. And on a micro-level, the multiple patterns made by the advancing and retreating waves do not map on to the music's beat. All of these discordances redound back upon us as we watch the video.

It is also worth noting that Maidza does not lip sync at any point in the course of the video. She remains sprawled in the same position for the entire length of the song. Although she is literally at the center of the image, the video is not organized around her point of view. Rather, the drone gives us an inhuman perspective. When the drone camera is at its lowest, we are close enough to see her eyes blinking as she stares at us; her tresses and her dress sway slightly in the wind. It almost feels as if we could touch her. But this moment of intimacy and reciprocity does not last. For most of the video, when the camera is higher in the sky, whether approaching or withdrawing, Maidza becomes just a feature of the landscape. Her white dress stands out against the variegated textures of the rock, the smoothness of the sand, and the pulsations of the waves. But our eyes are not drawn exclusively to her. Our gaze wanders, without guidance, over the whole extent of rocks, sand, and flowing water.

Another way to put all this is to say that the video is composed of multiple sonic and visual rhythms, which jostle one another and do not stack up together neatly. The scene as a whole provides an extended environment, or ambiance, within which the music unfolds; but within this framework, the details do not match up properly. We are pulled in different directions, and at different speeds, all at once. We might be tempted to describe this arrangement as an *alienation-effect*: a staple of modernist and postmodernist aesthetic practice. But such a categorization isn't quite right. In the video as a whole, as in the lyrics and the melody, the sense of alienation is oddly attenuated. Even though these multiple rhythms do not really fit together, we find ourselves *entrained* by all of them. This leads to a kind of scattering of attention: "my mind" is far away, as the song repeatedly insists. But nothing falls apart. Even as the rhythms seduce us in different directions and at different speeds, Maidza remains lying calmly on her rock throughout.

I am thinking here, in part, of Gilles Deleuze's distinction, in his book *The Fold*, between the Baroque world of Leibniz, in which a *pre-established harmony* excludes the co-existence of monads that are *incompossible* with one another, and the world of modern thinkers and artists, in which "bifurcations, divergences, incompossibilities, discords belong to the same motley world" (Deleuze 1993, 81). This distinction parallels the one that Deleuze makes, in his two *Cinema* volumes, between the classical movement image (Deleuze 1986) and the modernist time-image (Deleuze 1989). For Deleuze, classical cinema, like classical philosophy, measures time in terms of movement, whereas modernist cinema, like the philosophy of Kant and Bergson, releases time from its subordination to movement, and thereby liberates an experience of *duration*, or "time in its pure state" (Deleuze 1989, 17). Thanks to this opening of time, narrative closure gives way to the openings of "a process that at once affirms incompossibilities and passes through them" (Deleuze 1993, 81).

But is this still the case for digital audiovisual media today? The film theorist David Rodowick complains that digital media are unable to provide a true experience of Bergsonian and Deleuzian duration. This is because digital computation always brings us back to "the 'real time' of a continuous present" (Rodowick 2007, 171). Digital works physically exist as code, which is computationally rendered in "real time" when we open the file in order to watch or listen. For Rodowick, this means that digital works do not and cannot convey historical depth, or the thickness of indivisible duration. In digital production, "elements may be added, subtracted, or refashioned interactively because the data components retain their separate, modular identities throughout the 'editing' process" (Rodowick 2007, 167).

Rodowick echoes many other theorists who have similarly described how digital culture destroys the experience of duration, and undermines any possible understanding of history. Neoliberal capitalism operates a "time-space compression" (Harvey 1991, 260–83), enforces a "timeless time" (Castells 2010, 460–99), and compresses all happenings into an "eternal present" (Jameson 1994, 70). In a similar vein, other theorists have criticized the *presentism* of twenty-first-century speculative finance. Financial derivatives work "to objectify the future," colonizing it in and for the present, by pricing all its contingencies in advance (LiPuma and Lee 2004, 132). And the ubiquity of debt servicing, to whose sovereign requirements we are continually subjected, produces a "time in which the relationships between the past, present, and future are not fixed but open to constant adjustment" (Adkins 2018, 167). All these processes undermine the "pure state" of time as duration, compressing it to a point, and yet also filling it up with the detritus of "indeterminate movements of speculative time" (Adkins 2018, 167).

This is why I have emphasized the notion of a new audiovisual regime, the rhythm image, throughout this book. The sublime aesthetics of duration, as championed by Bergson, Deleuze, and Rodowick, is clearly no longer adequate to such compressed and contorted modes of temporality. Our digital culture has moved on to a new configuration, one that Deleuze did not fully anticipate. Just as the time-image displaced the movement-image as "the soul of the cinema" in the second half of the twentieth century (Deleuze 1986, 206), so today, in the early twenty-first century, the time-image has given way to something else, a third regime in which time is neither measured by movement, nor revealed in its "pure state" as duration. Rather, time becomes evident through its effects as pulsation and as force—or better, as the *superposition* of multiple (and often incompossible) pulsation-events and relations of force.

The ontology behind this description is not incompatible with Deleuze's own formulations, but it is something that he never worked through as explicitly as one might have wished. Deleuze's modernist sense of a "motley world" of divergences is retained in the audiovisual regime of the rhythm image. But these divergences can no longer be contained in the form of what Deleuze and Guattari, following Pierre Boulez, call "the 'nonpulsed time' of a floating music, both floating *and* machinic, which has nothing but speeds or differences in dynamic" (Deleuze and Guattari 1987, 262). We need George Clinton, rather than Boulez, if we are to make sense of this new articulation. In the regime of the rhythm image, time does not "float." Rather, it comes in syncopated pulses that overlap, yet without being hierarchically nested like Matryoshka dolls.

Already in the 1930s, inspired by quantum physics, Gaston Bachelard argued—against Bergson's insistence on the indivisibility of duration—for "a plurality of durations that have neither the same rhythm nor the same solidity in their sequence, nor the same power of continuity" (Bachelard 2000, 19). Of course, Bachelard did not anticipate twenty-first-century digital technologies; but his sense of multiple and incompatible temporal rhythms existing at once in quantum superposition does resonate with the way that digital audiovisual media are actually composed today, through the selection and compositing of multiple, qualitatively discrete elements.

Tkay Maidza's music video, with its modular, minimalist construction, demonstrates this process in a relatively simple and straightforward way. The video takes a single visual sequence of drone footage, repeating it reversed and re-reversed. This repetition cuts against the onward thrust of the song, but it also contrasts with the song's own structural repetitions. In turn, these formal dislocations resonate with the confusions narrated by the lyrics of the song. But although these tensions and contrasts are not resolved in any higher synthesis, they do not seem debilitating either. They are conditions that we must negotiate, like them or not.

In the course of the video, Tkay Maidza twice offers the viewer a brief sense of intimacy, but both times this offer is immediately withdrawn. Meanwhile, I am enraptured, as my eyes endeavor to trace the immanent, unstable patterns of waves crashing on the shore. This is also where my fatalistic sense of the arrow of time rubs up against the bliss of sheer reversibility. The water is never still; but as its modulating patterns unfold in time, they do not quite look the same backward and forward. But perhaps this perplexity, like the sense of being tracked and interrogated by a little fish, only adds piquancy to my feeling of subtle disorientation. I won't say that this video offers us an actual *way out* from what Deleuze calls the "snake's coils" of the control society (Deleuze 1995, 182); but it takes up the conditions imposed upon us by that society, and manages to twist them into three minutes of fugitive audiovisual bliss.

Afterword

The British singer Charli XCX released her song "Beg for You," with additional vocals by Rina Sawayama, as a single in early 2022. The song was then included in Charli's album *Crash* (whose title is perhaps an allusion to the novel by J. G. Ballard and the film by David Cronenberg—Davidson 2022). In "Beg for You," the singer implores a departing lover to stay with her a bit longer. There are two separate music videos for "Beg for You." The first one, directed by Angela Stephenson, is described as a "visualizer," though it might also be called a lyric video: it prints the words of the song over images of the two singers (Charli XCX 2022a). The second version, directed by Nick Harwood, is a full-fledged music video; it shows the singers in the desert, accompanied by backing dancers, performing some sort of strange ritual (Charli XCX 2022b). The two videos—together with the play between them, and their genealogical relation to earlier songs and videos—epitomize the metamorphoses of what I have been calling the rhythm image.

Harwood's video shows the two singers dancing in the California desert, dressed mostly in red, purple, and black. An article in *Vogue* lists the fashion designers (Mugler, Versace, Lemáine, and so on) whose clothes and shoes the singers wear in the video (Charli XCX 2022c). Designer labels always add to the commodified sheen of music videos; but I know far too little about fashion to comment on the brands listed in particular. The singers are accompanied by a group of female backing dancers, as well as by an older, bearded man dressed in white flowing robes and holding a tall staff (Vincent Castellanos, described in the credits as "cult leader"), and a figure with horns, entirely dressed in black, and wearing a black latex bunny mask (Aisha Hammond, described in the credits as "Henchwoman," though I cannot help thinking of her as a demonic figure). The landscape includes huge pylons and power lines, often crackling with bolts of electricity: a pile of rocks, one of which levitates into the air; and a circular pool, in front of symmetrical triangular monoliths, that serves as a sort of altar.

We first see all these figures walking down a road in the desert, toward the camera. After singing the first verse, and as she gets to the chorus, Charli goes down on her knees. She writhes back and forth, and eventually crawls through the dirt, desperately pleading to the song's addressee—or perhaps better to the camera, which observes her from above. Sawayama sings the second verse, mostly dancing in front of the pylons. Just as the song moves from the second chorus into the bridge, the horned figure hands a shard of broken glass to Charli. She cuts her palm with it, and lets her blood drip into the pool. The cult leader kneels by the pool and uses a gigantic spoon to take a sip of the reddened water. Just as the final chorus comes to its end, the backing dancers all fall down dead, like the victims of the Jonestown mass suicide. In a final tableau, Charli and Rina stand over the pool holding hands, while the white-robed man and the horned figure both kneel (see Figure 10.1). This is followed by a shot of a fire burning in the ritual space at night, and then a cut to the final credits.

The video is both sexy and sinister. Genna Rivieccio—the best commentator on the song, and on Charil XCX more generally—sarcastically suggests that the video enacts a cultic "ritual sacrifice" in order to appease PG&E, the monopoly provider of electric power to all of California (Rivieccio 2022b). PG&E has notoriously let the electrical grid decay in recent years, just as climate change has led to exacerbated periods of drought throughout the state. The predictable result has been frequent power outages, together with massive wildfires set off by sparks from the power lines. Given the patent unwillingness of governments, corporations, and the public to do anything to alleviate climate catastrophe and

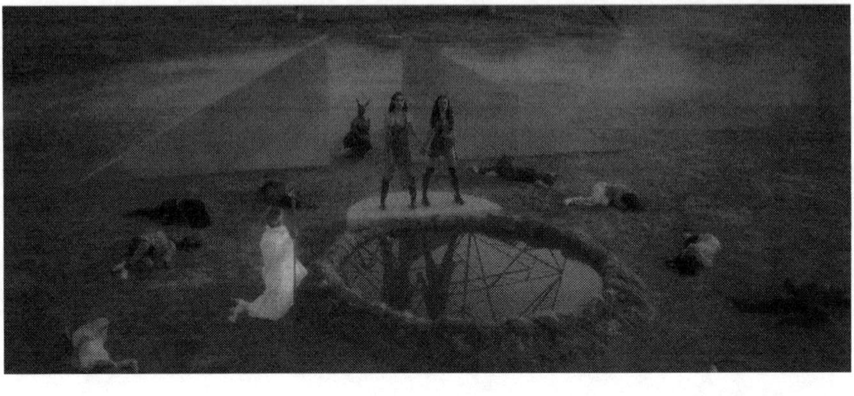

Figure 10.1 Charli XCX, "Beg For You feat. Rina Sawayama." Dir. Nick Harwood, 2022.

infrastructural collapse, ritual sacrifice and demonic intervention may well be our best bet.

Perhaps the prospect of environmental collapse works as an objective correlative for erotic despair. In its lyrics, "Beg for You" romanticizes emotional abandonment and self-abasement. The singers express desperation at being left behind. (The song is contrasted by other tracks on the album that express more ferocious and devouring erotic moods.) In any case, the previously released visualizer for "Beg for You" stays closer to the song's lyrics than the final video does. The visualizer depicts Charli and Rina—mostly in close-up, and both in white nightgowns—clinging to, cuddling, and caressing one another. The camera roves around the singers' faces and upper bodies, moving in and out, cutting frequently to extreme close-ups of just eyes or lips or fingers, sometimes going out of focus, and at other times overlaying multiple shots (see Figure 10.2).

The most steady light source in the visualizer is an illuminated circle behind the two singers. Sometimes the singers' faces are brightly lit from the front as well, but at other times not. The video has a relatively restricted color palette, with the greatest emphasis on the singers' similar skin tones (ethnically speaking,

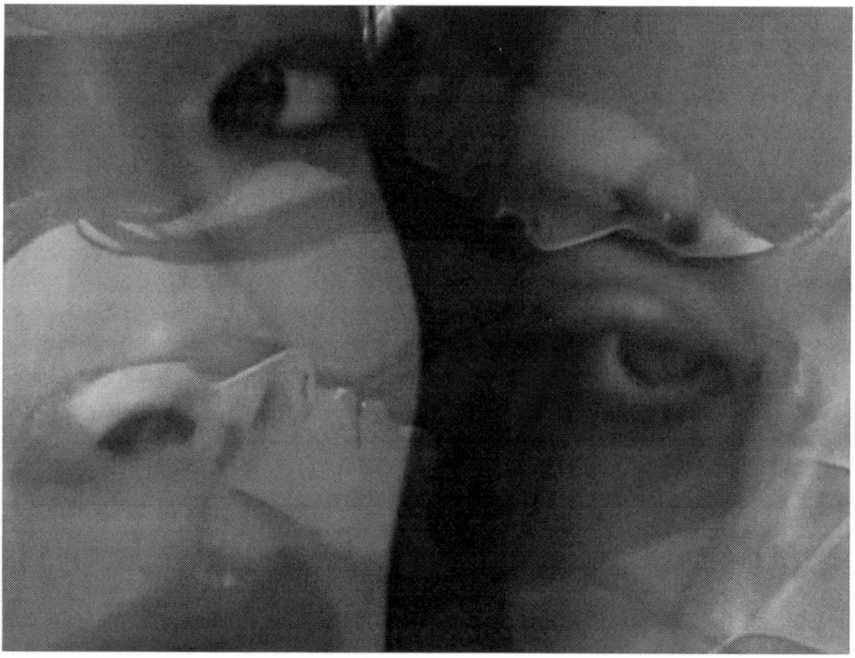

Figure 10.2 Charli XCX. "Beg For You (ft. Rina Sawayama) [Official Visualizer]." Dir. Angela Stephenson, 2022.

Charli is half white and half South Asian, while Rina is Japanese). Both women's facial expressions exhibit distress; they address their plaints directly to the camera (see Figure 10.3). Rivieccio says that the singers thus "perform a vanilla interpretation of lesbianic interaction" (Rivieccio 2022a). This seems accurate to me; what makes the interaction so "vanilla" is that the women mostly seem to be trying to comfort one another—rather than evincing positive desire either for one another or for the missing Other to whom their laments are addressed. But this scarcely makes the song seem restrained, or unmelodramatic, or particularly straight. Bradley Stern, discussing the song, notes that "yearning for more kisses from someone who isn't giving you the time of day is, canonically, queer" (Stern 2022). Indeed, Rina Sawayama describes herself as queer and pansexual (Tsjeng 2018), while Charli XCX is known to be queer-friendly, and has a large LGBTQ fan base (Daw 2019). Adding "featured artists" to pop music tracks is of course big business, so there is nothing inherently unusual about Sawayama making a guest appearance on the song and video. But the visualizer makes it particularly apparent, and therefore a bit strange, that both women are making

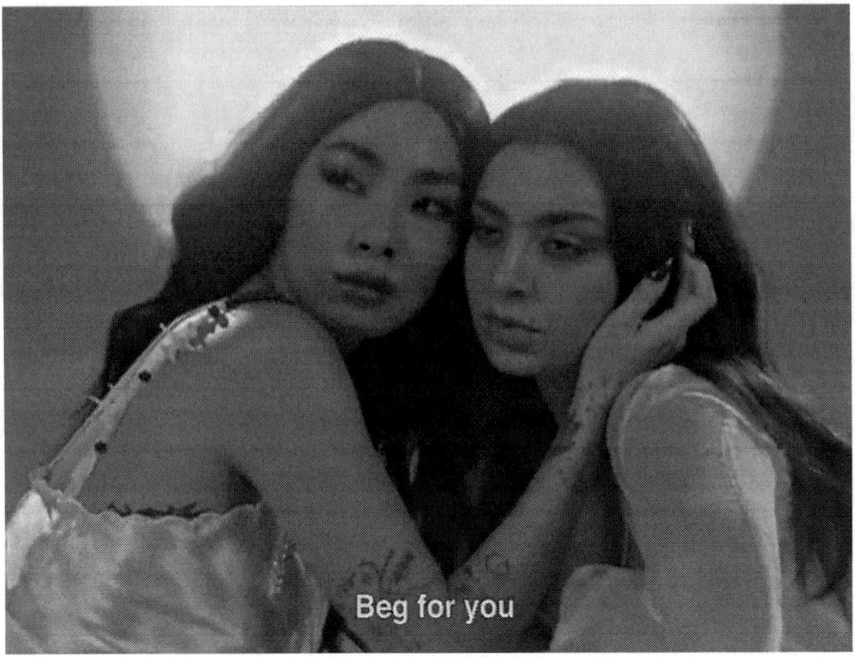

Figure 10.3 Charli XCX. "Beg for You (ft. Rina Sawayama) [Official Visualizer]." Dir. Angela Stephenson, 2022.

the same private plea. In highlighting the two women's closeness, the visualizer privileges their relationship to one another over that to their ostensible object(s) of affection.

Rivieccio adds to all this that there is something nostalgic and backward-looking about "Beg for You." This is because the song "takes us back to a time when yearning and burning for love instead of money felt more common," or even to a mythical past in which "actually being affected by another person" was possible without the mediation of posthuman cybernetic technologies. Naive sincerity is not something we cannot take at face value any longer, Rivieccio reminds us; especially now that "Grimes [has] assured us that AI would be taking over" (Rivieccio 2022a). This reading is supported, I think, by the way that the visualizer is shot in the antiquated 1.33:1 aspect ratio, used in Hollywood films prior to the 1950s, and in broadcast television prior to the adoption of high definition in the 1990s. Pop music often works by isolating a single emotion, and highlighting it with as great intensity as possible. In the case of "Beg for You," it is almost as if the feeling on display were being preserved under glass, heightened artificially in such a way that it will never be able to change or develop. This is the strategy of nostalgia, which seeks not so much to recover a past experience as to maintain it in its pastness. This is why nostalgia can operate even if the supposedly lost object that it mourns never actually existed, or never was actually possessed, in the first place. The visualizer brings us close to something that remains closed off to us. It is exquisite in the way that it gives us what Walter Benjamin called "the unique apparition of a distance, however near it may be" (Benjamin 2003, 255).

This distance is also expressed through the song's provenance. Charli XCX says in an interview, with considerable irony, that the song is a "sell-out"; she explains that she needed an "interpolation song"—one that was not just sampled, but entirely lifted from an older source—in order to provide "a truthful representation of what it's like to be a female pop artist signed to Atlantic Records" (Nix 2022). Indeed, against her usual procedure, "the track had been pitched to Charli rather than written with her in the room" (Jones 2022). As a result, the song is simultaneously heartfelt and inauthentic; or in Charli XCX's own words it "could be seen as a performance art piece or as a completely and utterly serious pop performance" (Charli XCX 2022c). For all these reasons, the song and its videos offer us a glimpse of heightened emotional expression; but they also frame this expression as an artifact and as a reconstruction. In maintaining such a contradictory stance, the song has a mainstream commercial sound, and yet it pushes at the limits of pop musical expression. It is worth noting that Rina Sawayama does something similar in her own solo work: as Dominique De Groen points out, the music video for Sawayama's song "XS" (Sawayama 2020) satirizes, and thereby acknowledges, the musical artist's inescapable status as a commodity (De Groen 2020).

The older song nostalgically interpolated by "Beg for You" is "Cry for You," by the Swedish singer Petra Marklund, aka September. "Cry for You" is a dance track recorded in 2005, but that only became an international hit in 2007–8 (Wang 2022). The song is a kiss-off anthem, with the singer gloatingly telling her ex that he will never see her again, and that she will not cry for him. There are two music videos for "Cry for You." The first one (September 2005) shows the singer at a photo shoot, interspersed with shots showing her breaking up with a male partner (this is why I am using the male pronoun for the ex in my description, even though gender is not specified in the lyrics). But the second, and more widely distributed, video has a science fiction scenario (September 2007). Marklund is portrayed singing and dancing as she appears on tall pedestals and on gigantic, pulsating video monitors. But she also appears as a character within the diegesis of the video. She is dressed in a black latex catsuit, and she runs in order to escape from a dystopian enclosure full of long, garishly lit corridors, dilating doors, marching clones, and guards shooting laser guns. All in all, the video recalls such 1970s science fiction movies as *THX 1138* and *Logan's Run*.

In "Beg for You," Charli XCX entirely inverts the meaning of "Cry for You." She changes the song from a triumphant cry of liberation into the plaintive expression of "a pink-hue of desire" (Wang 2022) that remains unfulfilled. The popping synthesizer sounds that carry the beat in "Beg for You" also make it sound less monolithic than "Cry for You" does. Or in the words of one discerning critic, "the accented aggression of the rhythmic drive in the sampled tune turns into something rhythmically coquettish in the later single" (Bushara 2022). As for the videos, Charli XCX inverts their visual themes as well. The businesslike representations of September's first video are replaced by mournful domestic enclosure in the visualizer. And the futuristic stylings of September's second video give way to an archaic ritual for binding electricity in the music video proper.

It is possible to continue tracing out these associations and borrowings almost indefinitely. For instance, despite a denial by the producer of "Cry for You," many listeners have felt that the song bears the melodic imprint of Bronski Beat's pioneering coming-out song from 1984, "Smalltown Boy" (Whosampled.com

2022). At least one commentator detects traces of "Smalltown Boy," and especially of the way that song "pulls at the heartstrings," in the plaintiveness of "Beg for You" as well (Rivieccio 2022a). This evidently amplifies the queer resonances of Charli's song and of both videos.

But instead of continuing to follow these threads, I will conclude this book by looking more broadly at the ramifications of what I have been calling the rhythm image, both in "Beg for You" and in the other songs and videos that I have discussed throughout the course of this book. Pop music is mostly about erotic desire and passion; and the longings it gives voice to are stifled and denied, at least as often as they are fulfilled. But if all these feelings are mundane and commonly shared, their expression is not in the least straightforward. Music videos amplify the emotions dramatized in their songs; but music videos also divert and transmute these emotions. This is equally true in terms of content, and in terms of visual and musical form. We see such processes at work in the two video iterations of "Beg for You." And we also see them at work in the ways that FKA twigs dramatizes her grief at abandonment in "cellophane" and "sad day," and in how The Weeknd gives a surreal, horror-film twist to his cycles of lust and abandonment in the series of videos for the songs from *After Hours*. More obliquely, we also see such expressive digressions in the intimations of catastrophe and entrapment that we find in the videos I have discussed for Massive Attack and for Bonobo, in the dysphoric affirmations of Moses Sumney as he struggles against the confines of normative gender roles, in the alien imaginings of Dawn Richard, in the divagations-in-place of Tkay Maidza, and in the continually shifting scenarios proposed to us by Tierra Whack.

All of these audiovisual expressions carve up the spacetime continuum in strange and unprecedented ways. Each video offers us what Deleuze and Guattari call "a bloc of sensations, that is to say, a compound of percepts and affects" (Deleuze and Guattari 1994, 164). These percepts and affects are drawn initially from concrete actuality—which may include, but need not be confined to, the life experience of the musical artist. But as constructions of sounds and images, and of their transmutations and modifications, they will evidently extend far beyond any such life experience. In any case, Deleuze and Guattari say, the important thing about such "blocs of percepts and affects" is that "the compound must stand up on its own"; this is even "the only law of creation" (Deleuze and Guattari 1994, 164).

In other words, each "bloc of sensations" must occupy and fill a certain determinate span of space and time; it must distinguish itself by individuating a specific portion of what Whitehead calls the "extensive continuum" (Whitehead 1978, 61ff.). Each "bloc" must therefore also be a sort of Leibnizian monad, offering its own unique perspective on the world we share in common:

> Just as the same city viewed from different directions appears entirely different and, as it were, multiplied perspectively, in just the same way it happens that, because of the infinite multitude of simple substances, there are, as it were, just as many different universes, which are, nevertheless, only perspectives on a single one, corresponding to the different points of view of each monad.
>
> (Leibniz 1989, 220)

There is evidently an enormous gap between the existential immediacies of each particular music video, and the way that I am now describing them all as Deleuzo-Guattarian blocs of sensation, or as Leibnizian monads. My own book evidently shares this problem, as it moves back and forth between close formal description, and sociological and philosophical generalizations. How can we bridge these gaps? I want to suggest that Deleuze's movement image and time image, together with the rhythm image that I am adding to his categorizations, are particular, historically embedded ways in which we can make these connections. Deleuze calls his effort to catalogue the various cinematic modes "a taxonomy, an attempt at the classification of images and signs" (Deleuze 1986, xiv). But each of the three "images" of the cinema in this classification works as something like what Kant calls a *schema*, or a "mediating representation" by means of which a "sensible intuition," or an object perceived by such an intuition, can be *subsumed* under a concept (Kant 1998, 271–2).

It is in this sense—or better, according to this procedure—that I group all the music videos discussed in the course of this book under the rubric of the rhythm image. The *occasions* presented in these videos are extraordinarily diverse, ranging from Charli XCX's plea to her departing lover to stay, to Tierra Whack's "Fuck Off" to her ex; or from the spare instrumentation and falsetto vocals of Moses Sumney's "Worth It" to the maximalism of The Weeknd's collaborations with Max Martin; or from the strictly delimited single camera movement of a drone in Tkay Maidza's "Where Is My Mind?" cover to the densely edited and composited visual simulations, and the overlapping musical samplings of Dawn Richard's "Calypso." But despite these differences, all the music videos that I have discussed in this book adhere to a temporal logic of polyrhythmic pulsations, in the course of which both narrated actions and extended durations are subordinated to generative, computational procedures of reproduction and transformation.

There is no last word here, because the incessant production, reproduction, appropriation, and remixing of audiovisual artifacts is not going to stop any time soon. This frenetic activity is propelled by the unceasing public demands of commodity production and consumption, but also by the stolen moments of audiovisual bliss—the private and shared joys of creativity and of reception—that they sometimes enable. Having started this book by citing a song by the Slits, I will conclude it by repeating the last line of the song: "Silence is a rhythm too."

Books and Articles Cited

Abel, Mark (2014). *Groove: An Aesthetic of Measured Time*. Boston: Brill.

Ableton.com (2016). "Bonobo: The Path to *Migration*". https://www.ableton.com/en/blog/bonobo-path-to-migration/.

Adkins, Lisa (2018). *The Time of Money*. Stanford: Stanford University Press.

Aku, Timmhotep (2019). "Moses Sumney Is the Last Man on Earth in 'Virile' Video". *Afropunk*, November 18, 2019. https://afropunk.com/2019/11/moses-sumney-virile-video/.

Alston, Trey (2020). "The Weeknd Channels His Inner Joker in Mind-Frying 'Blinding Lights' Video". *MTV*, January 21, 2020. http://www.mtv.com/news/3153297/the-weeknd-blinding-lights-video/.

Anderson, Chris (2008). "The End of Theory: The Data Deluge Makes the Scientific Method Obsolete". *Wired*, June 23, 2008. https://www.wired.com/2008/06/pb-theory/.

Aristotle (1995). *The Complete Works of Aristotle. The Revised Oxford Translation*. ed. Jonathan Barnes. Princeton: Princeton University Press.

Arnold, Gina, Daniel Cookney, Kirsty Fairclough, and Michael N. Goddard, eds. (2017). *Music/Video: Histories, Aesthetics, Media*. New York: Bloomsbury Academic.

Aswad, Jem (2020). "The Weeknd Goes Track-by-Track (Almost) on 'After Hours'". *Variety*, April 8, 2020. https://variety.com/2020/music/news/the-weeknd-after-hours-track-by-track–1234574136/.

Aswad, Jem (2021). "The Weeknd Reveals the Significance of His Full-Face Bandages, Ahead of Super Bowl (EXCLUSIVE)". *Variety*, February 3, 2021. https://variety.com/2021/music/news/the-weeknd-bandages-super-bowl-plastic-surgery–1234898743/.

Austerlitz, Saul (2007). *Money for Nothing: A History of the Music Video from the Beatles to the White Stripes*. New York: Continuum.

Bachelard, Gaston (2000). *The Dialectic of Duration*. Trans. Mary McAllester Jones. Lanham, MD: Rowman & Littlefield.

Balakrishnan, Sarah (2016). "Pan-African Legacies, Afropolitan Futures: A Conversation with Achille Mbembe". *Transition* 120, 28–37.

Bandcamp (2017). "*Migration*, by Bonobo". January 13, 2017. https://bonobomusic.bandcamp.com/album/migration.

Bataille, Georges (1988). *The Accursed Share. Vol. 1*. Trans. Robert Hurley. Brooklyn: Zone Books.

Bazin, André (2009). *What Is Cinema?* Trans. Timothy Bernard. Montreal: Caboose.

Beaver, Jacob (2020). "The Story within The Weeknd's New Album 'After Hours'". *The Cultured Nerd*, March 25, 2020. https://theculturednerd.org/2020/03/the-story-within-the-weeknds-new-album-after-hours/.

Bell, Daniel (1976). *The Cultural Contradictions of Capitalism*. New York: Basic Books.

Benjamin, Walter (2003). *Selected Writings*, Volume 4 (1938–1940). ed. Howard Eiland, Michael W. Jennings. Trans. Edmund Jephcott, and Others. Cambridge: The Belknap Press of Harvard University Press.

Bergson, Henri (1912). *An Introduction to Metaphysics*. Trans. T. E. Hulme. New York: Putnam.

Bergson, Henri (1946). *The Creative Mind: An Introduction to Metaphysics*. Trans. Mabelle L. Andison. Mineola: Dover.

Bergson, Henri (2014). *Laughter, an Essay on the Meaning of the Comic*. Trans. Cloudesley Brereton and Fred Rothwell. Eastford: Martino Fine Books.

Blanchot, Maurice (1995). *The Writing of the Disaster*. Trans. Ann Smock. Lincoln: University of Nebraska Press.

Blanco, Sebastian (2020). "Behind the Scenes as Mercedes-AMG GT Stars in The Weeknd's Video". *Car and Driver*, June 7, 2020. https://www.caranddriver.com/news/a32791487/mercedes-amg-gt-weeknd-blinding-lights-video/.

blankfist (2010). "Dancing on the Timeline: Slitscan Effect". http://videosift.com/video/Dancing-on-the-Timeline-Slitscan-Effect.

Bloom, Madison (2021). "The Weeknd's New 'Take My Breath' Video Pulled from IMAX Theaters Due to Epilepsy Concerns". *Pitchfork*, August 4, 2021. https://pitchfork.com/news/the-weeknds-new-take-my-breath-video-pulled-from-imax-theaters-due-to-epilepsy-concerns/.

Bogost, Ian (2006). *Unit Operations: An Approach to Videogame Criticism*. Cambridge: MIT Press.

Boltanski, Luc, and Eve Chiapello (2018). *The New Spirit of Capitalism*. 2nd edition. Trans. Gregory Elliott. New York: Verso.

Bolter, Jay David, and Richard Grusin (1999). *Remediation: Understanding New Media*. Cambridge: MIT Press.

Bordwell, David (2002). "Intensified Continuity: Visual Style in Contemporary American Film". *Film Quarterly* 55.3 (Spring 2002), 16–28.

Breihan, Tom (2009). "Album Review: Massive Attack, Splitting the Atom". http://pitchfork.com/reviews/albums/13574-splitting-the-atom/.

Breihan, Tom (2018a). "Tierra Whack Gamed the System". *Stereogum*, July 25, 2018. https://www.stereogum.com/2007168/tierra-whack-instagram-rap-star/franchises/status-aint-hood/.

Breihan, Tom (2018b). "Straight to Video: The Five Best Videos of the Week". *Stereogum*, August 24, 2018. https://www.stereogum.com/2011724/the-5-best-videos-of-the-week-336/franchises/straight-to-video/.

Breihan, Tom (2020). "Moses Sumney—'Me in 20 Years'". *Stereogum*, January 6, 2020. https://www.stereogum.com/2068946/moses-sumney-me-in-20-years/music/.

Brodsky, Rachel (2015). "Dawn Richard Does the 'Calypso' in Futuristic New Video". *Spin*, April 29, 2015. https://www.spin.com/2015/04/dawn-richard-calypso-video/.

Brookman, Jacob (2016). "Exclusive: The Photography Roots of Bonobo's Kerala, from Director Bison". http://www.bjp-online.com/2016/11/exclusive-the-photography-roots-of-bonobos-kerala-from-director-bison/.

Brooks, Clarissa (2019). "FKA twigs: We Are the Womxn". *WePresent*, website. https://wepresent.wetransfer.com/story/fka-twigs-we-are-the-womxn/.

Brow, Jason, and Jade Boren (2020). "The Weeknd's Fans Are Convinced That He Drops Multiple References to Bella Hadid in New Album". *Hollywood Life*, March 20, 2020. https://hollywoodlife.com/2020/03/20/the-weeknd-after-hours-album-bella-hadid-songs/.

Brown, Helen (2020a). "The Amen Break—How an Obscure 1960s B-side Became the Most Sampled Song in History". *The Financial Times*, April 13, 2020. https://ig.ft.com/life-of-a-song/amen-break.html.

Brown, Helen (2020b). "Moses Sumney: 'Men Are Entitled to Find What Socially Responsible Worth They Have'". *The Independent*, May 10, 2020. https://www.independent.co.uk/arts-entertainment/music/features/moses-sumney-interview-grae-album-gender-sexuality-lyrics-tour-a9504621.html.

Burberry (2020). Instagram, August 28, 2020. https://www.instagram.com/p/CecKM-qgN_C/.

Burns, Lori, and Stan Hawkins (2019). *The Bloomsbury Handbook of Popular Music Video Analysis*. New York: Bloomsbury Academic.

Burroughs, William S. (1987). *The Western Lands*. New York: Viking Press.

Burroughs, William S. (2013). *Naked Lunch: The Restored Text*. ed. James Grauerholz and Barry Miles. New York: Grove Press.

Bushara, Sarrah (2022). "'Beg For You' Review: Charli XCX and Rina Sawayama Offer Nothing New". *The Harvard Crimson*, February 8, 2022. https://www.thecrimson.com/article/2022/2/8/charli-xcx-rina-sawayama-beg-for-you-single-review/.

Butterfield, Aaron (2015). "Dawn Richard—*Blackheart* (Album Review)". *Breathe Heavy*, January 20, 2015. http://www.breatheheavy.com/dawn-richard-blackheart-album-review/.

Cabooter, James (2020). "The Weeknd Confesses He's a 'Lonely Pop Star' and Doesn't Like to Leave Home". *The Daily Star*, February 21, 2020. https://www.dailystar.co.uk/music/weeknd-confesses-lonely-pop-star–21550160.

Capper, Addison (2020). "Hiro Murai on Wushu Inspirations for FKA twigs' 'Sad Day'". *Little Black Book*, September 7, 2020. https://www.lbbonline.com/news/hiro-murai-on-wushu-inspirations-for-fka-twigs-sad-day.

Carle, Chris (2009). "Pixies Interview". https://www.ign.com/articles/2009/07/06/pixies-interview.

Casarino, Cesare (2011). “Three Theses on the Life-image (Deleuze, Cinema, Biopolitics)”. In *Releasing the Image: From Literature to New Media*, ed. Jacques Khalip and Robert Mitchell. Stanford: Stanford University Press, 156–67.

Castells, Manuel (2010). “The Rise of the Network Society”. In *The Information Age: Economy, Society, and Culture*. Second edition. Vol. 1. Cambridge: Blackwell, 1–597.

Cavell, Stanley (1979). *The World Viewed: Reflections on the Ontology of Film*. Enlarged edition. Cambridge: Harvard University Press.

Chalmers, Grace (2019). “Mary Magdalene: A Timeless Symbol of Strength and Rebirth in FKA twigs Recent Album MAGDALENE”. *Religion in Society* blog, December 10, 2019. https://onlineacademiccommunity.uvic.ca/sociologyofreligion/2019/12/10/mary-magdalene-a-timeless-symbol-of-strength-and-rebirth-in-fka-twigs-recent-album-magdalene/.

Charli, XCX (2022c). “Diary of a Pop Star: Charli XCX Takes Us behind the Scenes of Her New Video with Rina Sawayama”. *Vogue*, February 11, 2022. https://www.vogue.com/article/charli-xcx-diary-of-a-pop-star-beg-for-you-video.

Chinapen, Mark (2021). “The Story of The Weeknd’s After Hours”. March 24, 2021. https://medium.com/modern-music-analysis/the-story-of-the-weeknds-after-hours-cd42c391da71.

Chion, Michel (1994). *Audio-Vision: Sound on Screen*. First edition. Trans. Claudia Gorbman. New York: Columbia University Press.

Chion, Michel (2009). *Film, a Sound Art*. Trans. Claudia Gorbman. New York: Columbia University Press.

Chion, Michel (2019). *Audio-Vision: Sound on Screen*. Second edition. Trans. Claudia Gorbman. New York: Columbia University Press.

Christgau, Robert (2018). “Robert Christgau on G.O.O.D Music’s Good (and Less Good) Music”. *Vice*, July 13, 2018. https://noisey.vice.com/en_us/article/ev8nvz/robert-christgau-reviews-pusha-t-kanye-west-tierra-whack.

Christiansen, Steen Ledet (2019). “The Morph-Image: Four Forms of Post-Cinema”. In *Philosophy and Film: Bridging Divides*, ed. Christina Rawls, Diana Neiva, and Steven S. Gouveia. New York: Routledge, 49–63.

Christiansen, Steen Ledet (2021). “A MASSIVE Swirl of Pixels: Algorithms in Radiohead’s ‘Go to Sleep’”. In *Cybermedia: Explorations in Science, Sound, and Vision*. ed. Carol Vernallis, Holly Rogers, Jonathan Leal, and Selmin Kara. New York: Bloomsbury, 75–96.

Cliff, Aimee (2017). “In a World Obsessed with Romance, Moses Sumney Is Happy Alone”. *The Fader*, September 4, 2017. https://www.thefader.com/2017/09/04/moses-sumney-aromanticism-interview.

Clover, Carol (1992). *Men, Women, and Chain Saws: Gender in the Modern Horror Film*. Princeton: Princeton University Press.

Crawford, Anwyn (2010). “The Evolution of the Male Falsetto”. *Frieze* 133 (September 2010). https://www.frieze.com/article/evolution-male-falsetto.

Creative News (2020). "Hiro Murai Splits FKA twigs in Two for Spectacular Martial Arts Video". *Little Black Book*, August 28, 2020. https://www.lbbonline.com/news/hiro-murai-splits-fka-twigs-in-two-for-spectacular-martial-arts-video.

Cuby, Michael (2020). "The Weeknd Gets Bloodied Up in New 'Blinding Lights' Music Video". *Nylon*. https://www.nylon.com/the-weeknd-blinding-lights-video/amp.

Curto, Justin (2021). "How Many Red Suits Did the Weeknd Order for *After Hours*?". *Vulture*, November 23, 2021. https://www.vulture.com/2021/11/the-weeknd-over-18-red-suits-after-hours.html.

Daily News (2019). "Priti Patel Vows to 'End the Free Movement of People once and for All' after Brexit". October 1, 2019. https://www.youtube.com/watch?v=pwesFm0vSrg.

Davidson, Claire (2022). "Why Is Charli XCX so Obsessed with Cars?". *Vice i-D*, February 18, 2022. https://i-d.vice.com/en_uk/article/y3vq57/charli-xcx-cars-lyrics.

Davis, Nick (2013). *The Desiring-Image: Gilles Deleuze and Contemporary Queer Cinema*. Oxford: Oxford University Press.

Daw, Stephen (2019). "5 Reasons Why Charli XCX Is an Example for Queer Allies Everywhere". *Billboard*, September 3, 2019. https://www.billboard.com/culture/pride/charli-xcx-queer-ally–8529900/.

Dawndawndawn (2020). "An Interpretation of FKA twigs' 'Sad Day'". https://goingon.medium.com/an-interpretation-of-fka-twigs-sad-day-d3ac95fa1c2f.

De Groen, Dominique (2020). "Watch out for This—Opening Lecture by Dominique De Groen". *COLLATERAL Lecture Series on Music Videos*, December 16, 2020. https://www.facebook.com/watch/?v=3883136131699125.

DeLanda, Manuel (2002). *Intensive Science and Virtual Philosophy*. New York: Continuum.

DeLanda, Manuel (2016). *Assemblage Theory*. Edinburgh: Edinburgh University Press.

Deleuze, Gilles (1986). *Cinema 1: The Movement-Image*. Trans. Hugh Tomlinson and Barbra Habberjam. Minneapolis: University of Minnesota Press.

Deleuze, Gilles (1988a). *Bergsonism*. Trans. Hugh Tomlinson and Barbara Habberjam. New York: Zone Books.

Deleuze, Gilles (1988b). *Foucault*. Trans. Sean Hand. Minneapolis: University of Minnesota Press.

Deleuze, Gilles (1988c). *Spinoza: Practical Philosophy*. Trans. Robert Hurley. San Francisco: City Lights Books.

Deleuze, Gilles (1989). *Cinema 2: The Time-Image*. Trans. Hugh Tomlinson and Robert Galeta. Minneapolis: University of Minnesota Press.

Deleuze, Gilles (1990). *Logic of Sense*. Trans. Mark Lester. New York: Columbia University Press.

Deleuze, Gilles (1993). *The Fold: Leibniz and the Baroque*. Trans. Tom Conley. Minneapolis: University of Minnesota Press. (Translation modified).

Deleuze, Gilles (1994). *Difference and Repetition*. Trans. Paul Patton. New York: Columbia University Press.

Deleuze, Gilles (1995). *Negotiations 1972–1990*. Trans. Martin Joughin. New York: Columbia University Press.

Deleuze, Gilles (2003). *Francis Bacon: The Logic of Sensation*. Trans. Daniel W. Smith. New York: Continuum.

Deleuze, Gilles, and Félix Guattari (1983). *Anti-Oedipus*. Trans. Robert Hurley, Mark Seem, and Helen R. Lane. Minneapolis: University of Minnesota Press.

Deleuze, Gilles, and Félix Guattari (1987). *A Thousand Plateaus*. Trans. Brian Massumi. Minneapolis: University of Minnesota Press.

Deleuze, Gilles, and Félix Guattari (1994). *What Is Philosophy?* Trans. Hugh Tomlinson, and Graham Burchell. New York: Columbia University Press.

Denson, Shane (2020). *Discorrelated Images*. Durham: Duke University Press.

Derrida, Jacques (1973). *Speech and Phenomena: And Other Essays on Husserl's Theory of Signs*. Trans. David B. Allison. Evanston: Northwestern University Press.

DeVille, Chris (2018). "Tierra Whack Can't Be Pinned Down". *Stereogum*, July 27, 2018. https://www.stereogum.com/2006781/tierra-whack-cant-be-pinned-down/franchises/interview/.

Doane, Mary Ann (1980). "The Voice in the Cinema: The Articulation of Body and Space". *Yale French Studies* 60: 33–50.

During, Elie (2010). *Faux raccords: La coexistence des images*. Paris: Actes Sud.

Eisenstein, Sergei (1949). *Film Form: Essays in Film Theory*. Trans. Jay Leyda. New York: Harcourt, Brace and Company.

Emile, Chris (2021). Website: "A Choreographer's Exploration of Black Masculinity". http://chrisemile.com/.

Eshun, Kodwo (1998). *More Brilliant Than the Sun: Adventures in Sonic Fiction*. London: Quartet Books.

Eshun, Kodwo (2000). "Visions of Rhythm in the Kinematic Pneumacosm of Hype Williams". In *Machine Times*, ed. Arjen Mulder and Joke Brouwer. Rotterdam: V2.

Eshun, Kodwo (2003). "Further Considerations of Afrofuturism". *CR: The New Centennial Review* 3.2 (Summer 2003), 287–302.

Fagen, Lucas (2019). "What's up with FKA twigs' Voice on 'Magdalene'?". *City Pages*, November 14, 2019. http://www.citypages.com/music/whats-up-with-fka-twigs-voice-on-magdalene/564913742.

Fazi, Beatrice (2018). *Contingent Computation: Abstraction, Experience, and Indeterminacy in Computational Aesthetics*. London: Rowman and Littlefield.

Fisher, Mark (2013). "The Metaphysics of Crackle: Afrofuturism and Hauntology". *Dancecult* 5.2, Special Issue on Afrofuturism, 42–55.

FKA twigs (2019b). Twitter posting, April 24, 2019, 2:31 pm. https://twitter.com/FKAtwigs/status/1121119416815693825.

FKA twigs (2020b). Instagram posting, November 16, 2020. https://www.instagram.com/p/CHqgcLTpfyC/.

Foucault, Michel (1977). *Discipline and Punish: The Birth of the Prison*. Trans. Alan Sheridan. New York: Vintage Books.

Foucault, Michel (2008). *The Birth of Biopolitics (Lectures at the College De France)*. Trans. Graham Burchell. London: Palgrave Macmillan.

Galloway, Alexander R. (2005). *Gaming: Essays on Algorithmic Culture*. Minneapolis: University of Minnesota Press.

Galloway, Alexander R. (2014a). *Laruelle: Against the Digital*. Minneapolis: University of Minnesota Press.

Galloway, Alexander R. (2014b). "Rise of Nondiegetic Media". December 13, 2014. http://cultureandcommunication.org/galloway/rise-of-nondiegetic-media.

Galloway, Alexander R. (2021). *Uncomputable: Play and Politics in the Long Digital Age*. New York: Verso.

Galloway, Alexander R., and Mohammad Salemy (2013). "The Question of Interface". *Fillip* 18 (Spring 2013). https://fillip.ca/content/the-question-of-interface.

Gates, Marya (2021). "Movie References in The Weeknd's After Hours You Never Noticed". *MovieFone*, February 16, 2021. https://www.moviefone.com/2021/02/16/movie-references-in-the-weeknds-after-hours-you-never-noticed/.

Goodman, Steve (2009). *Sonic Warfare: Sound, Affect, and the Ecology of Fear*. Cambridge: MIT Press.

Goodwin, Andrew (1992). *Dancing in the Distraction Factory: Music Television and Popular Culture*. Minneapolis: University of Minnesota Press.

Gorbman, Claudia (1987). *Unheard Melodies: Narrative Film Music*. Bloomington: Indiana University Press.

Gowan, Peter (2001). "Neoliberal Cosmopolitanism". *New Left Review* 11 (September–October 2001), 79–93.

Gracie, Bianca (2021). "'Can't Feel My Face': The Weeknd's Smash Hit". June 8, 2021. https://www.udiscovermusic.com/stories/cant-feel-my-face-the-weeknd/.

Gunning, Tom (2006). "The Cinema of Attraction[s]: Early Film, Its Spectator and the Avant-Garde". In *The Cinema of Attractions Reloaded*, ed. Wanda Strauven. Amsterdam: University of Amsterdam Press, 381–8.

Hagglund, Martin (2008). *Radical Atheism: Derrida and the Time of Life*. Stanford: Stanford University Press.

Hansen, Mark B. N. (2015). *Feed Forward: On the Future of Twenty-First-Century Media*. Chicago: University of Chicago Press.

Haraway, Donna (1991). "A Cyborg Manifesto: Science, Technology, and Socialist-Feminism in the Late Twentieth Century". In *Simians, Cyborgs, and Women: The Reinvention of Nature*. New York: Routledge, 149–81.

Harvey, David (1991). *The Condition of Postmodernity: An Enquiry into the Origins of Cultural Change*. Hoboken: Wiley-Blackwell.

Hayles, N. Katherine (1999). *How We Became Posthuman: Virtual Bodies in Cybernetics, Literature, and Informatics*. Chicago: University of Chicago Press.

Hogan, Marc (2017). "Lorde's 'Green Light' Director Grant Singer Reveals Story behind the Video". *Pitchfork*, March 2, 2017. https://pitchfork.com/news/72018-grant-singer-talks-directing-lordes-green-light-video-shooting-on-16mm-film-and-the-power-of-familiarity/.

Horkheimer, Max, and Theodor Adorno (2002). *Dialectic of Enlightenment: Philosophical Fragments*. Trans. Edmund Jephcott. Stanford: Stanford University Press.

Horn, Olivia (2018). "Meet Tierra Whack, a True Hip-Hop Original". *Pitchfork*, June 28, 2018. https://pitchfork.com/features/rising/meet-tierra-whack-a-true-hip-hop-original/.

James, Robin (2008). "Robo-Diva R&B: Aesthetics, Politics, and Black Female Robots in Contemporary Popular Music". *Journal of Popular Music Studies* 20.4 (December 2008), 402–23.

James, Robin (2009). "Single Ladies = Robots". *It's Her Factory* blog, May 15, 2009. http://www.its-her-factory.com/2009/05/single-ladies-robots/.

James, Robin (2015). *Resilience and Melancholy: Pop Music, Feminisim, Neoliberalism*. Winchester: Zero Books.

James, William (1983). *The Principles of Psychology*. Cambridge: Harvard University Press.

Jameson, Fredric (1991). *Postmodernism, or, the Cultural Logic of Late Capitalism*. Durham: Duke University Press.

Jameson, Fredric (1994). *The Seeds of Time*. New York: Columbia University Press.

Jiayoowushu (2014). "Are Wushu 'Weapons' Real Weapons?: The Role of Apparatus in Modern Wushu". May 7, 2014. https://jiayoowushu.com/wushu-weapons-real/.

Jones, Marcus (2022). "Charli XCX Breaks down Her Rina Sawayama Duet 'Beg for You': 'It was a long time coming'". *Entertainment Weekly*, January 28, 2022. https://ew.com/music/charli-xcx-breaks-down-beg-for-you/.

Kameir, Rawiya (2020). "Moses Sumney Is Ready to Claim His Spotlight". *Pitchfork*, February 20, 2020. https://pitchfork.com/features/cover-story/moses-sumney-interview/.

Kant, Immanuel (1998). *Critique of Pure Reason*. Trans. Paul Guyer and Allen W. Wood. Cambridge: Cambridge University Press.

Kant, Immanuel (2000). *Critique of Judgment*. Trans. Paul Guyer and Eric Matthews. Cambridge: Cambridge University Press.

Kaplan, E. Ann (1987). *Rocking around the Clock: Music Television, Post Modernism and Consumer Culture*. London: Routledge.

Kent, Clarkisha (2019). "FKA twigs on the Healing behind Her Long-awaited Sophomore Album, Magdalene". *Yahoo! Money*, October 20, 2019. https://money.yahoo.com/fka-twigs-healing-behind-her-220018809.html.

Knight, David (2017). "Oscar Hudson on Bonobo's No Reason: There Are No VFX Whatsoever". *Promo News*, January 26, 2017. https://www.promonews.tv/interviews/oscar-hudson-bonobos-no-reason-there-are-no-vfx-whatsoever/45740.

Kornbluh, Anna (2019). *Marxist Film Theory and Fight Club*. New York: Bloomsbury.

Korsgaard, Mathias Bonde (2017). *Music Video after MTV: Audiovisual Studies, New Media, and Popular Music*. London: Routledge.

Kurzweil, Ray (2005). *The Singularity Is Near*. New York: Viking.

Latif, Nadia (2017). "It's Lit! How Film Finally Learned to Light Black Skin". *The Guardian*, September 21, 2017. https://www.theguardian.com/film/2017/sep/21/its-lit-how-film-finally-learned-how-to-light-black-skin.

Lazzarato, Maurizio (2019). *Videophilosophy: The Perception of Time in Post-Fordism*. Trans. Jay Hetrick. New York: Columbia University Press.

Lee, Kyoo E. (2002). "A Meditation on Knell, Funeral Melancholia and the Question of Self-Reflexivity". *Angelaki* 7.2 (August 2002), 93–105.

Leibniz, G. W. (1989). *Phiosophical Essays*. Ed. and Trans. Roger Ariew and Daniel Garber. Indianapolis: Hackett.

Levitt, Deborah (2018). *The Animatic Apparatus: Animation, Vitality, and the Futures of the Image*. Winchester: Zero Books.

LiPuma, Edward, and Benjamin Lee (2004). *Financial Derivatives and the Globalization of Risk*. Durham: Duke University Press.

Lordi, Emily (2020). "FKA twigs Has Reached New Heights". *The New York Times*, October 19, 2020. https://www.nytimes.com/interactive/2020/10/19/t-magazine/fka-twigs.html.

Lowe, Zane (2019). "FKA twigs and Zane Lowe 'MAGDALENE' Interview". YouTube, November 11, 2019. https://www.youtube.com/watch?v=FU88-ILTX5A.

Lyons, Patrick (2020). "When The Weeknd Called, Anton Tammi Answered". *GQ*, April 3, 2020. https://www.gq.com/gallery/anton-tammi-the-weeknd-after-hours-interview-2020.

Maher, Natalie (2018). "Tierra Whack on New Project 'Whack World,' Eating Chicken Wings with Andre 3000 & Why She Wants to Record in Tokyo". *Billboard*, August 27, 2018. https://www.billboard.com/articles/columns/hip-hop/8471508/tierra-whack-whack-world-andre-3000-interview.

Malabou, Catherine (2008). *What Should We Do with Our Brain?* Trans. Sebastian Rand. New York: Fordham University Press.

Mamo, Heran (2021a). "A Timeline of The Weeknd's Bloody 'After Hours' Character". *Billboard*, February 4, 2021. https://www.billboard.com/music/rb-hip-hop/the-weeknd-after-hours-character-timeline-9521577/.

Mamo, Heran (2021b). "The Greatest Hit: The New No. 1 Song of All Time". *Billboard*, November 23, 2021. https://www.billboard.com/music/features/the-weeknd-blinding-lights-billboard-cover-story-2021-interview-1235001282/.

Manovich, Lev (2001). *The Language of New Media*. Cambridge: MIT Press.

Marks, Laura U. (2000). *The Skin of the Film Intercultural Cinema, Embodiment, and the Senses*. Durham: Duke University Press.

Marks, Laura U. (2002). *Touch: Sensuous Theory and Multisensory Media*. Minneapolis: University of Minnesota Press.

Mbembe, Achille (2021). *Out of the Dark Night: Essays on Decolonization*. Trans. Daniela Ginsburg. New York: Columbia University Press.

McArtney, Tim (2021). "Dan Farber on the Power of Intent and Personal Connections". *Happy Mag*, June 8, 2021. https://happymag.tv/dan-farber-interview/.

McDermott, Maeve (2015). "11 Times The Weeknd Channeled Michael Jackson in His 'I Can't Feel My Face' Video". *USA Today*, July 28, 2015. https://www.usatoday.com/story/life/entertainthis/2015/07/28/the-weeknd-i-cant-feel-my-face-video/77535716/.

McLuhan, Marshall (1962). *The Gutenberg Galaxy: The Making of Typographic Man*. Toronto: University of Toronto Press.

McLuhan, Marshall (1964). *Understanding Media: The Extensions of Man*. Cambridge: MIT Press.

McLuhan, Marshall, and Quentin Fiore (1967). *The Medium Is the Massage*. New York: Bantam.

McLuhan, Marshall, and Eric McLuhan (1988). *Laws of Media: The New Science*. Toronto: University of Toronto Press.

Mignolo, Walter (2000). "The Many Faces of Cosmo-Polis: Border Thinking and Critical Cosmopolitanism". *Public Culture* 12.3, 721–48.

Mirowski, Philip (2001). *Machine Dreams: Economics Becomes a Cyborg Science*. Cambridge: Cambridge University Press.

Moten, Fred (2017). *Black and Blur (Consent Not to Be a Single Being)*. Durham: Duke University Press.

Moten, Fred (2018a). *Stolen Life (Consent Not to Be a Single Being)*. Durham: Duke University Press.

Moten, Fred (2018b). *The Universal Machine (Consent Not to Be a Single Being)*. Durham: Duke University Press.

Mufson, Beckett (2015). "Dive into a Rainbow Alien Disco in Richard's 'Calypso' Music Video". *The Creators Project* blog. April 30, 2015. http://thecreatorsproject.vice.com/blog/dive-into-a-rainbow-alien-disco-in-dawns-calypso-music-video.

Mulvey, Laura (1989). *Visual and Other Pleasures*. New York: Palgrave.

Mulvey, Laura (2006). *Death 24x a Second: Stillness and the Moving Image*. London: Reaktion Books.

Nix, Cole (2022). "Charli XCX Sells Out on 'Beg For You'". *Music Daily*, February 2, 2022. https://musicdaily.app/charli-xcx-sells-out-on-beg-for-you/.

O'Connor, Roisin (2017). "Bonobo Interview: Simon Green on New Album Migration, Living in LA, and Observing Britain from the Outside". *The Independent*, January 10, 2017. http://www.independent.co.uk/arts-entertainment/music/news/bonobo-new-album-migration-tour-uk-jon-hopkins-kerala-fabric-brexit-a7518876.html.

Pascual, Ashley (2021). "What Is MTV-Style Editing?". *Beverly Boy Productions*, May 6, 2021. https://beverlyboy.com/filmmaking/what-is-mtv-style-editing/.

Pasolini, Pier Paolo (2005). "The Cinema of Poetry". In *Heretical Empiricism*. Trans. Ben Lawton and Louise K. Barnett. Washington, DC: New Academia Publishing, 167–86.

Pearce, Sheldon (2020). "'I Definitely Rage against Being Classified as R&B': The Strange, Beautiful Music of Moses Sumney". *The Guardian*, February 29, 2020. https://www.theguardian.com/music/2020/feb/29/moses-sumney-interview-gray-aromanticism.

Pettman, Dominic (2015). *Infinite Distraction: Paying Attention to Social Media*. Cambridge: Polity Press.

Pisters, Patricia (2012). *The Neuro-Image: A Deleuzian Film-Philosophy of Digital Screen Culture*. Stanford: Stanford University Press.

Prigogine, Ilya, and Isabelle Stengers (1984). *Order Out of Chaos: Man's New Dialogue with Nature*. New York: Bantam.

Promonews (2020). "Behind the Video: Allie Avital on Moses Sumney's 'Me in 20 Years'". July 28, 2020. https://www.promonews.tv/interviews/behind-video-allie-avital-moses-sumneys-me-20-years/65827.

Rancière, Jacques (2006). *Film Fables*. Trans. Emiliano Battista. Oxford: Berg Publishers.

Reddit (2017). "Bonobo's New Music Video Is Subtle, Creepy, Frustrating and Brilliant". https://www.reddit.com/r/videos/comments/5aycto/bonobos_new_music_video_is_subtle_creepy/.

Remes, Justin (2015). *Motion(less) Pictures: The Cinema of Stasis*. New York: Columbia University Press.

Richmond, Scott (2016). *Cinema's Bodily Illusions: Flying, Floating, and Hallucinating*. Minneapolis: University of Minnesota Press.

Rindner, Grant (2020). "Why Bad Bunny, Rosalía and The Weeknd Are Going to Cliqua for Their Music Videos". *GQ*, December 4, 2020. https://www.gq.com/story/cliqua-the-weeknd-j-balvin-bad-bunny-rosalia-music-videos-interview.

Rivieccio, Genna (2022a). "Even Charli XCX and Rina Sawayama Have to Beg These Days (Just Not for Money)". *Culled Culture*, January 29, 2022. https://www.culledculture.com/charli-xcx-rina-sawayama-beg-for-you/.

Rivieccio, Genna (2022b). "A Ritual Sacrifice for PG&E: Charli XCX's 'Beg for You' Video". *Culled Culture*, February 25, 2022. https://www.culledculture.com/charli-xcx-rina-sawayama-beg-for-you-video/.

Roden, David (2014). *Posthuman Life: Philosophy at the Edge of the Human*. London: Routledge.

Rodowick, David (1997). *Gilles Deleuze's Time Machine*. Durham: Duke University Press.

Rodowick, David (2007). *The Virtual Life of Film*. Cambridge: Harvard University Press.

Rose, Steve (2015). "*Ex Machina* and Sci-fi's Obsession with Sexy Female Robots". *The Guardian*, January 15, 2015. http://www.theguardian.com/film/2015/jan/15/ex-machina-sexy-female-robots-scifi-film-obsession.

Ryce, Andrew (2015). "Dawn Richard: *Blackheart*". *Pitchfork*, January 16, 2015. http://pitchfork.com/reviews/albums/20104-blackheart/.

Sánchez, Sergio (2013). *Hacia una imagen no-tiempo: Deleuze y el cine contemporáneo*. Oviedo: Servicio de Publicaciones de la Universidad de Oviedo.

Serra, Emanuele (2020). "FKA twigs Sad Day behind the Scene". *3D Art*, September 5, 2020. https://www.3dart.it/en/fka-twigs-sad-day-behind-the-scene/.

Shaviro, Steven (2002). "The Erotic Life of Machines". *Parallax* 25 (October–December 2002), 21–31.

Shaviro, Steven (2003). *Connected, or, What It Means to Live in the Network Society*. Minneapolis: University of Minnesota Press.

Shaviro, Steven (2007). "Emotion Capture: Affect in Digital Film". *Projections* 2.1, 37–55.

Shaviro, Steven (2009). "The Singularity Is Here". In *Red Planets: Marxism and Science Fiction*, ed. Mark Bould and China Mieville. Middletown: Wesleyan University Press, 103–17.

Shaviro, Steven (2010). *Post-Cinematic Affect*. London: Zero Books.

Shaviro, Steven (2011). "Hyperbolic Futures: Speculative Finance and Speculative Fiction". *Cascadia Subduction Zone* 1.2 (April 2011), 3–5 and 12–15.

Shaviro, Steven (2015). *No Speed Limit: Three Essays on Accelerationism*. Minneapolis: University of Minnesota Press.

Shaviro, Steven (2016). "Post-Continuity: An Introduction". In *Post-Cinema: Theorizing 21st-Century Film*, REFRAME Books (2016), ed. Shane Denson and Julia Leyda. 51–64, http://reframe.sussex.ac.uk/post-cinema/1-2-shaviro/.

Shaviro, Steven (2017a). *Digital Music Videos*. Rutgers: Rutgers University Press.

Shaviro, Steven (2017b). "The Glitch Dimension: *Paranormal Activity* and the Technologies of Vision". In *Indefinite Visions: Cinema and the Attractions of Uncertainty*, ed. Martine Beugnet, Allan Cameron, and Arild Fetveit. Edinburgh: Edinburgh University Press, 316–33.

Simoneau, Nicholas (2015). "Focus on: KyttenJanae!". *Kaltblut*, March 17, 2015. http://www.kaltblut-magazine.com/focus-on-kyttenjanae/.

Singer, Leigh (2016). "The Enigmatic 'Pillow Shots' of Yasujiro Ozu". *BFI*, December 12, 2016. https://www2.bfi.org.uk/news-opinion/news-bfi/features/enigmatic-pillow-shots-yasujiro-ozu.

Skinner, Tom (2021). "The Weeknd Says 'Grand Theft Auto: Vice City' 'opened my eyes to a lot of '80s music'". *NME*, November 24, 2021. https://www.nme.com/news/music/the-weeknd-grand-theft-auto-vice-city-80s-music-3103875.

Snead, James A (1984). "Repetition as a Figure of Black Culture". In *Black Literature and Literary Theory*, ed. Henry Lous Gates. London: Methuen, 59–79.

Sobchack, Vivian (2004). *Carnal Thoughts: Embodiment and Moving Image Culture.* Berkeley: University of California Press.

Soja, Edward W. (1989). *Postmodern Geographies: The Reassertion of Space in Critical Social Theory.* New York: Verso.

Spinoza, Benedict de (2018). *Ethics.* Trans. Michael Silverthorne and Matthew J. Kisner. Cambridge: Cambridge University Press.

St. Félix, Doreen (2018). "Tierra Whack Stretches the Limits of One-Minute Songs". *The New Yorker*, July 1, 2018. https://www.newyorker.com/culture/culture-desk/tierra-whack-stretches-the-limits-of-one-minute-songs.

Sterbenz, Maeve (2016). "Movement, Music, Feminism: An Analysis of Movement-Music Interactions and the Articulation of Masculinity in Tyler, the Creator's 'Yonkers' Music Video". *MTO* (*Music Theory Online*) 23.2 (June 2016). https://mtosmt.org/issues/mto.17.23.2/mto.17.23.2.sterbenz.html.

Stengers, Isabelle (2011). *Thinking with Whitehead: A Free and Wild Creation of Concepts.* Trans. Michael Chase. Cambridge: Harvard University Press.

Stern, Bradley (2022). "Charli XCX & Rina Sawayama Flip September's 'Cry for You' for the LGBTs". *MuuMuse*, January 27, 2022. https://muumuse.com/2022/01/charli-xcx-rina-sawayama-beg-for-you.html/.

Stone, Bryony (2017). "We Go behind the Scenes of Bonobo's Trippy No Reason Video with Director Oscar Hudson". January 20, 2017. https://www.itsnicethat.com/articles/we-go-behind-the-scenes-of-bonobos-trippy-no-reason-video-with-director-oscar-hudson-200117.

Strauss, Matthew (2021). "The Weeknd's Director Alex Lill Unpacks the Singer's Eccentric String of *After Hours* TV Performances". *Pitchfork*, May 28, 2021. https://pitchfork.com/thepitch/the-weeknd-director-alex-lill-unpacks-the-singer-eccentric-string-of-after-hours-tv-performances/.

Strickland, Lloyd (2014). *Leibniz's Monadology: A New Translation and Guide.* Edinburgh: Edinburgh University Press.

Sumney, Moses (2020b). "Stateside Statelessness". In *Fight of the Century: Writers Reflect on 100 Years of Landmark ACLU Cases*, ed. Michael Chabon and Ayelet Waldman. New York: Avid Reader Press, 215–23.

Thaler, Richard H., and Cass R. Sunstein (2008). *Nudge: Improving Decisions about Health, Wealth, and Happiness.* New Haven: Yale University Press.

Tone Glow (2015). "Monthly Review: January 2015". http://toneglow.tumblr.com/post/109714211225/monthly-review-january-2015.

Tononi, Giulio (2008). "Consciousness as Integrated Information: A Provisional Manifesto". *The Biological Bulletin* 215.3 (December 2008), 216–42.

Tononi, Giulio (2012). *Phi: A Voyage from the Brain to the Soul.* New York: Pantheon.

Tsjeng, Zing (2018). "Singer Rina Sawayama Is Ready to Rep Her Pansexuality". *Vice*, August 14, 2018. https://www.vice.com/en/article/zmkgyx/rina-sawayama-comes-out-pansexual-interview.

Unterberger, Andrew (2018). "This Is a New Golden Age for Music Videos". *Billboard*, July 24, 2018. https://www.billboard.com/articles/columns/pop/8466248/music-video-golden-age.

Vain, Madison (2016). "Dawn Richard Details New Album: 'Why Not Celebrate Being a Woman?'" *Entertainment Weekly*, March 15, 2016. http://www.ew.com/article/2016/03/14/dawn-richard-interview.

van Zon, Harm (2010). "Edouard Salier: Massive Attack 'Splitting the Atom'". http://motionographer.com/2010/02/05/edouard-salier-massive-attack-splitting-the-atom/.

Vernallis, Carol (2004). *Experiencing Music Video: Aesthetics and Cultural Context*. New York: Columbia University Press.

Vernallis, Carol (2013). *Unruly Media: YouTube, Music Video, and the New Digital Cinema*. New York: Oxford University Press.

Vernallis, Carol (2022a). "Transmedia Director Joseph Kahn's Moments of Audiovisual Bliss". forthcoming.

Vernallis, Carol (2022b). *The Media Swirl*. Durham: Duke University Press.

Vernallis, Carol, Holly Rogers, and Lisa Perrott, eds. (2019). *Transmedia Directors: Artistry, Industry and New Audiovisual Aesthetics*. New York: Bloomsbury.

Walker, Alan (2009). *Hans von Bülow: A Life and Times*. Oxford: Oxford University Press.

Wang, Steffanee (2022). "Charli XCX and Rina Sawayama's 'Beg for You' Is Nostalgia Done Right". *Nylon*, February 1, 2022. https://www.nylon.com/entertainment/charli-xcx-rina-sawayamas-beg-for-you-review.

Wark, McKenzie (2012). "Preoccupying: McKenzie Wark". *The Occupied Times*, August 2, 2012. https://theoccupiedtimes.org/?p=6451.

Wark, McKenzie (2021). *Philosophy for Spiders: On the Low Theory of Kathy Acker*. Durham: Duke University Press.

Webb, Chris (2011). "Long Live Low Theory!—McKenzie Wark on the Legacy and Continued Relevance of Situationism". *Verso* blog, September 5, 2011. https://www.versobooks.com/blogs/690-long-live-low-theory-mckenzie-wark-on-the-legacy-and-continued-relevance-of-situationism.

Whitehead, Alfred North (1920). *The Concept of Nature*. Cambridge: Cambridge University Press.

Whitehead, Alfred North (1978). *Process and Reality: An Essay in Cosmology*. Corrected edition. New York: The Free Press.

Whosampled.com (2022). "Cry for You by September". https://www.whosampled.com/September/Cry-for-You/.

Wikipedia (2016). "Kerala". https://en.wikipedia.org/wiki/Kerala.

Wikipedia (2021a). "Black Secret Technology". https://en.wikipedia.org/wiki/Black_Secret_Technology.

Wikipedia (2021b). "Ancient to the Future". https://en.wikipedia.org/wiki/Ancient_to_the_Future.

Wikipedia (2021c). "Clarke's Three Laws". https://en.wikipedia.org/wiki/.Clarke's_three_laws.

Wikipedia (2021d). "Judith Beheading Holofernes". https://en.wikipedia.org/wiki/Judith_beheading_Holofernes.

Williams, Raymond (1974). *Television: Technology and Cultural Form*. London: Routledge.

Wittgenstein, Ludwig (2001). *Tractatus Logico-Philosophicus*. Trans. D. F. Pears and B. F. McGuinness. New York: Routledge.

Wittgenstein, Ludwig (2009). *Philosophical Investigations*. Revised fourth edition. Trans. G. E. M. Anscombe, P. M. S. Hacker, and Joachim Schulte. Hoboken: Wiley-Blackwell.

Womack, Ytasha (2013). *Afrofuturism: The World of Black Sci Fi and Fantasy Culture*. Chicago: Lawrence Hill Books.

Yeung, Vivian (2020). "FKA twigs Launches Sad Day Face Filter on Instagram". *Crack* Magazine, November 11, 2020. https://crackmagazine.net/2020/11/fka-twigs-launches-sad-day-face-filter-on-instagram/.

Younger, Briana (2018). "Tierra Whack, *Whack World*". *Pitchfork*, June 12, 2018. https://pitchfork.com/reviews/albums/tierra-whack-whack-world/.

Zabboo (2017). Review of Bonobo's *Migration*. *Metacritic*, January 14, 2017. https://www.metacritic.com/music/migration/bonobo.

Zuckerkandl, Victor (1973). *Sound and Symbol: Music and the External World*. Princeton: Princeton University Press.

Music and Videos Cited

41sttry (2009). “Dancing on the Timeline (Better Quality)”. https://www.youtube.com/watch?v=HmWljCI_4Ok.

AMathMonkey (2017). “Bonobo—Kerala [Edited to Remove Jump Cuts]”. https://www.youtube.com/watch?v=Sy5cbn3mKIM.

Beyoncé (2009). “Video Phone”. Dir. Hype Williams. https://www.youtube.com/watch?v=fMX4dcyr19E.

Björk (1999). “All Is Full of Love”. Dir. Chris Cunningham. https://www.youtube.com/watch?v=0cSjn4r4ddA.

blankfist (2010). “Dancing on the Timeline: Slitscan Effect”. http://videosift.com/video/Dancing-on-the-Timeline-Slitscan-Effect.

Bonobo (2016). “Kerala”. Dir. Dave Bullivant. https://vimeo.com/190146978.

Bonobo (2017). “No Reason”. Dir. Oscar Hudson. https://vimeo.com/199858222.

Calmatic (2018). “‘Insecure’ Music Video Director Calmatic Talks Success”. https://www.youtube.com/watch?v=7GGw_qnkOW0.

Charli XCX (2022a). “Beg for You (ft. Rina Sawayama) [Official Visualiser]”. Dir. Angela Stephenson. https://www.youtube.com/watch?v=h69otAKumSg.

Charli XCX (2022b). “Beg for You feat. Rina Sawayama”. Dir. Nick Harwood. https://www.youtube.com/watch?v=hw_Gtwdnp1Q.

Childish Gambino (2018). “This Is America”. Dir. Hiro Murai. https://www.youtube.com/watch?v=VYOjWnS4cMY.

Dawn Richard (2015a). “Tide: The Paradox Effect”. Dir. We Were Monkeys and Dawn Richard. https://www.youtube.com/watch?v=FszEaxrHGTs.

Dawn Richard (2015b). “Calypso”. Dir. Kytten Janae. https://www.youtube.com/watch?v=OT1ZtAo31J4.

FKA twigs (2013). “Papi Pacify”. Dir. FKA twigs and Tom Beard. https://www.youtube.com/watch?v=OydK91JjFOw.

FKA twigs (2014). “Two Weeks”. Dir. Nabil Elderkin. https://www.youtube.com/watch?v=3yDP9MKVhZc.

FKA twigs (2019a). “Cellophane”. Dir. Andrew Thomas Huang. https://www.youtube.com/watch?v=YkLjqFpBh84.

FKA twigs (2020a). “Sad Day”. Dir. Hiro Murai. https://www.youtube.com/watch?v=IxGDNRE-2c0.

FKA twigs (2021). “Tears in the Club”. Dir. Amber Grace Johnson. https://www.youtube.com/watch?v=cZTKjzAJLCk.

Grace Jones (2008). “Corporate Cannibal”. Dir. Nick Hooker. https://www.youtube.com/watch?v=Cc61C-VsTko.

Janelle Monáe (2008). "Many Moons". Dir. Alan Ferguson. https://www.youtube.com/watch?v=EZyyORSHbaE.

Janelle Monáe (2013). "Q.U.E.E.N". Dir. Alan Ferguson. https://www.youtube.com/watch?v=tEddixS-UoU.

Jimmy Kimmel Live! (2020). "The Weeknd Performs 'Blinding Lights'". January 23, 2020. https://www.youtube.com/watch?v=VJYpyC1SNPc.

Lil Nas X (2021). "Montero (Call Me by Your Name)". Dir. Tanu Muino and Lil Nas X. https://www.youtube.com/watch?v=6swmTBVI83k.

Lorde (2017). "Green Light". Dir. Grant Singer. https://www.youtube.com/watch?v=dMK_npDG12Q.

Madonna (1985). "Material Girl". Dir. Mary Lambert. https://www.youtube.com/watch?v=6p-lDYPR2P8.

Massive Attack (2009). "Splitting the Atom". Dir. Edouard Salier. https://www.youtube.com/watch?v=AzQZv30M5Aw.

Max Speedster (2020). "The Very First Two Hours of MTV (August 1, 1918)". https://www.youtube.com/watch?v=PJtiPRDIqtI.

Michael Jackson (1983). "Thriller". Dir. John Landis. https://www.youtube.com/watch?v=sOnqjkJTMaA.

Missy Elliott (2001). "Get Ur Freak On". Dir. Dave Meyers. https://www.youtube.com/watch?v=FPoKiGQzbSQ.

Moses Sumney (2016). "Worth It". Dir. Allie Avital. https://www.youtube.com/watch?v=-JeSL44Rrfw.

Moses Sumney (2019a). "Polly". Dir. Moses Sumney and Sam Cannon. https://www.youtube.com/watch?v=dta4heZacZE.

Moses Sumney (2019b). "Virile". Dir. Moses Sumney. https://www.youtube.com/watch?v=-Cq8zRq0G9I.

Moses Sumney (2020a). "Me in 20 Years" (lyric video). Dir. Josh Finck.

Moses Sumney (2020b). "Me in 20 Years". Dir. Allie Avital. https://vimeo.com/440814332.

Parliament (1978). "Mr Wigggles". From *Motor-Booty Affair*. https://www.youtube.com/watch?v=rnUgDW9N–A.

The Presets (2006). "Are You the One?". Dir. Kris Moyes. https://www.youtube.com/watch?v=NfsbqFbCtC0.

Rihanna (2008). "Disturbia". Dir. Anthony Mandler and Rihanna. https://www.youtube.com/watch?v=E1mU6h4Xdxc.

Rihanna (2010). "Rude Boy". Dir. Melina Matsoukas. https://www.youtube.com/watch?v=e82VE8UtW8A.

Rihanna (2015). "Bitch Better Have My Money". Dir. Rihanna and Megaforce. https://www.youtube.com/watch?v=B3eAMGXFw1o.

Rina Sawayama (2020). Dir. Ali Kurr. https://www.youtube.com/watch?v=TO2c06p6m5w.

Rosalía (2021). "La fama". Featuring The Weeknd. Dir. Director X. https://www.youtube.com/watch?v=e-CEd6xrRQc. "XS".

Scarface (2002). "On My Block". Dir. Marc Klasfeld. https://www.youtube.com/watch?v=DHyqs0PoBgE.

September (2005). "Cry for You" (first version). Director unknown. https://www.youtube.com/watch?v=pxu6iQ28arw.

September (2007). "Cry for You" (second version). Dir. Patric Ullaeus. https://www.youtube.com/watch?v=BqHYImUPjn8.

The Slits (1980). "In the Beginning, There Was Rhythm". https://www.youtube.com/watch?v=leOVkvGq8hs.

Tierra Whack (2018). "Whack World". Dir. Thibaut Duverneix. https://vimeo.com/272490132.

Tkay Maidza (2021). "Where Is My Mind? (Pixies Cover)". Dir. Tkay Maidza. https://www.youtube.com/watch?v=WFfGf1-y1Bs.

Tyler The Creator (2011). "Yonkers". Dir. Wolf Haley. https://www.youtube.com/watch?v=XSbZidsgMfw.

The Weeknd (2015a). "The Hills". Dir. Grant Singer. https://www.youtube.com/watch?v=yzTuBuRdAyA.

The Weeknd (2015b). "Can't Feel My Face". Dir. Grant Singer. https://www.youtube.com/watch?v=KEI4qSrkPAs.

The Weeknd (2019). "Heartless". Dir. Anton Tammi. https://www.youtube.com/watch?v=1DpH-icPpl0.

The Weeknd (2020a). "Blinding Lights". Dir. Anton Tammi. https://www.youtube.com/watch?v=4NRXx6U8ABQ.

The Weeknd (2020b). "After Hours (short film)". Dir. Anton Tammi. https://www.youtube.com/watch?v=oq9AgxHvGjw&t=1s.

The Weeknd (2020c). "In Your Eyes". Dir. Anton Tammi. https://www.youtube.com/watch?v=dqRZDebPIGs.

The Weeknd (2020d). "Until I Bleed Out". Dir. Anton Tammi. https://www.youtube.com/watch?v=i58MNnk6BhY.

The Weeknd (2020e). "Too Late". Dir. Cliqua. https://www.youtube.com/watch?v=Wh8DT09QCHI.

The Weeknd (2020f). "Save Your Tears/In Your Eyes (Live on the 2020 American Music Awards)". https://www.youtube.com/watch?v=f-g_SHNv5NI.

The Weeknd (2021). "Save Your Tears". Dir. Cliqua. https://www.youtube.com/watch?v=XXYlFuWEuKI.

Wild Beasts (2008). "Brave Bulging Buoyant Clairvoyants". Dir. OneInThree (Ross Cooper). https://www.youtube.com/watch?v=1bW6USsmR70.

Winsane (2017). "Bonobo—Kerala (without Video Cuts)". https://www.youtube.com/watch?v=EsUmw52LIOI.

Index